MACHINE CONVERSATIONS

THE KLUWER INTERNATIONAL SERIES
IN ENGINEERING AND COMPUTER SCIENCE

MACHINE CONVERSATIONS

edited by

Yorick Wilks
University of Sheffield
United Kingdom

KLUWER ACADEMIC PUBLISHERS
Boston / Dordrecht / London

Distributors for North, Central and South America:
Kluwer Academic Publishers
101 Philip Drive
Assinippi Park
Norwell, Massachusetts 02061 USA
Telephone (781) 871-6600
Fax (781) 871-6528
E-Mail <kluwer@wkap.com>

Distributors for all other countries:
Kluwer Academic Publishers Group
Distribution Centre
Post Office Box 322
3300 AH Dordrecht, THE NETHERLANDS
Telephone 31 78 6392 392
Fax 31 78 6546 474
E-Mail <services@wkap.nl>

Electronic Services <http://www.wkap.nl>

Library of Congress Cataloging-in-Publication Data

Machine conversations / edited by Yorick Wilks.
p. cm. -- (Kluwer international series in engineering and computer science ; SECS 511)
Includes bibliographical references and index.
ISBN 978-1-4419-5092-5
1. Human-computer interaction. 2. Natural language processing (Computer science) 3. Artificial intelligence. I. Wilks, Yorick, 1939- . II. Series.
QA76.9.H85M33 1999
004'.01'9--dc21 99-30264
CIP

Printed on acid-free paper.

Printed in the United States of America

Contents

Preface

Human-computer conversation is a technology that has reached the same stage of development as some better-known areas of language processing by computer, like machine translation (MT) and information extraction from texts (IE): it is an area of natural language processing (NLP) technology where new and striking developments come from effectively ignoring received theories and wisdoms. It is a truism in science as a whole that this can occur, but in artificial intelligence (AI), of which NLP is part, this often takes the form of striking out towards a practical implementation of a difficult task, with all the risks that such course of action entails. Recent examples would be the brief flowering of statistically based MT at the end of the 1980's, and the rapid growth of the IE movement at about the same time, a growth that continues.

Both those movements effectively ignored the current state of theory and any search for the foundations of the subject, in favour of what one could call having-a-go. This is an old AI tradition, sometimes called throwaway-AI, or more charitably rapid prototyping. It is widely condemned by theorists of all types, who point out yet again that climbing a tree cannot get one to the moon, even if it feels like a step in the right direction. Interestingly, too, both those movements were associated with the development of strong evaluation regimes, imposed by the sponsors of much of the work. Rapid improvements over time were seen, but then they began to fall off and it was again argued how much constant evaluation can stifle theoretical creativity and novelty, all of which is certainly true, though the criticism fails to capture how little such theorists had been interested in systems that were evaluable at all until this new pressure appeared.

Machine conversations with humans, as an area of research and development, shares another striking property with machine translation: both made rapid advances about twenty-five years ago and some doubt that the amount of theoretical and practical effort expended since have changed the situation very much. In MT it is clear that SYSTRAN, now well into its fourth decade, is still the most used system for large scale tasks and the one that still wins competitions against those embodying newer, more perspicuous, approaches.

In machine conversation, Colby's PARRY, devised at Stanford in the early Seventies, set a standard that has not been reached since, at least until recently. PARRY's position was, for most observers, hidden behind the greater publicity achieved by Weizenbaum's ELIZA, a much inferior conversationalist. Also, the fact that PARRY was designed to model a mental disorder (PARanoia) made it easier both to excuse its lapses and to dismiss its general significance for the area.

Four features of the machine conversation problem have brought us to the situation that motivated the essays in this book. First, dialogue analysis has now gathered a great deal of research attention (within linguistics proper and within AI-related work) under such titles as conversational analysis, dialogue acts, speech acts, conversation acts and so on, but virtually none of such work has contributed to any tradition of building real performing and robust conversational partners. That is a remarkable fact, though one not unknown before in the history of language processing, as I noted earlier. It is certainly a situation to make one sit back and ask calmly what has been the point of all that work if it has so few evaluable outcomes over twenty five years.

Secondly, one notes the resurgence within computational linguistics of empirical methods, methods driven by linguistic data (e.g. Charniak, 1993; and Wilks, 1996). This movement is now spreading to complex areas like language pragmatics and human conversation, partly (within the English language at least) because of the availability of the dialogue part of the British National Corpus, amounting to some two million words. One of the systems described here has built structures in part from analysis of those interchanges, and indeed from the corpus comprised of all the past Loebner competition dialogues (see below). Well-motivated empiricism, in addition to stamina and application, now seem to offer possible ways forward in this area and that is reflected in some of the papers here.

Thirdly, the need for such conversational agents has become acute with the widespread use of personal machines with which to communicate and the desire of their makers to provide natural language interfaces. There is good reason to believe that most, if not all, major hardware and software houses are working on some form of this problem, but the literature in the area shows little of proven practical help, only a welter of claims. Indeed, below the academic surface, work has continued in many places on such agents, developing a sort of craft-skill in how to program them, one that owes a great deal to AI conventions and to the approach embodied in Colby's PARRY. (Parkison et al., 1977) This is a theme developed in the book, but it can be summarized as: machine conversationalists have to have something to say, have to simulate having a story to tell, rather than just reacting to, disambiguating or otherwise processing what they receive.

For many this is a triviality, and the hard part is going from that to a craft skill that can express it in a program. I write "craft skill" in opposition to forms of theory that constantly reappear as new claims but with no method at all of tying the observation to any performance. Most recently, Poesio and Traum (1997) have developed a new fusion of Rochester speech-act techniques with an Edinburgh style of discourse-representation-theory, leading to a complex analysis of an interchange like:

A: There is an engine at Avon.

B: It is hooked to a boxcar.

which provides, over many pages, an analysis and representation capable of referring the "it" to the engine, as if there were serious alternatives, and then going on to talk of linking all this to a theory of what they call "conversational threads", which they concede was present many years ago in Schank's notion of script (Schank and Abelson, 1977). To anyone actively interested in machine conversation, all this is remarkable: the example dialogue is both artificial and unmotivated—why does B. say what he does?—and the linguistic pronoun issue has been a non-problem for a quarter century. The real problems, like conversational threads, however titled, are left always to some future time. Meanwhile, others, some of them represented in this book, are actually engaged with the construction of such conversation programs and the skills to develop them in a general and robust way. By way of historical analogy, some may recall that, only ten years ago, papers on computational syntax would spend pages discussing the parsing of a sentence like "Uthor sleeps", which could pose no conceivable problem; all such discussion has been swept into oblivion by the establishment of realistic parsing of real sentences evaluated in competitions like PARSEVAL.

The history of AI has shown the value and importance of such craft skills in all its areas from games to vision to language: the discovery of the underlying structures and principles to make something work, by experience. All formalisms and searches for justifiable *Anfangspuenkte* never replace this phase, and rarely add much later when tidying and refining is required. What they do is continue to is endlessly discuss the same examples in different forms as if the problems they present had not been cleared up decades before.

Fourthly and lastly, one must mention the role here of the Loebner competition, which has played the role of an evaluation process in machine conversations that DARPA has played in MT and IE. That an amateur with flair, with a notoriously eccentric personal web page, started this competition, rather than a staid government agency, has discredited it for some. Nonetheless, the Loebner competitions on human-machine conversation have been well conducted by the ACM and panels of experts and have certainly increased attention to, and activity in, the craft skills, and the 1997 Loebner winner is represented in this volume.

The drawback of the competition (and here it differs from MT and IE DARPA competitions) is that entrants bias their systems towards pretending to be people (it being the job of the competition judges to sort the people from the programs) and that is not necessarily a feature one will want in the future in useful machine conversationalists that are not pretending to be other than they are!

The papers in this volume came from an attempt to gather a collection of the best work available in the practical arts of machine conversation: not with the desire to exclude any theoretical claims but to keep the focus on the task and on performance. This had the effect of showing some of the first rate work going on in industry, quite apart from the academic tradition; it also brought out striking and relevant facts about the tone of machine conversations and what users want, and focused on non-linguistic aspects of these conversations that we, in the typing business, tend to ignore. Above all, it showed again the pioneering role of Ken Colby at Stanford in the 1970s, and this book is dedicated to him.

References

Charniak, E. 1993. Statistical Language Learning. MIT Press, Cambridge, MA.

Parkison, R.C., Colby, K.M. and Faught, W. 1977. Conversational language comprehension using integrated pattern-matching and parsing. Artificial Intelligence, 9: 111-134. Reprinted in Readings in Natural Language Processing, Grosz, B., Jones, K.S., Webber, B.L. (Eds.) (1986), Morgan Kaufman Publishers, Inc., Los Altos, CA.

Poesio, M. and Traum, D. 1997. Representing Conversation Acts in a Unified Semantic/Pragmatic Framework, In preprints of the AAAI Fall Symposia, Stanford, CA.

Schank, R. and Abelson, R. 1977. Scripts, Plans and Goals. Erlbaum, Hillsdale, NJ.

Wilks, Y. 1996. Special Issue of the Communications of the ACM on Natural Language Processing. January 1996.

Acknowledgements

Considerable thanks are due to David Levy, who thought of staging the original event that gave rise to this book at the Grand Hotel Villa Serbelloni at Bellagio, Italy, one of the world's finest spots, as Pliny knew long before us when he built his villa there. Also for substantial help and advice on the programme etc. from Louise Guthrie, and for great help with organizing from Gill Wells. An enormous debt of gratitude is due to Gillian Callaghan for much painstaking work on this volume. And to Roberta as always for everything.

Yorick Wilks
Sheffield

1 Dialogue Programs I have Known and Loved Over 33 Years

K.M. Colby

In the mid-1950s, when I first read about computers, it occurred to me that they might be used to provide some form of talk-therapy for the thousands of mentally ill warehoused in large mental hospitals receiving only custodial care. I envisioned some sort of large time-shared system running programs that could be communicated with in everyday natural language. But as we all have learned, it is a long way from an idea to its implementation.

In the late 1950s, Allen Newell paid me a visit. At the time I was practicing psychiatry in Northern California and trying to hand simulate a neurotic process with boxes of cards. Allen encouraged me to learn a programming language (IPL-V) and to get more involved in AI research. I decided to get into full-time research which meant academia. So after a year at the Center for Advanced Study in the Behavioral Sciences in Palo Alto, I joined the psychology department at Stanford and soon the Computer Science Department there.

And then I met Joe Weizenbaum. He was working for General Electric having contributed to the IRMA program which handled checking accounts for the Bank of America. We met through Ed Feigenbaum and even considered forming a company called Heuristics Inc. along with Ed and John Gilbert, the statistician at the Center for Advanced Study. Joe and I spent many hours together discussing the problems of talk-therapy programs in natural language. To change its mind, I was trying to communicate with my neurosis program using a form of Basic English, but it was hopelessly cumbersome.

Joe moved to MIT where, with the aid of the time-shared system MAC, he wrote the first up-and-running dialogue program ELIZA with me contributing many of the admittedly limited input responses characteristic of talk-therapy conversation. The first description of ELIZA appeared in the Harvard Review and was titled "Conversations With a Mechanical Psychiatrist". We soon had an ELIZA-like program running at Stanford called the "MAD DOCTOR"—not because it exhibited anger but in the British sense of the term "mad" meaning mentally ill. I saw the program as having a potential for psychotherapy.

But Joe did not. He objected strongly to using computers for therapy. He even said he was "shocked" by the publication of our paper (with James Watt and John

Gilbert) on the subject. In 1965, before publication, we sent Joe a copy of this paper and he requested that he write the section on ELIZA which we granted. It is hard to imagine how he could be shocked at a paper part of which was written, word for word, by himself. But Joe was not attacking just us. In a 1976 book, he objected to much of AI work as "immoral", "obscene", etc. My own interpretation is that in part he was striking back for being rejected by the AI group at MIT.

As an amusing aside, when Joe visited the Stanford area in the 1960s, he would often stay at our home - this of course before his anti-AI blasts. Our son Peter would give up his room to accommodate Joe. When Peter was a student at UC Santa Cruz, Joe gave a talk there. Afterwards Peter introduced himself to Joe and reminded him of how he had to give up his room on Joe's visits. In concluding their chat, Joe said to Peter "and give my regards to your mother". (!)

At the same time we were working on the talk-therapy program, I was interested in using programs to stimulate speech in non-speaking autistic children. In collaboration with Horace Enea and David Smith, we designed and ran many language-oriented programs which could hardly be called "dialogues" since they were quite rudimentary at the level of single words or short phrases. Some of the children began talking in response and some did not. These efforts have been taken up by Jill Lehman at Carnegie Mellon using the many advances in technology now available - animation, speech recognition, etc.

The next dialogue program was PARRY, a simulation of paranoid thought processes. Instead of having a program talk like a therapist, the goal was to have one talk like a paranoid patient. What we had learned from ELIZA and the MAD DOCTOR was that it might be possible to conduct a conversation using only word-meaning and that complex ontological designs (tree-structures categorizing world-knowledge with THING at the top and DOG at the bottom) were not necessary. Before he received his doctorate in linguistics, I had hired Roger Schank to work on the natural language problem. Roger worked with both Larry Tesler and David Smith but couldn't get along with either. He and I didn't see eye to eye about the usefulness of grammars in conversational language, so I let him go his own way in developing a conceptual dependency grammar. My main helper on PARRY was Sylvia Weber Russell who wrote the algorithm in LISP while I constructed the semantic data-base.

PARRY was designed to converse in the highly constrained situation of a first diagnostic psychiatric interview. As do human paranoids, he had a story to tell about how he was being persecuted, especially by the Mafia. If any of his "flare concepts", for example, were activated, he would reveal something about the Mafia. Hence any reference to gambling (or even Italy) would evoke part of his story. The importance of this point for machine conversation is that the participating program should have some sort of constraining anchor in the world so that its virtual person, or persons, can give direction to the flow of talk exchanges.

At Stanford, I had a Career Research Grant to do whatever interested me, but when President Nixon decided to abolish this luxury in the early 1970s, I realized I had to get a regular job and so accepted a professorship in psychiatry at UCLA. I brought William Faught and Roger Parkison with me and they both received their Stanford doctorates based on PARRY.

At Stanford, we had conducted a number of indistinguishability tests on the model with the help of Frank Hilf, a psychiatrist, and Hans Moravec, an AI graduate student. At UCLA we continued these tests and collected linguistic data from over 100,000 PARRY interviews on the ARPANET. Just when we were ready to try to "treat" PARRY by cognitive therapy, the project was defunded. (There is still no treatment for the paranoid mode). NIMH decided not to put any more money into AI. Such are the vagaries of grant funding.

In the mid 1970s an economist and population expert, Julian Simon, sent me a manuscript he was trying to get published describing his own depression and how he overcame it. He wondered if I could model depression as was done for paranoia. Still pursuing talk-therapy, I responded I would be more interested in developing a cognitive therapy program for depression. Roger Parkison and I had written a primitive Joe-the-Bartender program that could converse superficially about the weather, sports, etc. as bartenders do. While waiting for Simon's book to get published, son Peter and I developed the program 'Overcoming Depression' with a text mode based on Simon's work and a dialogue mode based on our own heuristic methods for making sense out of the tangles of conversational language in the interpersonal domain. Simon's book was finally published as Good Mood in 1993 and since then we have given away free over 1300 copies of the program to buyers of the book. Sad to say, Simon died recently. We will always be indebted to him for his emotional and financial support in our effort to make an end run around the social stigma associated with depression.

Like most prophecies, my initial vision of computer-based therapy was far off (even John McCarthy predicted we would be out of gasoline by the year 2000) because I did not anticipate the invention of personal computers in which a sufferer can treat himself at home with the help of a talk-therapy program. Because of innovation, it is difficult to predict - especially the future.

Risking prophecy again, I do not think computers as conversational agents have much of a future in psychotherapy. But they may have a great future commercially because people enjoy conversing with computers that tend to say odd but engaging and pertinent things. I view our dialogue mode as somewhat analogous to the Wright brothers' airplane. Once we get it off the ground (it now makes sense about 90% of the time), we can then worry about serving 150 people the shrimp cocktails at 600 miles per hour 35,000 feet above the earth.

Hence we continue to work on it every day.

2 Comments on Human-Computer Conversation

K.M.Colby

It was heartening to see so many men and women at the Villa Serbelloni eager to work on this seemingly insuperable and hence challenging problem of human-computer conversation. From the variety of issues, arguments, opinions, jokes, etc., I have selected a few that stand out in my memory. The order presented here does not reflect the order in which they occurred.

The term "theory" often appeared. There seem to be all sorts of theories. In physics, a "scientific" causal-explanatory theory consists of lawfully-related coherent abstract entities, with relevant variables specified and postulated about a system to account for the law-like generalization of its evidential phenomena. It states what a system is and what it must do. But can there be such a theory of conversational language which is convention-governed, providing room for choice, rather than physical-law governed? Since words and word-meanings are governed by conventions of linguistic communities, it is doubtful that a sound analogy with physical theories can be made. OED has recently added 3,000 new words to its vocabulary, which is not like discovering 3,000 new elementary particles. Conventions, as institutional facts, can be regular and systematic in a given period and have a clear enough specification that one can utilize an instrumental theory of heuristic devices and useful rules of thumb in constructing artifactual conversational agents.

In building programs that exhibit the skilled praxis of conversation, we can make progress using a background lore and rules of praxis much as did Gothic cathedral builders employing their practical-technological ingenuity and inventiveness long before there was a science of mechanics. Early in the 18th century, the British Parliament offered a large prize for a solution to the longitude problem since it was difficult for sailors to determine accurately where their ships were located once they lost the sight of land. Galileo, Newton and many physicists had been unable to solve the problem using astronomical theories. A man named John Harrison, with the help of his son, solved it by building a reliable clock, a chronometer, that could keep accurate time while withstanding the buffetings of a sea voyage. Perhaps one day there will be an adequate theory of conversational language. In the meantime, we are building a clock; we are not doing astronomy.

As artisanal engineers, we can proceed instrumentally using our heuristic native-speaker know-how-and-when knowledge of conversational interaction. One advantage of this "pure AI" (purely artifactual) approach is that we are free of the constraints imposed by a theory of how humans process conversational language.

A panelist expressed the view that since every word has a meaning, it may be a mistake to disregard or neglect words in an input as "fluff". But it seems to me that a simplification strategy with special purposes must ferret out and extract from otiose, redundant, superfluous and decoratively cluttered inputs what is important from what is not important for realizing these purposes. This strategy reduces the familiar signal-to-noise ratio characteristic of processing informational messages.

Another panelist sternly proclaimed that it was inhuman to use computers for conversation - a startling moral point to be made this late in the century when it seems clear that people want to talk to computers. We need not take human-human conversation as the gold standard for conversational exchanges. If one had a perfect simulation of a human conversant, then it would be a human-human conversation and not a human-computer conversation with its sometimes odd but pertinent properties. Before there were computers, we could distinguish persons from non-persons on the basis of an ability to participate in conversations. But now we have hybrids operating between persons and non-persons with whom we can talk in ordinary language. Pure machines can only be poked at but these new hybrids are interactive instruments that can be communicated with.

Yorick Wilks disagreed with what he took to be my position that a conversational program need not know anything. I should clarify my point by saying that the program needs knowledge but the question is in what format the knowledge is best represented for the program's purposes. An artifactual conversational modular processor is stipulatively defined as domain specific, informationally encapsulated, special purpose, and having fast, shallow outputs. Thus its knowledge can be efficiently represented in know-how-and-when production rules supplying information about potential action, i.e. what to do in a conversational context. In our module, the know-how rules can generate know-thats, e.g. creating conceptual patterns from the input, and the stored patterns represent know-that knowledge. This position may seem to revive the old and well-chewed procedural-declarative controversy in AI. If so, so be it. In a model of the human mind, declarative prepositional content is perhaps useful. But we are not modeling minds - we are constructing a new type of conversational artifact that can do its job without encyclopedic content.

My panel remarks addressed the problem of why there has been such slow progress in the field of conversational language, and I offered three reasons.

1. Institutional Obstacles - A field competes with rival fads and fashions. In my own experience, it has been very difficult to obtain funding in this area from government sources. I think the ultimate funding will come from the private sector when it realizes how much money can be made from conversing computers.

2. Research Traditions - In growing up in a research tradition our hero or heroine is inspired by, and becomes committed to, its methods, tools and view of the world. Thus in a logic-mathematical tradition, he becomes impressed by the precision of deductive logic, proof theory, the predicate calculus with an equal sign. etc. In a computer science tradition, he is taken with the elegance of Turing machines, recursion, and LISP. In linguistics, he becomes absorbed in parsing, grammars, etc. Then in approaching the problem of conversational language, he tries to use the tools of his research commitment. He underestimates the magnitude of the problem (a very large phase space), and when faced with a tool-to-task misfit, gives up and tries some other problem, preferring to retain the ontological allegiances of his research tradition.

3. Cognitive Laziness - We are all cognitively lazy. We would like to knock off the presenting problem with an X-bar grammar or a theorem-prover. But an adequate conversational language program must have a large semantic data base constructed to a great extent by hand. Machine readable thesauri and even Wordnet must still be added to, subtracted from, and modified by hand to suit the special purposes of the program. There is no escape from large amounts of sheer drudgery and dog-work. ("Hard pounding, this" - Duke of Wellington at Waterloo). This sort of grunt-work is neither magical nor macho programming leading towards a strong AI (somewhere North of the Future) characterized by flourishes of fanciful, unnecessarily complex, and over-elaborate structures so beloved by our hero who wants to show off his programming prowess.

A few "names" appeared in the discussion. I mentioned Chomsky's advice about transformational grammar, namely that it was ridiculous to use one to understand or generate natural language. These are performance phenomena whereas he is talking about competence, an innate language faculty of similar formal operations that delimit the range of natural language grammars. Most languages of the world have no S $\rightarrow$ NP + VP structure anyway.

It is canonical to refer to Wittgenstein about language but only his name was mentioned. Also missing were Grice's conversational rules (be brief, be clear, be relevant, be truthful).

To Searle's criticism that conversational programs do not really (he means consciously) understand language, David Levy's rejoinder was that for our pragmatic purposes, it makes no difference whether it is a "real" or "simulated" understanding as long as the program delivers the requisite simulated conversational goods.

My son Peter and I were naturally pleased to hear it stated by the panelist Gene Ball from Microsoft that ours was the best conversational program around. Ours represents a coarse-grained strategy at a level of analysis suitable for instrumental purposes in talk exchanges.

For me, the fundamental cognitive concept in all of this is "understanding". We try to understand the way the world works and we try to understand language.

Understanding (sense-making) represents an ontological category relating reality to technology. What we know, we know through the way it makes sense to us. When we write conversational programs, we are engaged in an artisanal technology of building artifactual special-purpose understanding systems. We are at a frontier where no one yet is quite at home. We are faced with insurmountable opportunities (sayeth Pogo) so let's get to it.

3 Human-Computer Conversation in A Cognitive Therapy Program

K.M.Colby

1 Background

I am neither a computational linguist nor an AI linguist nor a linguist of any kind. I am a psychiatrist interested in using computer programs to conduct psychotherapy - traditionally called talk-therapy, harking back to Socrates who remarked "the cure of the soul has to be effected by certain charms - and these charms are fair words".

About 30 years ago I tried to write a psychotherapy program but of course found the natural language problem to be formidable (Colby et al., 1966). The formal grammars and parsers of the time (phrase structure, ATN, etc.) did not give me what I was looking for. Formal operations were simply unable to handle the flux, slop, fluidity, zest and spunk of conversation. Even operating on the immaculate well-formed prose of narrative text, they were too fragile, unwieldy, brittle, slowed by unnecessary complexities, and generally too meticulous to be practical for conducting and sustaining the unruly, tangled, messy, elliptical, motley and cluttered hodgepodge of real-time, real-life conversations. Also these parsers took no account of who was saying what to whom for what purposes. Parsers depended upon a tight conjunction of stringent tests whereas, it seemed to me, what was needed was a loose disjunction of heuristic procedures to make sense out of highly idiolectic expressions characteristic of a talk-therapy context. To get a rough toe-hold on this large phase-space, I wanted a sturdy, robust, pliable, supple, flexible, rough-and-ready, extensible, error-tolerant, sense-making strategy to cut through a sea of noise with a low processing effort in satisfying the task-requirements of therapeutic conversation.

So, with the help of several diligent and courageous graduate students in AI at Stanford (Sylvia Weber Russell, Horace Enea, Lawrence Tesler, William Faught, Roger Parkison) I began to develop a different heuristic sense-making strategy for dealing with the sprawling patchwork melange and morass of idiolectic conversational language (Colby and Enea, 1967; Parkison et al., 1977). Since everyone seems to agree that context, however vague the concept, is important in language and my interests were psychiatric in nature, the psychosocial contexts of our program were those of diagnostic interviewing (as exemplified by interviews with PARRY, a simulation of paranoid thinking (Colby, 1981)) and, for the past few years, cognitive therapy (as currently exemplified by the program Overcoming Depression (Colby, 1995)).

The computer-simulation model PARRY passed several indistinguishability tests in which it was interviewed by expert mental health professionals (psychiatrists, psychologists, psychiatric nurses) who could not distinguish its linguistic behavior from that of paranoid patients at a statistically significant level. PARRY ran nightly on the ARPA network for many years and these interactions, numbering over 100,000 - often just playful or baiting in nature - nonetheless provided us with a rich source of words, phrases, slang, etc. for building a semantic database.

In the 1980s, joined by my son Peter, a highly inventive programmer, I began construction of a conversational Joe-the-Bartender type of program that discussed close interpersonal relationships (Colby et al., 1990). From this program (GURU) we constructed an artifactual cognitive module (domain specific, informationally encapsulated, fast, shallow) to serve as the dialogue mode of a cognitive therapy program for depression entitled Overcoming Depression, which henceforth I will term "the program". With the aid of my wife Maxine and my daughter Erin, we hand-crafted our own large semantic data-base using standard thesauri, several common frequency lists, slang dictionaries, Dear Abby and Ann Landers letters, a corpus of 70,000 words from 35 depressed women who described their life situations, the PARRY data, and the data from many users of the program itself under its years of development. I mention this family-run aspect of the project in passing because all of my several grant proposals to create this program failed to obtain funding from government, private, or university sources. So we founded a little company called Malibu Artifactual Intelligence Works with our own financial resources plus $23,000 from a friend. The program has been commercially available since 1991. Sometimes, when you develop a new field, you have to go it alone without institutional support.

Before getting into the details of the program, I would like to clarify a term I have used several times, i.e. sense-making (Colby et al., 1991). 1 realize this is an excursion into ontology but I will be brief. In person-to-person understanding, we try to make sense of what others say by extracting from their expressions, meaning relevant to our interests in a context. (More on meaning can be found in Electric Words by Wilks et al., (1996)). I take meaning or sense to be a fundamental dimension of reality running through all phenomena. This view is not unique, being shared by physicists or biologists like Wheeler, Bohm and even Crick. Making sense of what other people say is a practice involving extraction of meaningfulness of representational content from the meaning-forness (word-meaning) of language. I will have more to say about this type of sense-making in relation to the ontological status of deponent verbs in the Discussion. Let me now return to the practical perspective our approach to human-computer conversation is embedded in.

2 Computer-Based Cognitive Therapy for Depression

AI is noted for its interest in the workings of the mind. However it is not noted for its interest in one of the mind's main features - mental suffering and its relief. But that is our interest, mainstream or not.

A common example of mental suffering is the cognitive dysfunction of depression which afflicts 25% of the U.S. population at some time or other in their lives. There are roughly three treatments for depression; cognitive therapy, interpersonal therapy, and psychopharmacologic medication. These treatments have been systematically investigated in many controlled clinical trials and have been found to be about equally effective at a rate of 65-75%. The treatments are conducted by human mental health professionals. So why create a computer program? My main reason was to make an end-run around the social-stigma problem which is particularly troublesome in depression in which 65-70% of depressives do not even seek help, mainly because of social stigma. My goal was not to replace live therapists but rather to provide a therapeutic opportunity for depressives where none currently exists. The program does not threaten mental health professionals with unemployment.

Stigma comes from a Greek word meaning to physically brand a person with a mark of infamy or disgrace. A person so marked posed a risk to society, for example an escaped slave, someone not to be trusted. (Even today we hold up our right hand in court to show we are not branded). Although the situation is improving, in our society people with mental-emotional problems are still stigmatized in the workplace and by health insurance companies. Hence my idea was to provide a therapy opportunity in the form of a Personal Computer program that could circumvent social stigma in that the sufferer could engage in a treatment in the privacy and confidentiality of his own home. (Incidentally the method also avoids the negative side effects of some live therapists such as sexual involvements and financial exploitation). To my knowledge, ours is the world's first successful talk therapy program using conversational language. It has been used by thousands of people, attaining a 96% satisfaction rating from a sample of 142 out of 500 users responding to a survey questionnaire. This is by no means a controlled clinical trial but it is observational evidence supportive in the right direction and employing a commonly used global measurement of treatment outcomes. It should not be surprising that our program and chess-playing programs like Deep Blue are so successful. Both involve highly stereotyped situations.

The program is 5 megabytes in size with an interpreter, written by Peter Colby, of about 120K. The program is divided into a text mode and a dialogue mode. The text mode provides concepts and explanations based largely on theories and cognitive-remedial strategies described in a pre-publication manuscript of the book Good Mood: The New Psychology of Overcoming Depression by J. L. Simon (1993). The program can be viewed as an expert system designed to help the user become an expert on his own depression. It represents an educational technology for human improvement consisting of lessons designed for self-educative therapeutic learning. Each lesson combines a text mode and a dialogue mode in which the user can converse with the program in unrestricted everyday language.

I have said all this to provide a background context for the dialogue mode that is the central concern of this workshop and which I will now go into in some detail.

3 The Dialogue Mode

The dialogue mode in this program represents a specialized artifactual conversational module. It introduces a new type of conversational participant, a virtual person designed to engage in therapeutically relevant conversations by interpreting and responding appropriately to unrestricted natural language input in its own unique way. The user need not worry about this participant's good opinion as he might with a live therapist.

The purposes of the dialogue mode are to encourage free expression, to help the user bring forth his deepest thoughts and feelings, putting them into words that can be displayed, to be supportive, to foster internal dialogue, to arouse hope, to offer challenging questions and assertions, to excite interest, and to promote taking cognitive action. It is intended to function as a catalyst and complement to the cognitive-educational text.

In a sense, the program provides an ancillary "mind" for the user's mind to interact with. The conversational talk-therapy responses are designed to facilitate confidential free expression and exploration on the part of the user, to mobilize relevant concepts, and to orient his attention towards aspects of his life-situations and thinking processes that he may not have considered.

"I offer you explanations of yourself, theories about yourself, authentic and surprising news of yourself." (Borges).

I will sketch some workings of this dialogue module under the headings of A. Semantic Data-base, Patterns and Output Responses.

3.1 Semantic Data-Base

The data-base consists of two parts (1) a conceptual lexicon or thesaurus of about 40,000+ expressions (words, phrases, idioms, colloquialisms, etc) and (2) a set of 11,000+ conceptual patterns. The thesaurus consists of 500+ semantic categories or types to which token expressions are assigned. The assignments were made by ourselves with the aid of standard thesauri, books, etc. Thus, as native speakers, we assigned token-expressions to semantic types in accordance with our own negotiated conventions regarding the best translations (for our teleonomic purposes) from the user's output idiolect into the conceptual idiolect of the module under construction. For example, we assigned the word "procrastinate" to the concept 'avoidl' by the psychologic inference that someone who procrastinates is avoiding something. (A semantic category is identified here by an arbitrary label consisting of letters followed by a number). The concept labels look like English words but they are only convenient mnemonics for the program's authors trying to keep track of matters that can become quite complicated.

I mentioned that a token expression, single or multiple word, is assigned to a semantic category. In certain cases, however, it is a useful heuristic trick to assign an expression to an entire higher-level semantic pattern. For example, we consider the single-word elliptical input "Right" to be an affirmation of a yes-no question or an assertion. It is assigned to the pattern (you1 correct1) and the output response is directed by the rules for this pattern - which brings us to the topic of patterns.

3.2 Patterns

The stored semantic patterns are skeletal, schematic formulas consisting of strings of semantic categories (concepts) organised in the form of a condition-action production system with a pattern on the left-hand side (LHS) and its associated output responses on the right-hand side (RHS). The sequences of concepts in a semantic pattern are situation-indicators consisting minimally of an individual and a property including relational properties. The patterns have no numerical weights or attenuation factors.

The user's input serves as a blueprint or recipe for constructing semantic conceptual patterns. A semantic category type is substituted for each natural language token that the program is designed to care about. In the interest of simplification, we are willing to take risks, pay the price of making sacrifices, and accept blindnesses. Hence, many expressions in the input are disregarded and bypassed as irrelevant (not worth processing), e.g. articles, most adverbs, punctuation, meaningless strings such as "the thing is that". Our intuitive judgments about the relevance to a context-set is the central decision-making problem here.

The program attempts to cull, distill, glean, winnow out, extract nuggets or kernels of meaning by constructing patterns. The program pairs word-tokens with semantic categories and assembles or links them into conceptual patterns, i. e. patterns that have meaning for the idiolect of the program. The stored patterns serve as types with the constructed patterns acting as tokens to possibly fit the types. Depending on the length of the input (which is often paragraphic in size), a cluster of semantic patterns is assembled. Each pattern constructed from the input is compared for similarity to a LHS pattern stored in the data-base. If a concordance is found, the stored LHS conceptual pattern becomes a potential candidate for producing a RHS output response.

The interpreter for the production system constructs patterns by substituting concept labels for the input tokens according to the assignment functions in the thesauric data-base. By ignoring and excluding "don't cares" as non-relevant, the left-to-right concatenated patterns are much simpler than the natural language input sequences. The strategy here is consonant with the natural science strategy of abstraction and simplification by stripping away unessential details. A great range and diversity of manifest patterns of phenomena are pared down by many-to-few transforms and are converted into a much smaller set of stringent underlying patterns in order to make the problem more tractable.

From the set of concordant patterns constructed and fitted, a best-fit pattern is selected as most pertinent and preferred according to a variety of criteria. If there is a tie in the selection process, a random selection of the best-fit is made from the ties constructed. If none of the constructed patterns fit, the program is in a PUNT situation. (In US football, it is a joke that whereas you have four downs, when you don't know what to do on third down, you punt). In this sort of breakdown, the program has two options for recovery. First, it can offer a question or assertion about the topic under discussion or second, it can return to the text mode of the program to the point where it left off to enter the dialogue mode. If he wishes, the user can abort the return to the text and return to the dialogue mode by pressing a special key.

The program has a memory stack for anaphoric reference and for keeping track of topics under discussion. Once a specific LHS pattern is selected, it is time for an associated RHS response to be produced.

3.3 Output Responses

Each LHS pattern of a production rule is linked to a list of 3-10 RHS responses. These responses are ordinary language expressions of three syntactic and five semantic types. The syntactic response types are Questions, Requests, and Assertions. The semantic response types refer to Beliefs, Causes, Feelings, Desires, and Actions.

The RHS responses are partially ordered in respect to semantic intensity from milder to stronger as the dialogue proceeds. By the term 'stronger" here we mean the output expression points more directly to the user's personal intentional system.

Each RHS response is made up of a formula of constants and variables with a list of options for the variable placeholders. For example, in the assertion "You feel your wife nags you", the word "feel" has been randomly selected from the list "feel", "think", "believe", the word "wife" from the list "wife", "spouse", "mate", and the word "nags" from "nags", "berates", "criticizes". These lists are roughly synonymic but sometimes contain a contrast class or a "goes-with" expression. These constant-variable formulae allow the generation of a great variety of output surface expressions with holding power, an ability to keep the conversation going. Currently the program can generate about 600,000 responses in this way.

The meaningful content of the responses stem from our own psychologic inferences. The program does not reason from premise to conclusion on its own. To repeat, it is a specialized artifactual cognitive module, domain specific, informationally encapsulated, fast and shallow. It is a psychologic inference engine grinding out its authors' inferences. It succeeds partly because of its designed ignorance. The activity- specific knowledge structures are appropriate to their use.

They are not connected to explicitly tokened approximative descriptive propositional- content for reasonings. The inferences are implicit in the procedures and control logic of the program. For example, in the database there are no explicit declarative statements of propositions in the syllogistic form:
Premise #1: S is an F
Premise #2: (All, Most, Some) Fs are G
Conclusion: Therefore, S is a G

Premise #l corresponds to a fact, a situation involving an individual and a property. But the generalization of Premise #2 is absent from the data-base. The generalizations "honored" by Premise #2 reside entirely in the program authors' minds and are simply installed in the production rules in which implications are exhibited rather than described. I stress this point because many other programs explicitly declare their general inference rules in a world-knowledge data-base. Why don't we? Because we are following the venerable AI heuristic "don't do any more than you have to". The strategy of a specific applicational module is reflected in the words of the Rolling Stones and Immanuel Kant - "it may not get you all you want but it may get you all you need". For our special modular purposes, prepositional encyclopedic world-knowledge qualifies as a candidate for Ockham's razor.

To illustrate this procedure of a program knowing what to do rather than figuring out what to do, consider that a given input can serve as the premise for an indefinite and unbounded number of inferences. Suppose the user's input is:
USER - My wife is very beautiful.

What might such an expression imply? (I have read somewhere that the singular noun phrase "my wife" has 16 meanings).
"Every utterance is deficient - it says less than it wishes to say. Every utterance is exuberant - it conveys more than it plans." Ortega y Gasset

The obvious superficial implications of the expression are that the user is a man, the user has a wife, the user is a husband, the user speaks English and so on. Which implications do we decide to care about? What is of semantic import here? The program might assert:

1. You are proud of having a beautiful wife.
2. Her physical appearance is of great importance to you.
3. Perhaps you worry she may be too attractive to other men.

Assertion (1) points to the user's speech act whose illocutionary force is a positively valued expression of his wife's merit. Assertion (2) points to the salience of physical appearance for the user. Assertion (3) points to a possible negatively-valued emotional concern with many potential jealousy ramifications. How do we decide on these particular implications?

It is to be noted that the module responds to the user's construal of his situations as he describes them. The module does not judge truth-conditions - is his wife really beautiful? It needs no predicate calculus for "proving" anything. Nor does it try to figure out the user's communicative intentions or meanings, i.e. the conceptual categories he uses to assign linguistic expressions. The module does not learn from experience. The modular processor does not provide or support an explanatory linguistic theory or model of what human users do in conversation. It lacks an ontological design of a tree structure carving up reality into types of entities the world contains such as found in CYC or Wordnet.

Our sense-making approach represents a form of mathematical engineering designed to produce effects we want to produce. The module is simply a practical tool, a communicative instrument whose operations were designed by us to serve our special teleonomic purposes. We, the authors, judiciously decided what output expressions would be relevant to collaboration with the user's efforts to change his way of thinking in order to alleviate his depression. The RHS responses derive from many years of experience with the properties and regularities of talk-therapy conversations. Judgments regarding how well we have achieved our aims can be arrived at by exercising the program yourselves in the demonstration sessions.

Here is an example of the dialogue mode in Lesson #1:

```
PROGRAM -  We were talking about your depressed
feelings. What else can you tell me about them?
USER - I have been down in the dumps now for six
months.
PROGRAM -  It must be a burden to feel so depressed.
USER - It is. I feel like I'm drowning in a swamp.
PROGRAM -  What in particular depresses you?
USER - Mornings. I can't get out of bed in the
morning.
PROGRAM -  It must be hard to get up when you have
nothing to look forward to.
USER - Right. I hate the idea of going to work.
PROGRAM -  What in particular don't you like about
your work?
USER - I have a dead-end job. I don't know which way
to turn.
PROGRAM -  What makes you feel you can't do anything
about your situation?
USER - I feel helpless to change anything.
PROGRAM -  Some of your feeling of helplessness comes
from a misconception that there is nothing you can do
on your own to improve your condition.
```

In my judgment, the current dialogue mode is good but not great. It is good to a first approximation. It is not as great as we are trying to get it to be. It has its shares of slippage, stumbles, faltering, glides, blindnesses, and outright irrelevant clanks that we continuously work on. There will always be room for improvement well into the next century.

4 Discussion

Numerous questions have been raised about our modular strategy. For example, does this module "understand" natural language? Much depends on who is asking the question and what one means by "understand". Often the issues are only terminological. If Searle, of Chinese Room fame, is asking the question, I would answer "No - it does not understand in your sense. It only behaves as if it understands, which is good enough to get the job done". Our modular processor can carry on conversations without having explicit propositional content-representations of what is being talked about.

To someone else, I might answer that the module has a type of restricted know-how understanding in that it knows how to react to the meaning-fors, the convention-governed word-meanings, of linguistic input but does not consult propositional content-carrying meaningful states of a representational system. The modular processor uses "she" as an anaphoric reference to wife but it does not contain the propositional knowledge that a wife is a woman. This know-that knowledge is only implicit in the control structures.

How does the module know what to do? We have designed it to do what it does, e.g. form patterns, fit them, and momically respond with the RHS of a production rule. It has skill in dealing with words properly in this context. Since its know-how knowledge of what to do is installed implicitly in condition-action production rules, its knowledge is not available for more general use, for example, by a central inference processor with encyclopedic knowledge or by other modules.

Is the dialogue mode a simulation of a human cognitive therapist? No - it is not intended to represent a simulation or imitation of a human therapist. At times the responses resemble those of a human but that is only because the program's authors simulate themselves in designing cogent responses, i. e. responses consistent with the interpretation that the program has a therapeutic intent. Recall my mention of the virtual person in the dialogue mode. This conversational participant says many things a human therapist would never say, e.g. "I am sure my programmers would be glad to hear that" in response to a user compliment. Who is this "I" and "my"? It is a conversational participant with a particular character and set of attitudes that we have constructed. One might view its presence as a type of theater, thus lending the flavor of an art-form to the program.

Is our modular artifact intelligent? Yes and no. It selects the right thing to do at the right time under the circumstances and under time constraints. But it obviously is not a complete or general intelligent agent.

Early on I alluded to an ontological point about sense-making and deponent verbs. These verbs, such as "think", derive from Latin passives with an active sense. Do I think or is there something in me that thinks? Nowadays we seldom use the archaic "methinks" but we still say "it occurred to me".

What is agent and what is patient? Is thinking something I do or something that happens to me? Or both? What agent deserves the deictic "I"? Does our module think, or are we building only a talker rather than a thinker? Does it make sense, or is it just a proxy, a stand-in for its authors' sense-making? These are deep metascientific questions about the knowing subject, subjectivity, and intentionality that we can leave philosophers of mind to struggle with.

5 Conclusion

In this account, I have sketched the background and workings of a specialized dialogue module designed to conduct and sustain a cognitive therapy conversation for users suffering from depression. It contributes to a program that does effective therapeutic work in the world. I have pointed out some aspects of, not only what the dialogue module does, but also what it does not and cannot do. The module operates in unrestricted colloquial natural language typical of a talk-therapy context. The dialogue mode is not designed for idle conversation. Talk about the weather does not attempt to influence the weather but therapy talk about a user's thinking attempts to influence that thinking. The dialogue mode is teleologically job-oriented, and job-committed towards cognitive therapy with all the advantages, shortcomings, and sacrifices of such an approach.

As a final exhortation about human-computer conversations in general, whether casual, computer-as-companion, or job-oriented, I would urge everyone to see to it that the computer participants try to become interesting, spontaneous, stimulating, engaging, arousing, enabling, enjoyable, encouraging, captivating, surprising, fascinating, thoughtful, informative, illuminating, humorful and even exhibit some esthetic merit.

References

Colby, K.M., Watt, J. and Gilbert, J. 1966. A computer method for psychotherapy. Journal of Nervous and Mental Disease, 142 : 148-152.

Colby, K.M. and Enea, H. 1967. Heuristic methods for computer understanding of natural language in context restricted on-line dialogues. Mathematical Biosciences, I : 1-15.

Colby, K. M. 1981. Modeling a paranoid mind. Behavioral and Brain Sciences, 4 : 515-560.

Colby, K.M., Colby, P.M. and Stoller, R.J. 1990. Dialogues in natural language with GURU, a psychologic inference engine. Philosophical Psychology, 3 : 171-186.

Colby, K.M., Gould, R., Aronson, G. and Colby, P.M. 1991. A model of common sense reasoning underlying intentional nonaction in stressful interpersonal situations and its application in the technology of computer psychotherapy. Journal of Intelligent Systems, 1 : 259-272.

Colby, K.M. 1995. A computer program using cognitive therapy to treat depressed patients. Psychiatric Services, 46 : 1223-1225.

Parkison, R.C., Colby, K.M. and Faught, W. 1977. Conversational language comprehension using integrated pattern-matching and parsing. Artificial Intelligence, 9: 111-134. Reprinted in Readings in Natural Language Processing, Grosz, B., Jones, K.S., Webber, B.L. (Eds.) 1986. Morgan Kaufman Publishers, Inc., Los Altos, CA.

Simon, J.L. 1993. Good Mood: The New Psychology of Overcoming Depression, La Salle,

Illinois, Open Court Press.
Wilks, Y.A., Slator, B.M. and Guthrie, L.M. 1996. Electric Words: Dictionaries, Computers and Meanings. MIT Press, Cambridge, MA.

4 Architectural Considerations for Conversational Systems

G. Görz, J. Spilker, V. Strom and H. Weber

1 Conversational Requirements for Verbmobil

Verbmobil[1] is a large German joint research project in the area spontaneous speech-to-speech translation systems which is sponsored by the German Federal Ministry for Research and Education. In its first phase (1992-1996) ca. 30 research groups in universities, research institutes and industry were involved, and it entered its second phase in January 1997. The overall goal is develop a system which supports face-to-face negotiation dialogues about the scheduling of meetings as its first domain, which will be enlarged to more general scenarios during the second project phase. For the dialogue situation it is assumed that two speakers with different mother tongues (German and Japanese) have some common knowledge of English. Whenever a speaker's knowledge of English is not sufficient, the Verbmobil system will serve him as a speech translation device to which he can talk in his native language.

So, Verbmobil is a system providing assistance in conversations as opposed to fully automatic conversational systems. Of course, it can be used to translate complete dialogue turns. Both types of conversational systems share a lot of common goals, in particular utterance understanding - at least as much as is required to produce a satisfactory translation, processing of spontaneous speech phenomena, speech generation, and robustness in general. A difference can be seen in the fact that an autonomous conversational system needs also a powerful problem solving component for the domain of discourse, whereas for a translation system the amount of domain knowledge is limited by the purpose of translation, where most of the domain specific problem solving - except tasks like calendrical computations - has to be done by the dialog partners.

A typical dialogue taken from the Verbmobil corpus is the following:

<SIL> GUTEN TAG HERR KLEIN
<SIL> K-ONNEN WIR UNS AM MONTAG TREFFEN
<SIL> JA DER MONTAG PA-ST MIR NICHT SO GUT
<SIL> JA DANN TREFFEN WIR UNS DOCH AM DIENSTAG
<SIL> AM DIENSTAG HABE ICH LEIDER EINE VORLESUNG
<SIL> BESSER W-ARE ES BEI MIR AM MITTWOCH MITTAGS
<SIL> ALSO AM MITTWOCH UM ZEHN BIS VIERZEHN UHR HABE ICH ZEIT
<SIL> DANN LIEBER GLEICH NACH MEINEM DOKTORANDENTREFFEN
<SIL> WOLLEN WIR UNS NICHT LIEBER IN MEINEM B-URO TREFFEN
<SIL> NA JA DAS W-URDE GEHEN
<SIL> JA HERR KLEIN WOLLEN WIR NOCH EINEN TERMIN AUSMACHEN
<SIL> VIELLEICHT GINGE ES AM MITTWOCH IN MEINEM B-URO
<SIL> DAS IST DER VIERZEHNTE MAI
<SIL> AM MITTWOCH DEN VIERZEHNTEN PA-ST ES MIR NICHT SO GUT
<SIL> AM DIENSTAG IN DIESER WOCHE H-ATTE ICH NOCH EINEN TERMIN
<SIL> ALSO DANN AM DIENSTAG DEN DREIZEHNTEN MAI
<SIL> VORMITTAGS ODER AM NACHMITTAG
<SIL> JA MACHEN SIE DOCH EINEN VORSCHLAG
<SIL> JA DANN LASSEN SIE UNS DOCH DEN VORMITTAG NEHMEN
<SIL> JA GUT TSCH-U-S
<SIL> = "silence".

2 Prosody and Spontaneous Speech Phenomena

To cope with spontaneous speech, prosody plays a decisive role. Integration of prosody into a speech-to-speech translator as an additional speech language interface is a current topic of research. Within the Verbmobil project, the experimental system INTARC was designed which performs simultaneous speech-to-speech translation (cf. Görz et al., 1996; Amtrup et al., 1997). In INTARC, particular emphasis has been put on the issues of *incrementality* and (top-down) *component interaction* in order to take into account expectations and predictions from higher level linguistic components for lower level components. For this purpose time synchronous versions of traditional processing steps such as word recognition, parsing, semantic analysis and transfer had to be developed. In part completely new algorithms had to be designed in order to achieve sufficient processing performance to compensate for the lack of right context in search. The use of prosodic phrase boundaries became essential to reduce search space in parsing and semantic analysis.

A further goal was robustness: If a detailed linguistic analysis fails, the system should be able to produce an approximately correct output. For this purpose, besides the main data flow the system has a second template-based transfer strategy as a supplement, where a rough transfer is performed on the basis of prosodically focused words and a dialogue act detection.

Furthermore, various spontaneous speech phenomena like pauses, interjections, and false starts are covered by INTARC's dialogue turn based unification grammar (cf. Kasper and Kreiger, 1996; Kasper and Kreiger, 1996a).

3 Incremental, Interactive, and Time Synchronous Processing

The general design goals of the INTARC system architecture were time synchronous processing as well as incrementality and interactivity as a means to achieve a higher degree of robustness and scalability. Interactivity means that in addition to the bottom-up (in terms of processing levels) data flow the ability to process top-down restrictions considering the same signal segment for all processing levels. The construction of INTARC 2.0, which has been operational since fall 1996, followed an engineering approach focussing on the integration of symbolic (linguistic) and stochastic (recognition) techniques which led to a generalization of the concept of a "one pass" beam search. Fig. 1, which is a screen shot of INTARC's user interface, gives an overview of the overall system architecture.

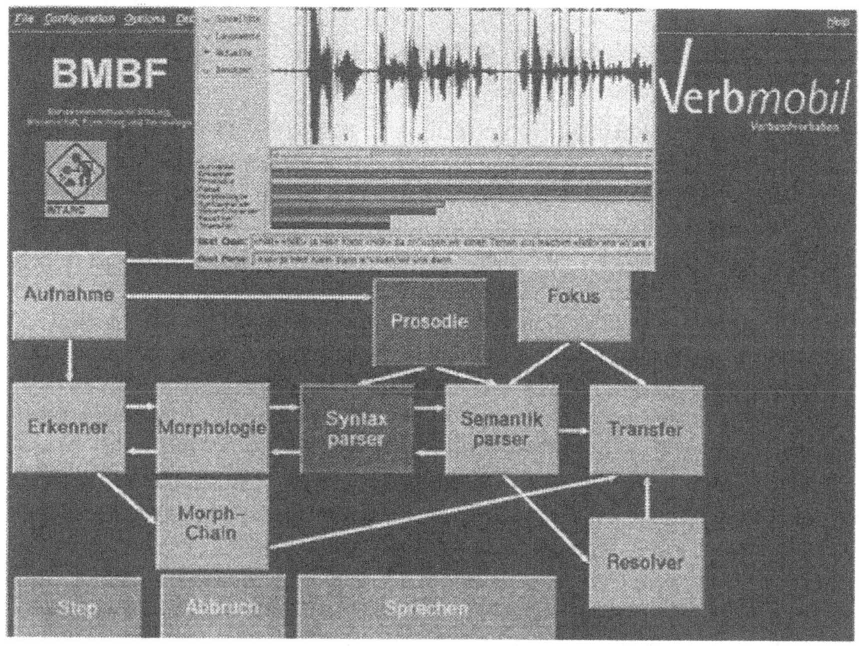

Figure 1: The architecture of INTARC 2.0

To enable component interaction, we designed the communication framework ICE (Amtrup, 1995; Amtrup and Benra, 1996) which maps an abstract channel model onto interprocess communication. Its software basis is PVM (Parallel Virtual Machine), supporting heterogeneous locally or globally distributed applications. The actual version of ICE runs on four hardware platforms and five operating systems with interfaces to eight programming languages or dialects.

4 Interactions between Recognizer, SynParser, SemParser, and Prosody

To understand the operation of INTARC, we start with an overview of its syntactic parser component (SynParser). Whereas the dialogue turn based grammar of the system is a full unification grammar written in HPSG, SynParser uses only the (probabilistically trained) context-free backbone of the unification grammar - which overgenerates - *and* a context-sensitive probabilistic model of the original grammar's derivations. In particular, the following preprocessing steps had to be executed:

1. Parse a corpus with the original unification grammar *G* to produce an ambiguous tree bank *B*.
2. Build a stripped-down (type skeleton) grammar *G'* such that for every rule *r'* in *G'* there is a corresponding rule *r* in *G* and vice versa.
3. Use an unsupervised reestimation procedure to train *G'* on *B* (context sensitive statistics).

The syntactic parser (SynParser) is basically an incremental probabilistic search engine based on (Weber, Spiker and Görz, 1997) (for earlier versions cf. Weber, 1994; Weber, 1995)), it receives word hypotheses and phrase boundary hypotheses as input. The input is represented as a chart where frames correspond to chart vertices and word hypotheses are edges which map to pairs of vertices. Word boundary hypotheses (WBHs) are mapped to connected sequences of vertices which lie inside the time interval in which the WBH has been located. The search engine tries to build up trees according to a probabilistic context free grammar supplied with higher order Markov probabilities. Partial tree hypotheses are uniformly represented as chart edges. The search for the *n* best output trees consists of successively combining pairs of edges to new edges guided by an overall beam search strategy. The overall score of a candidate edge pair is a linear combination of three factors which we call decoder factor, grammar factor and prosody factor. The decoder factor is the well-known product of the acoustic and bigram scores of the sequences of word hypotheses covered by the two connected edges. The grammar factor is the normalized grammar model probability of creating a certain new analysis edge given the two input edges. The prosody factor (see next section) is calculated from the acoustic WBH scores and a class based tetragram which models sequences of words and phrase boundaries.

So, SynParser performs purely probabilistic parsing without unifications. Only n best trees are transmitted to the semantic parser component (SemParser) to be reconstructed deterministically with unification. SemParser uses a chart for representation and reuse of partial analyses. On failure, it issues a top-down request to SynParser. Because we make heavy use of structure sharing (to depth n) for all chart edges we were able to achieve polynomial runtime. So, the main processing steps along the path recognizer - SynParser - SemParser are the following:

- The *recognizer (decoder)* performs a beam search producing a huge lattice of word hypotheses.
- *SynParser* performs a beam search on this lattice to produce a small lattice of tree hypotheses.
- *SemParser* executes the unification steps in order to pick the best tree that unifies.
- Incremental bottom-up and top-down interaction of syntactic and semantic analysis are achieved by chart reconstruction and revision in SemParser.
- Furthermore, bottom-up input from recognizer is provided via a morphology module (MORPHY (Althoff et al., 1996)) for compound nouns.

First experiments resulted in a runtime of approximately 30 times real time (on a SuperSparc) and a recognition rate for *words in valid trees* of approximately 50%. Current work is focussing on fine tuning for word recognition, morphology, syntactic and semantic parsing.

In the following we describe the interactions between the components mentioned.

- **Interaction Recognizer-SynParser (cf. Hauenstein and Weber, 1994)**
  - The (left-hand side connected) word graph is being transmitted by endpoints bottom up.
  - Possible path extensions are being transmitted by starting points top down.
  - This leads to the following *effects*:
  - A dynamic modification of language perplexity for recognition;
  - Data reduction and search is being moved (partially) from recognizer to parser.
  - Top-down interactions make only sense if there are strong model restrictions (narrow domain).

- **Interaction SynParser-SemParser (cf. Kasper et al., 1996)**
  - Probabilistic Viterbi parsing of word graphs with G' in polynomial time (without unifications).
  - Packing and transmission of n best trees(only trees with utterance status!) per frame in O(#treenodes) time complexity.
  - Protocol with powerful data compression.
  - Trees are being reconstructed by SemParser by means of G deterministically. On failure a top-down request for the next best tree is being issued.
  - On failure, a top-down request for the next best tree is being issued.
  - Structure sharing (to depth n) for all edges results in *polynomial runtime*
  - This yields a preference for the longest valid utterance.

A 100% tree recognition rate results in unification grammar parsing in cubic time. So, in our case lattice parsing is tree recognition (decoding):

- For each new frame, a vertex and an empty agenda of search steps are created.
- All word hypotheses ending in the actual frame are read in as edges and all pairs of edges which can be processed are being scored and pushed on the agenda for that frame.
- The score is a weighted linear combination of log probability scores given by the models for acoustics, bigram, grammar and prosody.
- As in an acoustic beam recognizer all steps down to a given offset from the maximum score are taken and all others are discarded.
- The procedure stops when the word recognizer - which supplies word hypotheses with acoustic scores - sends an end of utterance signal.

The interaction protocol implies that the first tree to be transmitted is the best scored one: SynParser constructs its chart incrementally, always sending the best hypotheses which have utterance status. SemParser reconstructs the trees incrementally and reports failures. While SemParser is working - which may lead to a rejection of this tree - SynParser runs in parallel and finds some new trees. The failure messages are ignored as long as SemParser is still constructing trees. If SemParser becomes inactive, further hypotheses with a lower score are sent. SemParser utilizes its idle time to reconstruct additional trees which may become important during the analysis ("speculative evaluation"). i.e., if the estimation of an utterance improves over time, its subtrees are in general not accessible to SemParser, since they have never got a high score. With speculative evaluation, however, we often find that they have already been constructed, which helps to speed up parsing. Since our grammar is turn-based, this situation is not the exception, but in fact the normal case. Hence, this strategy guarantees that the utterance spanned by the trees increases monotonously in time.

A second phase is entered if SynParser has reached the end of the word lattice. In the case that SemParser has accepted one of the previous trees as a valid reading, SynParser is being informed about the success. Otherwise SemParser calls for further tree hypotheses. The selection criteria for the next best hypothesis are exactly the same as in the first phase: “Long” hypotheses are preferred, and in the case of equal length the one with the best internal score is chosen. i.e., in the second phase the length of a potential utterance decreases. If none of the requested trees are accepted, the process stops if SynParser makes no further trees available. This parameter controls the duration of the second phase.

Depending on the choice which trees are sent, SynParser directs the behavior of SemParser. This is the essential reason why SemParser must not perform a search over the whole set of received hypotheses.

The stepwise reduction of the length of hypotheses guarantees that the longest possible valid utterance will be found. This is particularly useful to analyze utterance parts when no fully spanning reading can be found.

To summarize, the advantages of this protocol are that no search must be performed by SemParser, that the best tree which covers the longest valid utterance is being preferred (graceful degradation) and that dynamic load-balancing is achieved.

5 Issues in Processing Spontaneous Speech: Prosody and Speaker Style

5.1 Prosody

The decisive role of prosody for processing spontaneous speech has already been mentioned. Now we describe the integration of prosodic information into the analysis process from an architectural viewpoint. The **interaction Parser-Prosody** can be summarized as follows:

- Bottom-up hypotheses on the word boundary class are time intervals; they are attached incrementally to word lattice nodes.
- A prosodic score is computed from the word path, a trigram for words and phrase boundaries and an acoustic score for phrase boundaries (maximized).
- Prosody detectors are based on statistical classifiers, having been trained with prosodically labeled data.
- No use of word information is made; time assignment is done through syllabic nucleus detection.

- Recognition rates are: for accents 78%, for phrase boundaries 81%, and for sentence mood 85%

The prosody module consists of two independently working parts: the phrase boundary detector (Strom, 1995) and the focus detector (Petzold, 1995).

The data material investigated consists of spontaneous spoken dialogues on appointment scheduling. A subset of 80 minutes speech has been prosodically labeled: Full prosodic phrases (B3 boundaries) are distinguished from intermediate phrases (B2 boundaries). Irregular phrase boundaries are labeled with B9, and the default label for a word boundary is B0. The B2 and B3 boundaries correspond roughly to the linguistic concept of phrase boundaries, but are not necessarily identical (cf. Strom, 1996).

In the phrase boundary detector, first a parameterization of the fundamental frequency and energy contour is obtained by calculating eleven features per frame: F0 is interpolated in unvoiced segments and decomposed by three band pass filters. F0, its components, and the time derivatives of those four functions yield eight F0 features which describe the F0 contour at that frame globally and locally. Furthermore three bands of a short-time FFT followed by median smoothing are used as energy features.

The phrase boundary detector then views a window of (if possible) four syllables. Its output refers to the syllable boundary between the second and the third syllable nucleus (in the case of a 4-syllable window). Syllables are found by a syllabic nucleus detector based on energy features derived from the speech signal. For each window a large feature vector is constructed.

A Gaussian distribution classifier was trained to distinguish between all combinations of boundary types and tones. The classifier output was then mapped on the four classes B0, B2, B3, and B9. The a posteriori probabilities are used as confidence measure. When taking the boundary with maximal probability the recognition rate for a test set of 30 minutes is 80.76%, average recognition rate is 58.85%.

The focus detection module of INTARC works with a rule-based approach. The algorithm tries to solve focus recognition by global description of the utterance contour, in a first approach represented by the fundamental frequency F0. A reference line is computed by detecting significant minima and maxima in the F0 contour. The average values between the maximum and minimum lines yield the global reference line. Focus accents occur mainly in the areas of steepest fall in the F0 course. Therefore, in the reference line the points with the highest negative gradient were determined first in each utterance. To determine the position of the focus the nearest maximum in this region has been used as approximation.

The recognition rate is 78.5% and the average recognition rate is 66.6%. The focus detection module sends focus hypotheses to the semantic module and to the module for transfer and generation.

In a recent approach, phrase boundaries from the detector described above where integrated in the algorithm. After optimization of the algorithm even higher rates are expected.

As mentioned in the last section, one of the main benefits of prosody in the INTARC system is the use of prosodic phrase boundaries inside the word lattice search.

When calculating a prosody factor for an edge pair, we pick the WBH associated with the connecting vertex of the edges. This WBH forms a sequence of WBHs and word hypotheses if combined with the portions already spanned by the pair of edges. Tests for the contribution of the prosody factor to the overall search lead to the following results: For a testset with relative simple semantic structure the use of the detected phrase boundaries increased the word recognition rate[2] from 84% to 86% and reduced the number of edge pairs (as a measure for the run time) by 40%. For the 'harder' Verbmobil dialogues prosody raised the word recognition rate from 48.2% to 53.2% leaving the number of edge pairs unchanged.

In INTARC, the transfer module performs a dialog act based translation. In a traditional deep analysis it gets its input (dialog act and feature structure) from the semantic evaluation module. In an additional path a flat transfer is performed with the best word chain from the word recognition module and with focus information.

During shallow processing the focus accents are aligned to words. If a focus is on a content word a probabilistically selected dialog act is chosen. This dialog act is then expanded to a translation enriched with possible information from the word chain.

Flat transfer is only used when deep analysis fails. First results show that the 'focus-driven' transfer produces correct - but sometimes reduced - results for about 50% of the data. For the other half of the utterances information is not sufficient to get a translation; only 5% of the translations are absolutely wrong.

While the deep analysis uses prosody to reduce search space and disambiguate in cases of multiple analyses, the 'shallow focus based translation' can be viewed as directly driven by prosody.

5.2 Speaker Style

A new issue in Verbmobil's second phase are investigations on speaker style. It is well known that system performance depends on the perplexity of the language models involved. Consequently, one of the main problems is to reduce the perplexity of the models in question. The common way to approach this problem is to specialize the models by additional knowledge about contexts. The traditional n-gram model uses a collection of conditional distributions instead of one single probability distribution. Normally, a fixed length context of immediately preceding words is used. Since the length of the word contexts is bound by data and computational resources, practicable models could only be achieved by restricting the application domain of a system. Commonly used n-gram models define $P(w|C,D)$ where C is a context of preceding words and D is an application domain. But also finer grained restrictions have been tested in the last decade, e.g. a cache-based n-gram (Kuhn and DeMori, 1990).

Intuitively, every speaker has its own individual speaking style. The question is whether it is possible to take advantage of this fact. The first step towards specialized speaker models is to prove whether sets of utterances sorted by speakers show significant differences in the use of syntactic structure at all. So, first of all the whole corpus has been tagged with POS-categories grounded on syntactic properties of words (for tagger and POS-categories see Schmid, 1995). Using the whole corpus, we determined an empirical distribution D_{all} over these categories. In order to separate the corpus in typical and non typical speakers we checked the distribution D_s of every speaker s against D_{all} using the Chi-square test. While we can't say anything about the usage of syntax by non-typical speakers, there is evidence that typical speakers make a similar use of syntax in a rough sense. With a significance level of 0.01 the test rejects 23.6% of the speakers.

Using this first partitioning, bi- and trigram models were estimated on the basis of the typical speakers and on the whole corpus in comparison. On a test set of normal speakers only the specialized models showed a slightly higher perplexity than the more general models. In contrast to this the specialization explored with automatic clustering using the K-means method shows a slightly better perplexity on most of the test set speakers. As a distance measure we take difference of two bigrams. The relatively small improvement with specialized models due to the small amount of data. Even partitioning of the corpus into few classes leads to a lot of unseen pairs among the specialized bigrams. Hence a general model trained on a larger amount of data could produce better results.

Using the results of the experiments above as a guideline we chose a clustering procedure using a different clustering criterion. The procedure is adapted from automatic word clustering (Ueberla, 1994; Martin, Liermann and Ney, 1995). The goal of the procedure is to find a partition such that the perplexity of the specialized models is being minimized. To reduce the parameter problem we used a class-based n-gram instead of the word-based bigram. Class-based n grams estimate the probability of a word sequence $w_1 \ldots w_n$

by

$$\prod_{i=1}^{n} P(w_i | C(w_i)) * P(C(w_i) | C(w_i - 1)) \quad \text{bigram class model}$$

or

$$\prod_{i=1}^{n} P(w_i | C(w_i)) * P(C(w_i) | C(w_i - 2) C(w_i - 1)) \quad \text{trigram class model}$$

where $C(w)$ denotes the class of word w. $P(w_i|C(w_i))$ is called the lexical part and $P(C(w_i)|C(w_{i-1}))$ resp. $P(C(w_i)|C(w_{i-2})C(w_{i-1}))$ the grammatical part of the model. We performed three different experiments to get an impression how speaking style affects the lexical and grammatical part:

1. 2POS test: $P(w_i|C(w_i))$ is assumed to be invariant. Only the grammatical part $P(C(w_i)|C(w_{i-1}))$ is adapted to every cluster.
2. 3POS test: $P(w_i|C(w_i))$ is assumed to be invariant. Only the grammatical part $P(C(w_i)|C(w_{i-1})C(w_{i-2}))$ is adapted to every cluster.
3. POS/word: Both parts are considered.

First clustering tests showed good results:

The best result was achieved by adapting both parts of the class model. This fact corresponds with the intuitive expectation that speaking style influences the selection of words and grammar rules.

	Reduction
2POS	6.5%
3POS	1.9%
POS/word	10%

Table 1: Reduction of test set perplexity

6 Recognition Results for INTARC 2.0

For INTARC 2.0, a series of experiments has been carried out in order to also compare empirically an incremental and interactive system architecture with more traditional ones and to get hints for tuning individual components and their interactions.

Basically, we tested three different module configurations:

DM Decoder, Morphy (acoustic word recognition)

DMP Decoder, Morphy, Lattice Parser (word recognition in parsed utterances)

DMPS Decoder, Morphy, Lattice Parser, Semantic Module (word recognition in understood utterances)

These configurations correspond to successively harder tasks, namely to recognize, to analyze and to "understand".

We used the NIST scoring program for word accuracy to gain comparable results. By doing this we gave preference to a well known and practical measure although we know that it is in some way inadequate. In a system like INTARC 2.0, the analysis tree is of much higher importance than the recovered string. With the general goal of spontaneous speech translation a good semantic representation for a string with word errors is more important than a good string with a completely wrong reading. Because there does not yet exist a tree bank with correct readings for our grammar, we had no opportunity to measure something like a "tree recognition rate" or "rule accuracy".

The word accuracy results in DMP and DMPS can not be compared to word accuracy as usually applied to an acoustic decoder in isolation, whereas the DM values can be compared in this way. In DMP and DMPS we counted only those words as recognized which could be built into a valid parse from the beginning of the utterance. Words to the right, which could not be integrated into a parse, were counted as deletions - although they might have been correct in standard word accuracy terms. Our evaluation method is much harder than standard word accuracy, but it appears to be a good approximation to "rule accuracy". What cannot be parsed is being counted as an error. The difference between DMP and DMPS is that a tree produced by the statistical approximation grammar can be ruled out when being rebuilt by unification operations in semantic processing. The loss in recognition performance from DMP and DMPS corresponds to the quality of the statistical approximation. If the approximation grammar had a 100% tree recognition, there would be no gap between DMP and DMPS.

The recognition rates of the three configurations were measured in three different contexts. The first row shows the rates of normal bottom-up processing. In the second row, the results of the phrase boundary detector are used to disambiguate for syntax and semantics. The third row shows the results of the system in top-down mode; here no semantic evaluation is done because top-down predictions only affect the interface between SynParser and Recognizer.

	DM	DMP	DMPS
Word Accuracy	93.9%	83.3%	47.5%
WA with phrase boundary	93.9%	84.0%	48.6%
WA in TD-Mode	94.0%	83.4%	--

Table 2: Recognition rates

7 Conclusions

Splitting composite nouns to reduce the recognizer lexicon shows good results. Search and rebuilding performed by the morphology module is implemented as a finite state automaton, so there is no great loss in performance. Incremental recognition is as good as the standard decoding algorithms, but the lattices are up to ten times larger. This causes a performance problem for the parser. So we use an approximation of an HPSG-Grammar for search such that syntactic analysis becomes more or less a second decoding step. By regarding a wider context, we even reduce the recognition gap between syntax and semantics in comparison with our previous unification-based syntax parser (see Weber, 1994; Weber, 1995). For practical usability the tree-recognition rate must be improved. This can be achieved with a bigger training set. The dialogues we used contained only 83 utterances. Further improvement can be achieved by a larger context during training to get a better approximation of the trees built by the unification grammar.

Prediction of words seems to have no influence on the recognition rate. This is a consequence of the underlying domain. Since the HSPG grammar is written for spontaneous speech, nearly every utterance should be accepted. The grammar gives no restrictions on possible completions of an utterance. Restrictions can be only obtained by a narrow beam-bound when compiling the prediction table. But this leads to a lower recognition rate because some correct words are pruned.

Acknowledgements

We are grateful to all our colleagues within the Verbmobil subproject on "Architecture" from the universities of Bielefeld, Bonn, Hamburg, and from DFKI Saarbruecken without whose contributions within the last four years this article could not have been written.

References

Althoff, F., Drexel, G., Lüngen, H., Pampel, M. and Schillo, Ch. 1996. The Treatment of Compounds in a Morphological Component for Speech Recognition. In: Gibbon, D. (Ed.): Natural Language Processing and Speech Technology. Results of the 3rd KONVENS Conference, Berlin: Mouton de Gruyter.

Amtrup, J. 1995. ICE-INTARC Communication Environment: User's Guide and Reference Manual. Version 1.4. Verbmobil Technical Document 14, Univ. of Hamburg.

Amtrup, J., Benra, J. 1996. Communication in large distributed AI systems for natural language processing. Proc. of COLING-96, Kopenhagen, 35-40.

Amtrup, J., Drexel, G., Görz, G., Pampel, M., Spilker, J. and Weber, H. 1997. The parallel time-synchronous speech-to-speech system INTARC 2.0. Proc. of ACL-97.

Carter, D. 1994. Improving Language Models by Clustering Training Sentences. Proc. of ANLP '94, Stuttgart, Germany. Extended version in http://xxx.lanl.gov/cmp-lg/.

Görz, G., Kesseler, M., Spilker, J. and Weber, H. 1996. Research on Architectures for Integrated Speech/Language Systems in Verbmobil. Proc. of COLING-96, Kopenhagen.

Hauenstein, A., Weber, H. 1994. An investigation of tightly coupled time synchronous speech language interfaces. Proceedings of KONVENS-94, Vienna, Austria. Berlin: Springer.

Kasper, W. and Krieger, H.-U. 1996. Integration of prosodic and grammatical information in the analysis of dialogs. In: Görz, G., Hölldobler, S. (Ed.): Proceedings of the 20th German Annual Conference on Artificial Intelligence, KI-96, Dresden. Berlin: Springer (LNCS).

Kasper, W. and Krieger, H.-U.1996. Modularizing codescriptive grammars for efficient parsing. Proc. of COLING-96, Kopenhagen, 628-633.

Kasper, W., Krieger, H.-U., Spilker J. and Weber, H. 1996. From word hypotheses to logical form: An efficient interleaved approach. In: Gibbon, D. (Ed.): Natural Language Processing and Speech Technology. Results of the 3rd KONVENS Conference, Berlin: Mouton de Gruyter, 77-88.

Kuhn, R. and DeMori, R 1990. A cache-based natural language model for speech recognition. IEEE Transactions on Pattern Analysis and Machine Intelligence, 12(6).

Martin, S., Liermann, J., Ney, H. 1995. Algorithms for Bigram and Trigram Word Clustering. Proc. EUROSPEECH-95, Madrid, 1253-1256.

Petzold, A. 1995. Strategies for focal accent detection in spontaneous speech. Proc. 13th ICPhS Stockholm, Vol. 3, 672-675.

Schmid, H. 1995. Improvements in Part-of-Speech Tagging with an Application to German. http://www.ims.uni-stuttgart.de/Tools/DecisionTreeTagger.html.

Strom, V. 1995. Detection of accents, phrase boundaries and sentence modality in German with prosodic features. Proc. EUROSPEECH-95, Madrid, 1995, 2039-2041.

Strom, V. 1996. What's in the 'pure' prosody? Proc. ICSLP 96, Philadelphia.

Ueberla, J.P. 1994. An Extended Clustering Algorithm for Statistical Language Models, E-Print Archive Nr. 9412003, http://xxx.lanl.gov/cmp-lg/

Weber, H. 1994. Time Synchronous Chart Parsing of Speech Integrating Unification Grammars with Statistics. Speech and Language Engineering, Proceedings of the Eighth Twente Workshop on Language Technology, (L. Boves, A. Nijholt, Ed.), Twente, 107-119.

Weber, H. 1995. LR-inkrementelles probabilistisches Chartparsing von Worthypothesen-mengen mit Unifikationsgrammatiken: Eine enge Kopplung von Suche und Analyse. Ph.D. Thesis, University of Hamburg, Verbmobil Report 52.

Weber, H., Spilker, J., Görz, G. 1997. Parsing N Best Trees from a Word Lattice. In: Nebel, B. (Ed). Advances in Artificial Intelligence. Proceedings of the 21st German Annual Conference on Artificial Intelligence, KI-97, Freiburg. Berlin: Springer (LNCS).

Notes

[1] This work was funded by the German Federal Ministry for Research and Technology (BMFT) in the framework of the Verbmobil Project under Grant BMFT 01 IV 101 H / 9. The responsibility for the contents of this study lies with the authors.

[2] Only words that are part of a valid parse from the beginning of a turn are counted as recognized.

5 Conversational Multimedia Interaction

M.T. Maybury

1 Co-operative Multimedia Interfaces

More effective, efficient and natural human computer or computer mediated human-human interaction will require both automated understanding and generation of multimedia. Fluent conversational interaction demands explicit models of the user, discourse, task and context. It will also require a richer understanding of media (i.e., text, audio, video), both in its use in the interface to support interaction with the user as well as its use in access to content by the user during a session. Multimedia dialogue prototypes have been developed in several application domains including CUBRICON (for a mission planning domain) (Neal and Shapiro, 1991), XTRA (tax-form preparation) (Wahlster, 1991), AIMI (air mission planning) (Burger and Marshall, 1993), and AlFresco (art history information exploration) (Stock et al., 1993). Typically, these systems parse mixed (typically asynchronous) multimedia input and generate coordinated multimedia output. They also attempt to maintain coherency, cohesion, and consistency across both multimedia input and output. For example, these systems often support integrated language and deixis for both input and output. They extend research in discourse and user modeling (Kobsa and Wahlster, 1989) by incorporating representations of media to enable media (cross) reference and reuse over the course of a session with a user. These enhanced representations support the exploitation of user perceptual abilities and media preferences as well as the resolution of multimedia references (e.g. “Send this plane there” articulated with synchronous gestures on a map).

The details of discourse models in these systems, however, differ significantly. For example, CUBRICON represents a global focus space ordered by recency whereas AIMI represents a focus space segmented by the intentional structure of the discourse (i.e., a model of the domain tasks to be completed). While intelligent multimedia interfaces promise natural and personalized interaction, they remain complicated and require specialized expertise to build. One practical approach to achieving some of the benefits of these more sophisticated systems without the expense of developing full multimedia interpretation and generation components, was achieved in AlFresco (Stock et al., 1993), a multimedia information kiosk for Italian art exploration. By adding natural language processing to a traditional hypermedia system, AlFresco achieved the benefits of hypermedia (e.g. organization of heterogeneous and unstructured information via hyperlinks, direct manipulation to facilitate exploration) together with the benefits of natural language parsing (e.g. direct query of nodes, links, and subnetworks which provides rapid navigation). Providing a user with natural language within a hypertext system helps overcome the indirectness of the hypermedia web as well as disorientation and cognitive overhead caused by large amounts of typically semantically heterogeneous links representing relations as diverse as part-of, class-of, instance-of or elaboration-of. Also, as in other systems previously described (e.g. CUBRICON, TACTILUS), ambiguous gesture and language can yield a unique referent through mutual constraint. Finally, AlFresco incorporates simple natural language generation which can be combined with more complex canned text (e.g. art critiques) and images. Reiter, Mellish and Levine (1995) also integrated traditional language generation with hypertext to produce hypertext technical manuals. While practical systems are possible today, the multimedia interface of the future may have facilities that are much more sophisticated. These interfaces may include human-like agents that converse naturally with users, monitoring their interaction with the interface (e.g. key strokes, gestures, facial expressions) and the properties of those (e.g. conversational syntax and semantics, dialogue structure) over time and for different tasks and contexts. Equally, future interfaces will likely incorporate more sophisticated presentation mechanisms. For example, Pelachaud (1992) characterizes spoken language intonation and associated emotions (anger, disgust, fear, happiness, sadness, and surprise) and from these uses rules to compute facial expressions, including lip shapes, head movements, eye and eyebrow movements, and blinks. Finally, future multimedia interfaces should support richer interactions, including user and session adaptation, dialogue interruptions, follow-up questions, and management of focus of attention.

2 Intelligent Multimedia Browsing

An important element of future interaction is intelligent and intuitive interfaces to complex information spaces. For example, consider a visionary demonstration of interaction on the Internet prototyped for ARPA by MITRE, whose architecture is illustrated in Figure 1 (Smotroff, Hirschman and Bayer, 1995). The prototype addressed some limitations of Mosaic: disorientation in a web of hypertext, poor indexing of document collections, and untailored information presentation (ironically problems which remain today). The MITRE team augmented the existing X-Mosaic infrastructure with an event queue to manage interactions.

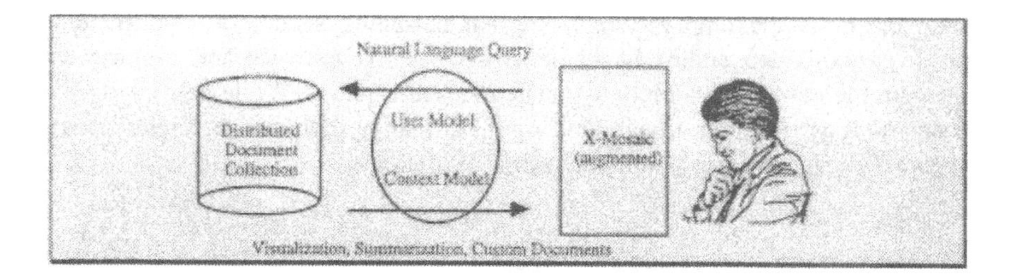

Figure 1: Intelligent Mosaic

More significantly, they adapted and integrated natural language processing and distributed document visualization capabilities to support the process of information exploration and retrieval from a database of joint venture documents representing different sources on joint ventures (e.g. Mead, Prompt, Wall Street Journal). First, a natural language understanding system for full-text understanding was applied to the document collection to generate database templates representing the joint venture objects and relationships represented in the content of the documents[1]. MITRE further integrated Carnegie Mellon University's Phoenix natural language parser to provide a natural language front-end to the document collection. Successful hits against a user query were then displayed in a visualization tool, essentially a matrix, with columns representing different information sources and rows representing a rank-ordered set of the most relevant documents. Color and size were used to emphasize individual document relevance. This adaptation of University of Maryland's TREEMAP visualization software further enabled the user to interatively refine their query, resulting in an updated color and size encoded visualization of the distributed document space. The user could either retrieve the full text of the document or request a summary of the document, generated automatically from the underlying database templates by MITRE's TEXPLAN system for natural language generation. A user model adapted output to user characteristics (e.g. their age, preferred language) and a discourse model interpreted queries in the context of their use (e.g. anaphoric expressions such as "the ones that are from Japan" are resolved automatically). Custom collections of documents could be generated on the fly based on a user query along with custom views (e.g. a table of contents page resulting from an ad-hoc collection of documents). A visionary facility for converting sources from one media to another (e.g. from a full-text article to a multimedia presentation) was also simulated.

An important aspect of the above demonstration was the ability to search on the content of the information, that is on the people, places, organizations, relationships, events and so on, mentioned in the document. Because automating this remains difficult, it was actually simulated by searching on the object-oriented answer keys developed for the Message Understanding Conference, which is focused on automated information extraction technology. Both automated extraction and machine translation of foreign documents remain important needs.

Also important is the ability to perform content-based search on multimedia sources (e.g. text, video, audio). In the demonstration, the user was able to retrieve video by simple keyword search of associated closed-captions. While this interface was primarily passive, other researchers are investigating more active, agent-based systems that engage the user in a mixed-initiative dialogue.

3 Visualizing Text with Graphics: FISH

Just as we can allocate information to particular media to support generation of more effective mixed media, so too we can exploit the properties of information and associated media to support other kinds of tasks, such as design or information retrieval ones. One application of information encoding using graphical devices is used in a tool called Forager for Information on the SuperHighway (FISH) (Smotroff, Hirschman and Bayer, 1995; Mitchell, 1996).

FISH supports the visualization of large, physically or logically distributed document collections. Figure 2a illustrates the application of FISH to three Wide Area Information Server (WAIS) databases containing information on joint ventures from the Message Understanding Conference (MUC) . Figure 2b

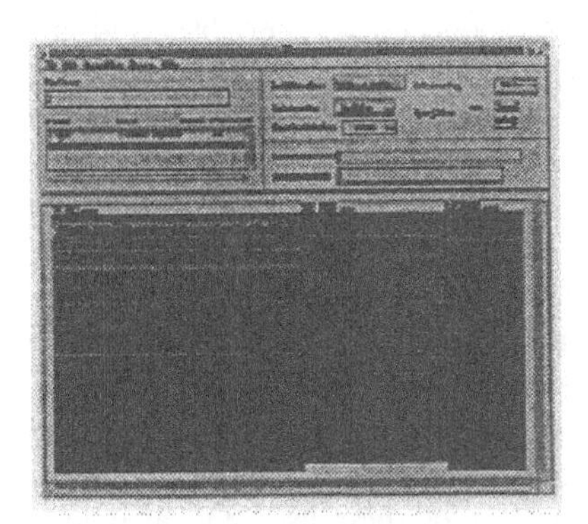

Figure 2a. WAIS FISH

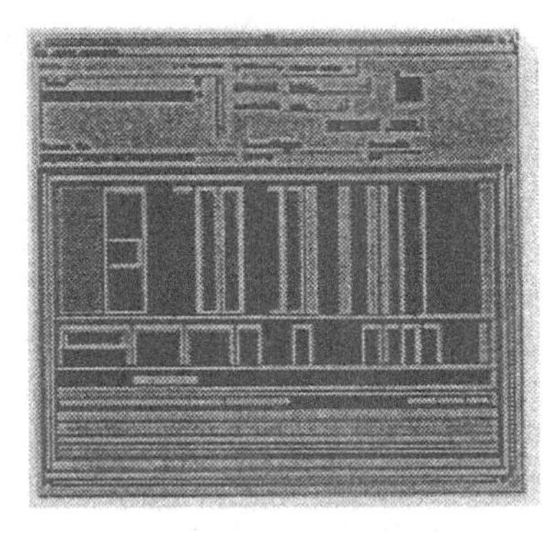

Figure 2b. NPR FISH

illustrates the application of FISH to visualize e-mail clustered by topic type for a moderator supporting a National Performance Review electronic town hall.

The traditional WAIS interface of a query box and a list of resulting hits is replaced by the interface shown in Figure 2, which includes a query box, a historical list of queries, and a graphically encoded display of resulting hits. Motivated by the University of Maryland's TreeMap research for hierarchical information visualization, FISH encodes the measure of relevance of each document to a given query (or set of compound queries) using both color saturation and size, the latter in an iterative fashion. In WAIS, the relevancy of a document to a given keyword query is measured on a scale from 1-1000 (where 1000 is the highest relevancy) by the frequency and location of (stems of) query keywords in documents.

In the example presented in Figure 2a, each database is allocated screen size in proportion to the number of and degree with which documents are relevant to the given query. For example, the MEAD database on the left of the output window is given more space than the PROMT database because it has many more relevant documents. Similarly, individual documents that have higher relevancy measures for a given query are given proportionally more space and higher color saturation. In this manner, a user can rapidly scan several large lists of documents to find relevant ones by focusing on those with higher color saturation and more space. Compound queries can be formulated via the "Document Restrictions" menu by selecting the union or intersection of previous queries (in effect an AND or OR Boolean operator across queries).

In Figure 2, the user has selected the union of documents relevant to the query "Japan" and the query "automobile", which will return all documents which contain the keywords "Japan" or "automobile". Color coding can be varied on these documents, for example, to keep their color saturation distinct (e.g. blue vs. red) to enable rapid contrast of hits across queries within databases (e.g. hits on Japan vs. hits on automobile) or to mix their saturation so that intersecting keyword hits can be visualized (e.g. bright blue-reds could indicate highly relevant Japanese automobile documents, dark the opposite). In the example in Figure 2a, blue encodes Japan, red Automobile; the color coding is set for mixed saturation, the union of the relevant document sets for those two keywords is selected, and the order (from top to bottom in the display) is used to encode the WAIS relevancy ranking.

4 Broadcast News Navigator

The explosion of multimedia information on our world wide information web is demanding more sophisticated tools to segment, browse, retrieve, extract, summarize and customize information captured in natural language text (written or typed), spoken language, graphics, imagery, and video or combinations thereof. One principal advantage of automatically generated presentations is that they include explicit representation of the underlying presentation semantics and intention. In contrast, most existing electronic documents do not. Even given richer document markup semantics, manually index materials remains time consuming and error-prone. Document markup may be as straightforward as typing hyperlinks (e.g. part-of, example-of, elaboration-of) or as detailed as identifying the entities and relations in text or images (e.g. objects, attributes, events, states, processes) to support detailed information extraction and query. For example, in navigating the World Wide Web, one cannot pose a query such as "Find me all video clips in the last six months from foreign broadcasts of no longer than 20 seconds long that show Boris Yeltsin and detail his heart condition".

To address this problem we have created the Broadcast News Navigator (BNN) TM, the user interface of which is illustrated in Figure 3. Unlike previous research (Shahraray and Gibbon, 1995; Stevens et al., 1994) BNN enables topic and story based browsing and retrieval of news. The application furthermore supports access to a knowledge base of facts extracted from performing a number of multistream analyses on broadcast news programs. Analysis tools process the imagery, audio and textual streams and store the gathered information in a relational and a video database management system. For example, image-processing algorithms are used to identify visual scene changes and to select the most meaningful keyframes for use during summarization. This selection is performed by taking advantage of the discourse structure of the news. For example, keyframes for a typical story containing a reporter segment are selected from the center of the reporter segment. For audio analysis, we utilize speaker change detection algorithms and silence detection to detect story changes. Finally, our most extensive processing is linguistic and operates on the closed caption textual stream. By integrating multistream analysis results using a time-enhanced finite state machine (Maybury et al., 1997), we are able to automatically detect commercials, story segments, and named entities.

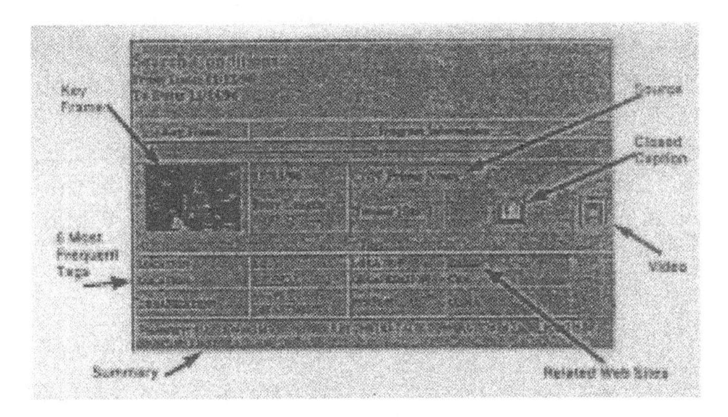

Figure 3. Viewing Story Segments that Meet Query Criteria

5 Discourse Analysis for Story Segmentation

Human communication is characterized by distinct discourse structure (Grosz and Sidner 1986) which is used for a variety of purposes including mitigating limited attention, signaling topic shifts, and as a cue for shift in interlocutor control. Motivated by this and after more general purpose text segmentation algorithms (Mani et al., 1997; Hearst, 1994) failed because of the short news segments in our corpus, we investigated the use of discourse structure to analyze broadcast news.

We identified three parallel sources of redundant segmentation cues that can be correlated and exploited to achieve higher precision segmentation information within the closed caption stream: structural analysis, closed caption operator cues, and discourse cues. Together they provide and recall. For example, structural analysis of CNN Prime News reveals a series of segments such as:

- Broadcasts always start and end with the anchor and a distinctive visual icon
- A preview or highlight of the day's news follows the broadcast start
- Commercials serve as story boundaries
- Each reporter segment is preceded by an introductory anchor segment and together they form a single story
- Weather is characterized by distinct visuals and meteorological language
- "coming up" segments signal subsequent reports

Other broadcast agencies such as the Jim Lehrer News Hour or ABC World News Tonight have similar characteristic structures (Maybury et al., 1997). This is important as this can be exploited to turn a monologue into an interactive news program in which a user can query and customize the news to their interests. For example, a user wishing to browse a one hour Jim Lehrer newscast need only to view a four minute opening summary and a 30 second preview of the major stories. Similarly, sponsor messages can be eliminated.

As we report in Maybury et al., (1997) and Mani et al., (1997), we have developed linguistic patterns which detect cues which signal the above program structure and have achieved performance in the 90+% range measured in terms of precision and recall of story segments. This, in spite of the fact that closed caption text presents a number of challenges, including errors created by upper case text and during transcription (e.g. errors of transposition, substitution and omission).

6 Named Entity Extraction

In addition to detecting segments and summarizing stories (for search or browsing), it is also important to extract information from video, including who did what to who, when, where and how, to support subsequent conversation. BNN enables a user to view a visualization of proper names (e.g. people, organizations, locations) extracted from closed captions associated with a broadcast video (see Figure 4). To achieve this, we have applied a proper name tagger from the Alembic System (Aberdeen et al., 1995). This trainable system applies the same general error-reduction learning approach used previously for generating part-of-speech rules designed by Brill (1995) to the problem of learning phrase identification rules.

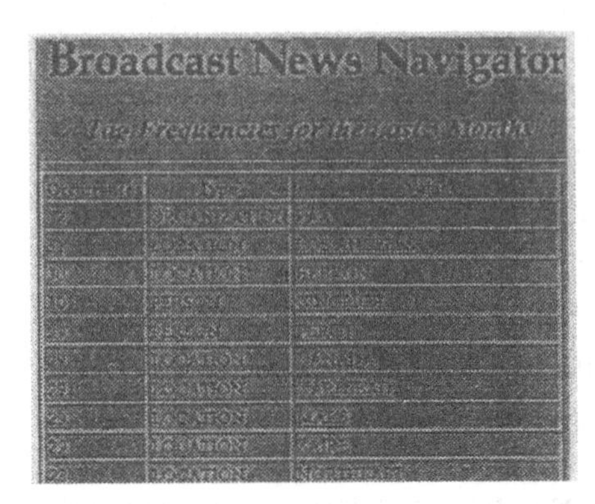

Figure 4. Named Entity (Metadata) Visualization

Figure 5 illustrates initial precision and recall results of applying the phrase finder to detect people, organization, and locations in the closed caption transcripts for five ABC World News Tonight programs. These results are promising given that we are applying a part of speech and named entity tagger trained previously on scientific texts to a new genre of language (broadcast news) with no modification to either the lexicon or grammatical rules, despite the significant differences in language, grammar, noisy data, and upper case only text.

Whereas some broadcasts contain embedded summaries (e.g. Jim Lehrer), others (e.g. ABC) contain no such summary. In collaboration with Mani (Mani 1995; Maybury, 1995), we have been experimenting with several heuristics for text summarization. The first is simply to pick the first N words in a document or segment, assuming that the text was created in journalistic style. Since we are extracting proper names out of the text, however, another strategy is to use the most frequently occurring named entity within each segment to serve as its label. We still have the remaining problem of choosing not only a sample video frame and perhaps also a representative set of key frames (e.g. a video clip). Perhaps most challenging, we need to choose the most visually informative and/or pleasing keyclip. Other research is investigating similar retrieval and display challenges in audio broadcasts (e.g. Brown et al., 1995).

As systems become more sophisticated in their ability to extract content from multimedia sources, this will enable the application of user and discourse models to tailor this output to the user, both in terms of selecting content, realizing it (e.g. choosing shading and shape encoding versus colors for color blind users), and ensuring appropriate cross media coordination (e.g. between audio descriptions and labels in a related graphic).

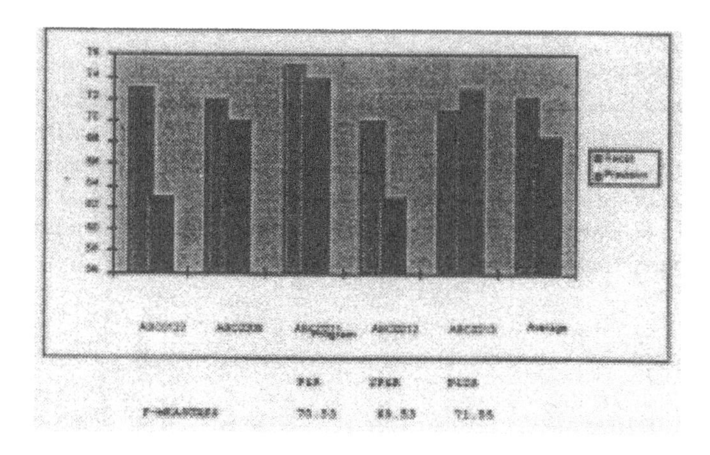

Figure 5. Named Entity Extraction Performance

7 Enabling Conversation

Currently, BNN users can interactively define a news program by indicating natural language phrases and/or providing temporal queries to indicate the information of interest. Unlike the Intelligent Mosaic application, there is not explicit model of conversation (other than that in the story segmentation modules).

An important area for further research is to capture a model of the conversation a user is having with the news videobase to, for example, manage error correcting subdialogues. We are currently measuring not only segmentation and extraction accuracy, but also efficiency measured in time to perform an information seeking task and we hypothesize interactive conversational capability would positively effect this.

8 Conclusions

This paper reports on two efforts to provide conversational interaction with information sources. The first is an early extension of a world wide web browser. The second is supporting interaction with a richly semantically indexed broadcast news repository. These discourse structure and content analyses are an important step toward enabling more sophisticated customization of automatically generated multimedia presentations that take advantage of advances not only in user and discourse but also in presentation planning, content selection, media allocation, media realization, and layout (Maybury, 1993).

Acknowledgments

John Burger and Ralph Marshall developed the AIMI system. Rich Mitchell and colleagues created FISH. Andy Merlino created the Broadcast News Navigator and Inderjeet Mani its summarization component. Ira Smotroff, Lynette Hirschman, and colleagues created the visionary information access system briefly described in Section 2. Marc Vilain and John Aberdeen provided part of speech and proper name taggers, and David Day for trained these on the broadcast news domain. CNN is a registered trademark of Cable News Network.

References

Aberdeen, J., Burger, J., Day, D., Hirschman, L., Robinson, P. and Vilain, M. 1995. Description of the Alembic System Used for MUC-6, Proceedings of the Sixth Message Understanding Conference. Advanced Research Projects Agency Information Technology Office, Columbia, MD.

Brill, E. 1995. Transformation-based Error-Driven Learning and Natural Language Processing: A Case Study in Part of Speech Tagging. Computational Linguistics, 21(4).

Brown, M.G., Foote, J.T., Jones, G.J.F., Sparck-Jones, K. and Young, S.J. 1995. Automatic Content-Based Retrieval of Broadcast News, Proceedings of ACM Multimedia. San Francisco, CA, p.35-44.

Dubner, B. 1996. Automatic Scene Detector and Videotape logging system, User Guide, Dubner International, Inc., Copyright 1995.

Grosz, B. J. and Sidner, C. 1986. Attention, Intentions, and the Structure of Discourse. Computational Linguistics 12(3):175-204.

Hearst, M. A. 1994. Multi-Paragraph Segmentation of Expository Text, ACL-94, Las Cruces, New Mexico.

Kobsa, A. and Wahlster, W. (eds.) 1989. User Models in Dialog Systems. Berlin: Springer-Verlag.

Mani, I. 1995. Very Large Scale Text Summarization, Technical Note, MITRE Corporation.

Mani, I., House, D., Maybury, M. and Green, M. 1997. Towards Content-based Browsing of Broadcast News Video. In Maybury, M. (ed.) Intelligent Multimedia Information Retrieval, AAAI/MIT Press, 241-258.

Maybury, M. T. (ed.) 1993. Intelligent Multimedia Interfaces. Menlo Park: AAAI/MIT Press. (http://www.aaai.org/Publications/Press/Catalog/maybury.html)

Maybury, M. T. 1995. Generating Summaries from Event Data. International Journal of Information Processing and Management: Special Issue on Text Summarization 31(5): 735-751.

Maybury, M. T. (ed.) 1997. Intelligent Multimedia Information Retrieval. Menlo Park: AAAI/MIT Press. (http://www.aaai.org:80/Press/Books/Maybury-2/)

Maybury, M., Merlino, A. and Morey, D. 1997. Broadcast News Navigation using Story Segments, Proceedings of the ACM International Multimedia Conference, Seattle, WA, November 8-14, 381-391.

Michell, R. 1996. Forager for Information on the Super Highway (FISH). Unpublished Manuscript.

[MUC-6] Proceedings of the Sixth Message Understanding Conference. Advanced Research Projects Agency Information Technology Office, Columbia, MD, 6-8 November, 1995.

Pelachaud, C. 1992. Functional Decomposition of Facial Expressions for an Animation System. In Catarci, T., Costabile, M. F. and Levialdi, S. (eds). Advanced Visual Interfaces: Proceedings of the International Workshop, Singapore: World Scientific Series in Computer Science, Vol 36: 26-49.

Reiter, E., Mellish, C. and Levine, J. 1995. Automatic Generation of Technical Documentation. Applied Artificial Intelligence 9(3):259-287

Shahraray, B. and Gibbon, D. 1995. Automated Authoring of Hypermedia Documents of Video Programs. Proceedings of ACM Multimedia. San Francisco, CA, p. 401-409.

Smotroff, I., Hirschman, L. and Bayer, S. 1995. Integrating Natural Language with Large DataspaceVisualization, to appear in Adam, N. and Bhargava, B. (eds), Advances in Digital Libraries, Lecture Notes in Computer Science, Springer Verlag.

Stevens et al., 1994. Informedia - Improving Access to Digital Video, Interactions, October, pp. 67-71.

Stock, O. and the ALFRESCO Project Team. 1993. ALFRESCO: Enjoying the Combination of Natural Language Processing and Hypermedia for Information Exploration. In Intelligent Multimedia Interfaces, ed. M. Maybury, 197-224. Menlo Park: AAAI/MIT Press.

Wahlster, W. 1991. User and Discourse Models for Multimodal Communication. In Sullivan, J. W. and Tyler, S. W. (eds). Intelligent User Interfaces. Frontier Series. New York: ACM Press, 45-67.

Notes

[1] As then current information extraction techniques had low precision and recall, this was simulated in the prototype by using the templates manually generated by domain experts to be used as answer keys in the Message Understanding Conference evaluation.

6 The SpeakEasy Dialogue Controller

G. Ball

The SpeakEasy dialogue controller interprets conversational scripts that control how a computer character interacts with a user. The scripts are written in a simple imperative programming language with special features designed to simplify the authoring of natural conversations. This paper explains the requirements for a conversational scripting language, based on experience with Microsoft's Peedy the Parrot prototype. It then illustrates how those requirements have been addressed in the design of SpeakEasy. The interpreter has been packaged as an ActiveX object, and used in conjunction with the Microsoft Agent animated character to implement a series of Web guides which can lead a user on a tour of a portion of the World Wide Web.

1 Background: Peedy The Parrot

Interaction with computers by means of a spoken dialogue is likely to become commonplace in the not too distant future. Many of the required technologies (including speech recognition, natural language processing, speech synthesis, and animation) have reached a sufficient level of maturity that the creation of an integrated conversational assistant has become feasible.

The Persona project at Microsoft Research created a limited prototype of such an assistant in 1994, called "Peedy the Parrot" (Ball et al., 1997). The Peedy prototype integrated real components (i.e. it wasn't just a mock up), but in very limited forms. The language forms that it could handle were restricted to just a few hundred variations of a dozen or so basic requests. Similarly, the task domain (selecting and playing music CD's) supported only a tiny database. These limitations, while representing significant challenges for future research, were largely a matter of scale.

A more fundamental problem with Peedy was the level of effort and expertise required to author extensions to the system. In order to add a new command to Peedy's repertoire, researchers had to:

- extend the speech recognition vocabulary and grammar to include acceptable paraphrases of the request,
- modify custom English parsing rules to ensure that those paraphrases would be recognized as variations of a single request type,
- add database queries or application commands to support the new operation,
- extend the dialogue state machine to fit the new command into a conversational sequence,
- author new 3D animations as necessary to illustrate Peedy carrying out the new request,
- write Peedy's verbal responses in the new conversational sequence,
- record any new phrases that Peedy might need to speak, along with the corresponding 'beak sync' scripts, and
- debug the entire sequence, including all interactions with existing operations.

These tasks were complex enough, and required enough specialized knowledge, that it quickly became impractical to extend the prototype to cover additional interactions. Before conversational assistants can become a practical interface technique, it must be possible for a wide variety of application designers to be able to define and extend their behaviors.

Therefore, simplifying the authoring process has been a major goal of our continuing work on conversational assistants.

2 Authoring Conversational Interfaces

We are working toward the creation of a conversational interface platform, in which much of the structure and capability of a conversational assistant is provided in an application-independent fashion. Our design attempts to encapsulate all of the application-specific information required by the interface in a dialogue script, which is a program-like description of the possible interaction sequences that the user and assistant might traverse. This script specifies exemplars of utterances that the user might generate, as well as defining the assistant's reaction (which also depends on the current conversational state).

The input exemplars will be used by the Natural Language Processing system to generate conceptual representations of the expected inputs, which are then matched against user utterances in order to detect acceptable paraphrases. The exemplars are also used to update the vocabulary and grammar of the speech recognizer, so that better recognition accuracy can be achieved on the most likely input utterances. The character's output is presented using a general text-to-speech synthesizer and a graphical character with a limited collection of pre-authored animations. Thus the dialogue script can specify the complete conversational behavior of a character.

3 Dialogue Script Requirements

The ease of dialogue authoring largely depends upon the appropriateness of the capabilities in the dialogue script representation. At least the following list of requirements need to be easily achievable:

- The assistant must be able to react promptly and appropriately to both verbal input and other events. A character that demonstrates awareness of many aspects of its environment is likely to be more believable.
- The timing of dialogue interactions is especially important. The script must be able to conveniently describe the desired interaction timing, and to react to the pacing of user responses.
- The author should be able to list a number of possible new dialogue initiatives and have the choice of conversational direction at a particular time be controlled by a combination of constraints and chance.
- Verbal responses to the user will seem more natural if they include linguistic variation and stay consistent with the personality and mood of the assistant. It should be easy to specify both probabilistic and deterministic (based on context) control of output phrasing.
- Inappropriate repetition in the assistant's dialogue is especially disconcerting. The dialogue script must have an effective and convenient mechanism for detecting and avoiding it.
- During assistant 'monologues', users need to be able to control the pacing of the tour, ideally by means of the same non-linguistic signals that are used in human conversation.
- Awareness of recent conversational events is an important part of the capabilities of a convincing dialogue partner. The dialogue script needs to have access to an easily referenced conversational history in order to respond appropriately.
- Finally, the behavior of the assistant when it fails to respond successfully is very important. The script should be able to specify a sequence of responses to be generated when the user's input is totally unrecognizable or the assistant has run out of appropriate things to say.

4 The Speakeasy Scripting Language

The SpeakEasy dialogue controller interprets conversational scripts that determine how a computer character will interact with a user. These scripts are written in a simple imperative programming language that was designed to address the requirements detailed in the previous section. The language is somewhat reminiscent of Expect (Libes, 1994), in that it is designed for the creation of scripts that recognize and respond to externally generated textual messages. This section describes the SpeakEasy language and explains how individual language features support the specialized requirements of conversational interaction.

4.1 Scenarios to scripts

The starting place for the design of a human-computer dialogue is often a scenario. By generating an example of a typical interaction, the designer can focus on the key features of the program in "normal" use. For example,

Figure 1 shows a brief interaction between a user and a computer assistant acting as a guide to the World Wide Web.

```
User: Is there anything new available at Slate?
Comp: There's a new column by Nathan Myhrvold
defending human cloning.
User: Please show that to me now.
Comp: Here it is.
User: Has anyone argued the other point of view?
Comp: Sure. Here's an...
```

Figure 1. A conversational scenario

This scenario can be turned directly into a SpeakEasy script that will carry out that conversation (exactly) with a user, waiting for the user to say each of their "lines" and then responding accordingly. This script, shown in Figure 2, also includes a command to show the appropriate Web page at the proper point in the interaction.

```
[Is there anything new available at Slate?]
say "There's a new column by Nathan Myhrvold defending
human cloning."
[Please show that to me now.]
show "http://www.slate.com/CriticalMass/97-03-
13/CriticalMass.asp"
say "Here it is."
[Has anyone argued the other point of view?]
say "Sure. Here's an ..."
```

Figure 2: The scenario of Figure 1 in SpeakEasy

Conditionals

Of course, scripts must be able to respond appropriately to a variety of user utterances in addition to the "typical" one. The basic SpeakEasy conditional statement looks like a normal programming language if statement (Figure 3), but from the middle of the contest, which accounts for the small number of its dialogues. `crl'` and `tut'` are revisions of `crl` and `tut`, respectively. These two revisions appear successful because these two systems outperform the others systems in terms of dialogues with people.

However, machine-machine dialogues among the same set of systems lead to a rather different comparison, as shown in Table 7. This table is organized in the

	naist-ob	crl'	atr'	tut'	naistl'	total=score
nasit-ob	2093	260	1316	256	0	6413
crl'	0	1784	644	1125	0	5739
atr'	0	0	1293	0	0	5140
tut'	164/395	142	694	451	0	2539
naistl'	0	0	0	0	0	0

Table 7: Machine-Machine Dialogues in October 1997

same way as Table 5. Since a common set of ten tasks is used for each pair of dialogue systems (that is, each slot of the table), each system is involved in 100 dialogues, where a dialogue in which the system talks to itself is counted twice. So the total point is equal to the overall score, which is 100 times the average point. Here a system wins a positive number of points in a dialogue when its partner obtains the right path --- the same way of grading as for people. Two systems won different points only when `tut'` is the first speaker and `naist-ob` is the second, as indicated by the two figures in the corresponding slot: they won 164 points and 395 points in total there, respectively.

Note that the difference in ranking between human-machine dialogues and machine-machine dialogues is much greater between Table 6 and 7 than between Table 4 and 5. This suggests that machine-machine dialogues cannot be an appropriate basis on which to evaluate dialogue systems. In contrast, human-machine dialogues appear to be a stable basis for evaluation, because the ranking among dialogue systems is nearly equal among Table 3, 4 and 6. Table 3 and 4 show almost the same ranking. `tut` and `naist-ob` are exchanged between the two sessions, but the differences between the two systems are small in both cases, and the overall better scores in the latter session in Table 4 may be because it is a contest. Similarly, the ranking between `atr'` and `naist-ob` is preserved in Table 6. Still better performance of the systems here is probably accounted for by higher incentives of the human talkers involved. In fact, the First Dialogue Contest (Table 4) included 463 dialogues, whereas the Second (Table 6), 728. A major cause of this increase may be the greater amount of award in the Second Dialogue Contest. In the First Dialogue Contest, it was announced that the best three human talkers would win 15,000, 10,000, and 5,000 yen, whereas in the Second, the awards were 30,000, 20,000 and 10,000 yen. Moreover, none of the best three talkers contacted the organizers to actually get their awards in the First Dialogue Contest, whereas the best three talkers all received their awards in the second contest. This suggests that the participants in the latter contest had stronger overall incentives than in the former.

active until it executes a return statement or blocks waiting for additional user input.

For example, in Figure 5, the conversation starter "What time is it?" will result in a new context that responds to the question (note that $(daytime) is replaced with the value of the variable 'daytime' which holds the current time of day) and then immediately terminates. Thus, a time request can be handled at any point without interfering with the active conversation. Conversation starters can also jump into the middle of scripts that can also be executed from other paths. The second example in Figure 5 shows how a direct request for information can transfer control into a discussion of the requested topic (conversation starters do not effect script execution when encountered in normal program flow).

```
// *[] designates a conversation starter
*[What time is it?]
  say "It is $(daytime)."
  return
...
say "Are you interested in user interfaces?"
if [yes]
  *[Tell me about user interfaces.]
  say "The user interface group...
elseif
...
```

Figure 5: SpeakEasy conversation starters

The example in Figure 6, uses "*show" to indicate that transferring to the designated Web page should be considered a conversation starter as well. That is, if the user independently navigates to that URL, the script will generate a response to that user "utterance".

```
*show "http://research.microsoft.com/~geneb/home.htm"
  say "He should get a new picture, shouldn't he?"
return
```

Figure 6: Web transfers as conversation starters

When a conversation starter creates a new context, previously active contexts (which are blocked waiting for user input) are still available to respond to input directed to them. In this way the user can return to the earlier conversation at will.

Events that do not match any active input patterns need to be handled as well: SpeakEasy generates a special event "No_Match" when such an input occurs. As Figure 7 shows, a context that responds to this event can adapt its behavior depending on the frequency of misunderstandings.

The example also shows how labels (:FailLoop) and jump statements can be used to produce loops, so that the third and subsequent responses to "No_Match" will be "I'm really sorry, but I still don't understand".

```
[No_Match]
say "Sorry, I didn't understand '$(LastUtterance)'"

[No_Match]
say "I still don't understand."

:FailLoop
   [No_Match]
   say "I'm really sorry, but I still don't
understand."
jump FailLoop
```

Figure 7: Handling inputs that don't match a pattern

Events and Timeouts

In many situations, achieving a natural conversational interaction depends largely on timing. SpeakEasy provides several events that help the script author control the rhythm of the interaction. In Figure 8, after requesting the display of a Web page, the script waits for either the Web_Slow event or the Web_Done event to occur. If Web_Slow is generated (after a settable timeout), the character can comment on the responsiveness of the server.

After the page arrives (Web_Done), the character makes a comment, and when finished speaking (Speak_Done) instructs the MS Agent animated character to gesture toward a particular location on the screen. Do commands cause SpeakEasy to report an event to the controlling application, which can then interpret the rest of the command appropriately. This makes it easy to control application-specific actions from a script, and to synchronize them properly with the conversation.

The final line of Figure 8 causes SpeakEasy to wait 30 seconds before proceeding, unless the user specifically says "Go on." or "Go ahead."

```
show "http:// ..."
if [Web_Slow]
   say "Boy this server is pokey."
   [Web_Done]
   say "Well it finally arrived."
elseif [Web_Done]
   say "Here's the page, note the..."
endif
[Speak_Done]
do gestureat 200, 200
[Go on.] [Go ahead.] [>30]
```

Figure 8: External events and timeouts

Output variability

The illusion of natural conversation with a computer assistant can be destroyed very easily by exact repetition of phrasing in the computer's responses. As we've seen, SpeakEasy does not attempt to support the generation of natural language, instead the character's utterances are authored as part of the dialogue script.

However, the language does provide some support for authors who wish to add random or contextual variability to their character's speech.

When SpeakEasy string constants are evaluated, they are examined for substrings of the form **$(expr)**, which are then replaced by the value of the enclosed expression. Thus, in figure 9, the name of the site in the first say statement comes from the variable **Web_Suggestion** that was assigned to earlier.

Figure 9 also illustrates the use of a probabilistic expression to generate variation in output messages. The variable Site is assigned the following string constant (^^ is a line continuation sequence, and string constants can be enclosed in either double quotes or pairs of single quotes.):

```
$(| 30%: "site" | 30%: "pages"
| 20%: "WWW site" | 100%: "Web pages")
```

This is an example of the SpeakEasy cond—an expression of the form (| e_1:v_1 | e_2:v_2 | e_3:v_3) where each expression en is evaluated in turn until one is found to be non-zero, and the value of the cond is then the corresponding v_n. The expression n% is a primitive SpeakEasy expression that pseudo-randomly evaluates to true n times out of 100. Thus the first say statement in Figure 9 will produce the output "Would you like to visit the Microsoft Research site?" 30% of the time, and "Would you like to visit the Microsoft Research Web pages?" with probability (1-0.3)* (1-0.6)* (1-0.2)*1.0 = .224, or approximately 22 times out of 100.

The second half of Figure 9 illustrates the use of a context variable, **Happiness**, to select among alternative phrasings in order to reflect the current emotional state of the character. Another mechanism for controlling repetition in SpeakEasy is the *historical variable*, which will evaluate to true only once within a specified length of time. In figure 10, the expressions of the form **(< name : interval >)** will evaluate to true unless they have returned true within the specified interval. Thus, (<TellJoke:20m>) returns true when first evaluated, and then returns false anytime it is referenced during the next 20 minutes. Similarly, (<ChessNuts:1y>) and (<JokeOfDay:1d>) remain false for 1 year and 1 day respectively, after once returning true.

```
Web_Sugggestion = "Microsoft Research"
Site = "$(|30%: "site" |60%: "pages" ^^
           |20%: "WWW site" ^^
           |100%: "Web pages")"
Say "Would you like to visit the $(Web_Suggestion)
$(Site)?"
I_Will = "$(| Happiness>80 : ^^
        "Great, I'd love to" ^^
            | Happiness>50 : ^^
        "Sure, I'd be pleased to" ^^
            | Happiness>20 : "OK, I will" ^^
            | Happiness>0 : ^^
        "Since you insist, I guess I can" )"
say "$(I_Will) show it to you."
```

Figure 9: Output variability

```
if (<TellJoke:20m>)
   Say "Would you like to hear a joke?"
   if [P_yes]
      if (<ChessNuts:1y>)
         say "Did you hear about the chess experts..."
      elseif (<JokeOfDay:1d>)
         show "http://joke/of/the/day"
      endif
   endif
endif
```

Figure 10: Historical variables

5 Status and Future Work

The SpeakEasy interpreter has been implemented as an ActiveX control (written in Visual Basic 5.0) that can be included as a component in Visual Basic programs or downloaded as an active object in a World Wide Web page. A few prototype examples of conversational interfaces have been built using SpeakEasy to control the Microsoft Agent. Microsoft Agent (Trower, 1996) is another ActiveX control (available on the Microsoft web site) which displays an animated character (initially a genie) that can listen (using speech recognition within small collections of possible inputs) and speak (using text to speech and speech balloons). One of these prototypes, is a guide that can give a tour of the Microsoft Research web site.

As mentioned earlier, we intend to integrate SpeakEasy with a broad coverage natural language processing system and a large vocabulary continuous speech recognition system, each under development by other groups within Microsoft Research. We then plan to evaluate the degree to which it is possible to script natural conversations in limited domains, without requiring users to learn and restrict themselves to a specialized command language.

In many application domains, conversations largely consist of users specifying commands for the application to carry out. These commands may have many required and/or optional parameters, each of which can be specified by a variety of English paraphrases. Negotiating the settings of those parameters may require many conversational interactions, which can occur in nearly any order. The declaration of a conversational frame would allow SpeakEasy to automatically handle those interactions, reporting only the final values of the parameters. Such a mechanism is currently under design.

References

Ball, G. et al., 1997. Lifelike Computer Characters: The Persona Project at Microsoft. In Software Agents (eds. Bradshaw, J.) AAAI/MIT Press, Menlo Park, CA.

Libes, D. 1994. Exploring Expect A Tcl-based Toolkit for Automating Interactive Programs. O'Reilly and Associates.
Microsoft Corporation. 1997. Visual Basic 5. http://www.microsoft.com/vbasic/
Trower, T. 1996. Microsoft Agent. http://www.microsoft.com/intdev/agent/ Microsoft Corporation.

7 Choosing a Response Using Problem Solving Plans and Rhetorical Relations

P. Barboni and D. Sestero

1 Introduction

In building a system capable of natural language interaction with a human being, a key issue is how the context (dialogic and pragmatic) constrains the structure of the ongoing dialogue[1]. In fact, the context provides the basis both for the recognition of an agent's goals and plans and for the construction of an answer that "makes sense".

In the analysis of linguistic context, previous research has identified several kinds of relationships between sentences; these relationships can be understood in terms of different kinds of knowledge: domain (e.g. in Dialogue 1, A refers to a domain plan, C to a constraint on it, and D to an alternative plan for a related[2] goal); rhetorical (in Dialogue 1, C is clearly intended as a justification for B, and E as an enablement allowing the user to perform D; furthermore, BC and DE stand in a relation of contrast, while A and the complex BCDE constitute a question-answer pair); and problem-solving (in Dialogue 1, the user is asking A because there is a problem-solving plan saying that in order to reach a goal, an action having the goal among its effects can be selected; for what concerns the goal of obtaining an exchange with professor Verdi, meeting him is such an action. On the other hand, the system is suggesting D as an alternative action because it has the goal "minimize the time spent by the professor talking with students outside his office hours" and is performing a problem-solving plan that tries to balance this goal against the user's one).

A: May I meet Professor Verdi?
B: No, you cannot,
C: because he does not receive now;
D: but you can send him an e-mail
E: at verdi@di.unito.it.

Dialogue 1

As can be seen from the previous example, the structure and content of the system answer are made out of the interaction of various layers of knowledge. Previous research in generation focused on the relationship between discourse and domain knowledge (Appelt, 1985; McKeown, 1985; Paris, 1988; Cawsey, 1993), on the rhetorical and pragmatic goals of the explainer (Mann and Thompson, 1988; Hovy, 1988b; Moore, 1995), or on the illocutionary aspects of a two-party exchange between an information seeker and an information provider, modeling their conversational tactics and strategies, and mutual role expectations (Stein and Maier, 1995). On the recognition side, some attention has been devoted to the problem-solving activity of an information-seeking agent and the way he moves when considering possible future courses of actions (Ramshaw, 1989; Carberry et al., 1992). Although these studies gave important insights about an agent's plans and goals, we argue that none of them provides an explicit account of the relationship between the goals of the interactants and their response behavior. For example, in Dialogue 1 these approaches cannot explain why the system chooses to provide Professor Verdi's e-mail address rather than his office hours.

A linguistic approach to dialogue would consider it like an object whose structure can be analyzed. On the other hand, a cognitive approach allows to view conversation like an interpersonal activity controlled by shared social rules and motivated by private mental states of the interlocutors (Bara, 1990). The rational agent approach (see Russell and Norvig, 1995; Wooldridge and Jennings, 1995; Allen, 1996) allows us to model dialogue exactly as such an activity, by providing the agent's perspective on it: the agent reconstructs goals and plans of its interlocutors by observing their (linguistic) behavior, and responds to this interpretation of reality by producing physical and/or linguistic actions, where we are especially interested in the latter.

Our consultation system[3] evaluates possible courses of action according to a number of context-related factors, including user's and system's goals, complexity of the candidate action, its applicability in the current situation, and user's knowledge of it. In such a way it is possible to obtain a broad range of behaviors, resulting in the production of flexible responses. In particular, given some general goals of the system (like "maintain a good face", or "provide consulence"), and some specific ones related to the domain of interest (like the above-mentioned one regarding professor-time scheduling), a *main content selection* phase considers how possible alternative courses of action realize to a lesser or greater extent the system's goals and the user's expectations. A subsequent *structuring* phase decides which rhetorical strategies are best suited to convey the previously selected material, what additional material is needed, and the structure to impose over it. The same mechanism is used to plan the system's behavior in both phases: a problem-solving plan layer represents explicitly the reasoning activity of a rational agent interacting through natural language with another agent in a restricted domain and the process of selecting a reasonable act.

In summary, the original contributions of this work are:

1. The development of a framework for rational action that fits both domain-related and linguistic actions, keeping into account the relationships existing between the two; in particular that:
   - agents communicate in order to synchronize their efforts;
   - agents communicate in order to obtain information that would enable them to choose a course of action.
2. The design of the generation module of an autonomous system able to participate in dialogues with its users, so far as the content selection (what to say) and structuring of the text (how to organize the material) are concerned. The linguistic behavior of the system is affected by several factors including explicit user's and system's goals and intentions, the current state of the world, and the knowledge the interlocutors are equipped with. In particular, the coupling of a set of rhetorical strategies specialized to cope with information about actions with the plans describing the mental activity of the autonomous agent sheds light on the relationships between content selection and text structuring in information-providing dialogues.
3. To show how the problem-solving plans (describing the mental activity of the autonomous agent) can be directly interpreted in order to direct the system actions without making use of a traditional planner. This is the consequence of having represented in a declarative way an important piece of knowledge (namely, the knowledge about how to satisfy a goal in a cooperative inter-agent context), making it available to both the plan recognition and text planning processes.

2 Related work

Recently, various models have been proposed to deal with plan recognition and sentence planning in dialogue.

First of all, we would like to characterize our view of what constitutes the problem-solving level of plans and contrast it with related works, notably that of Carberry and her collaborators. Carberry and Chu-Carrol (1995) structured a cycle of actions for modeling collaborative activities adopting a tripartite dialogue model that deals with intentions at three levels: domain, problem solving and discourse. The first one contains the domain plan being constructed for later execution; the problem-solving level registers agents' intentions about how to construct the domain plan, and the discourse level contains the communicative plan initiated to further their mutual problem-solving intentions. These authors use the problem-solving layer to mediate between the domain and the linguistic ones rather than as truly meta-knowledge (see (Wilensky, 1981)).

For us, the problem-solving plans describe the activity of a rational agent trying to satisfy a goal, possibly interacting with other agents. We view them as meta-plans with respect to domain and linguistic ones since they take domain and linguistic goals and actions as arguments. These two aspects imply that, from the generation point of view, the problem-solving plans play the role of a planner. All we need to build the partially instantiated plans that constitute the output of the system is an interpreter of the plan representation language. On the other hand, using Carberry's framework for generation purposes requires to apply some planner to each of the three layers, which results in a considerable complexity.

Furthermore, having encoded in a declarative form all the knowledge responsible for rational, goal-oriented behavior of an agent interacting with another one, we have it available also for plan recognition purposes. Sharing the same knowledge between the interpretation and generation phases seems reasonable both from an engineering and cognitive point of view.

Another point that worth mention is that Carberry and her collaborators focus on the detection and resolution of the conflicts arising between two agents involved in building a shared plan. On the contrary, we are more concerned with a cooperative system, able to adopt goals and choose linguistic and domain actions in order to achieve them.

In our approach linguistic plans include speech acts and rhetorical relations where the latter express coherent ways to link speech acts in a discourse (Mann and Thompson, 1988). Hovy (1988a) showed how rhetorical relations can be operationalized by means of a plan library but he conflated intentional and rhetorical structure (see the discussion in (Moore and Pollack, 1992)). Also in (Carberry et al., 1993) it is claimed that rhetorical relations, though necessary, are not sufficient to structure a text. On the other hand, our use of rhetorical relations guided by the problem-solving plans on the basis of the communicative intentions arising during the planning process and the *interpersonal goals* set up, allows to track the different levels of intentions behind a linguistic act. Furthermore, this fact together with the agent-based perspective on the dialogue blurs the long debated distinction between illocutionary and perlocutionary speech acts resulting in an overall simplification of the model[4].

Moore (1995) works out the conflation of intentional and rhetorical structure by allowing a many to many mapping of intentions on rhetorical relations. Her system PEA, designed to aid users in enhancing LISP programs by suggesting transformations that improve their readability and maintainability, is concerned with explanatory dialogues. It doesn't possess natural language understanding capabilities: the user can react by pointing to the portion of text not understood or typing predefined sequences of words in order to have extra information. On the contrary we are concerned with dialogues: in our system the input is interpreted, a user model dynamically updated, and goals not explicit in the text are inferred.

Furthermore, on the basis of this input, our system can perform an action in the domain or provide information about the action execution. This information may be either about the action itself (in which case it is communicated to enable the user to successfully perform the plan), or it may concern the problem-solving process (in which case it is communicated to keep the synchronization between the agents). For such a task, having a set of communicative strategies that consider all possible things to say would be redundant, and this is the main reason for clearly separating linguistic and domain knowledge.

To provide a flexible explanation, when the first reply is not satisfactory, PEA uses a set of selection heuristics to choose among different explanation strategies. These heuristics refer either to the user acquaintance with the concepts involved, giving high scores to plans that avoid making assumptions on user's knowledge or mental state, or to features of the communicative plans, like their coherence with the previous dialogue, specificity and verbosity. We have adopted scoring criteria resembling Moore's ones in our *Explore* problem-solving plan with some important differences. First, while her heuristics are essentially discourse based, ours take more into account the current situation as needed to allow the planning agent to choose the action it considers the best. Second, while Moore's heuristics implicitly encode the linguistic behavior of the system, we made explicit all the system's goals. In particular, the system has some basic goals (like *provide-consulence*, *maintain-good-face*, or *preserve-resource-integrity*) and is able to derive new ones, related to the current situation, from these and the ones recognized from the user's utterance by means of some intention-acquisition heuristics (implemented in the *interpersonal goal manager*). This allows on the one hand the intention acquisition and response generation components to reason indifferently on domain and linguistic goals, and to the other hand to easily introduce pragmatic goals affecting the choice of different linguistic means. Furthermore, Moore's heuristics come into play only when the previous system's explanation didn't satisfy the user while our scoring criteria are used throughout the action selection process.

Cawsey (1993) takes into account the crucial aspect of interactivity in human explanatory dialogue. Her system EDGE plans tutorial explanations on structure and behavior of electric circuits and covers aspects like conversation management (e.g. handling user interruptions), topic shift and generation of meta-comments (e.g. "We'll be getting to this argument in a moment").

Though Cawsey uses discourse plans to model different interactions between system and user, she doesn't have a general mechanism to make the discourse dependent on the available content and the participants' goals. On the other hand we achieve a more flexible result by making the problem-solving plans direct the system behavior, entrusting the rhetorical strategies with the task of including all the information relevant for achieving a particular set of goals, and structuring it in order to make an understandable contribution to the dialog.

Similar considerations apply to the work of (Belkin et al., 1995), (Stein and Maier, 1995). These authors propose a model of the interactions occurring between the user and an information-retrieval system. Their work is influenced by the Conversation for Action model, proposed by Winograd and Flores (1986), which was developed for computer-supported negotiations between humans. They extended and refined this action model for the genre of information-seeking dialogues in the context of human-computer interaction applying some concepts of Systemic Linguistic approaches to discourse modeling (Fawcett et al., 1988). Also, concepts of Mann and Thompson's Rhetorical Structure Theory were used and applied to multiparty discourse. Finally, these authors used scripts as prototypical cases of information-seeking dialogues characterizing the most usual, or most effective, or in some sense standard means by which the user and the system interact to achieve classes of information-retrieval goals.

Although their model accomplish several functions, like: (i) to define the available and regular conversation moves (e.g. requesting or offering information, rejecting offers and withdrawing commitments), (ii) to specify the role changes that occur in the course of the dialogue, for example in situations where the information seeker temporarily takes the role of the information provider, and (iii) to decompose the dialogue in a hierarchical structure, it remains focused on the illocutionary aspects of a two-party exchange between an information seeker and an information provider. In this respect, our proposal has the advantage of situating the linguistic activity in the much more general framework of rational action, where linguistic and rhetorical knowledge are related with domain knowledge according to the needs of agents' coordination and planning of activity.

3 Overall architecture

Figure 1 shows the architecture of our dialogue agent as far as the pragmatic part is concerned. Input sentences from the user are first syntactically and semantically analyzed by the GULL natural language interpreter (Lesmo and Lombardo, 1993). The semantic representation is given in input to the plan recognizer that extracts the user's goals and plans and builds a hierarchical structure (the *Context Model*, following (Carberry, 1988)) representing the inferred user's plan (Ardissono, Lombardo, and Sestero, 1993), (Ardissono, Boella, and Sestero, 1996). Furthermore, a user model is dynamically updated on the basis of the meaning of the input and the goals recognized.

Ardissono and Sestero (1996) discuss some techniques used for integrating the plan recognition and user modeling component in order to:

1. Infer the user's beliefs from both the sentences he utters and the information stored in the domain plan library, hence obtaining rich and flexible user models;
2. Restrict the set of hypotheses on the user's goals and plans to the most plausible ones on the basis of the current assumptions about the user.

The context model constitutes the input for the response production process that we can articulate into the following phases:

- *Intention acquisition*, where the agent sets up some new goals that he wants to achieve as a consequence of the interpretation of the input sentence. In fact, a cooperative agent is supposed to take into account what has been said by its interlocutor, adhere to the linguistic expectation if there is one, and adopt[5] possible high-level goals that could have been inferred from the dialogue context. Of course, in a planning agent the intention acquisition phase does not complete before the formulation of the plan: the hierarchical plan formation process itself implies the posting of progressively more refined goals. However, it should be clear that the intention acquisition problem is worth to be studied per se, since it involves issues of interactions and choice among different agents' goals.

- *Content selection*, where the propositional contents to be included in the response are selected on the basis of the communicative intentions the agent has towards its interlocutor. We considered at least 6 factors that, in turn, determine these intentions:

  - The desire to increase the ability of the other agent to achieve common goals. It is the case of goals posted to make true the *knowledge preconditions* (Moore, 1985) of an action to be executed by another agent. For example, this situation occurs when an expert (Information Provider or IP) is giving advice to a novice (Information Seeker or IS), in this case the common goal is the one the IP adopted. Another example is when a request to another agent was made, like in: "Would you light the stove? You have to open the gas valve, then push the red button"?

  - The desire to increase the other agent's desire to cooperate. In other words, the attempt to induce the other agent to adhere to an agent's goal?

  - The decision to request the other agent to perform some action in the domain

  - The need of obtaining information useful to choose a course of action (e.g. the IP's question for clarification in Dialogue 2)

  - The need to keep the synchronization among agents acting together to a common task (e.g. the acknowledgement in the exchange: "I would like a paper copy of this document" "The document 'foo.doc' is being printed; you can find it on printer 'laser-II' in room 10").

Note that the first factor is closely related to what assumptions about the other agent are contained in the user model; the subsequent two depend upon social knowledge concerned with the relationships that exist between our agent and the rest of the world, and they exploit mechanisms of politeness (e.g. indirect speech acts) and argumentative structures; the last three are part of the activities involved in making and executing a plan in a two-agent context.

- *Structuring*, where the selected contents are mapped on a coherent text. This phase is possible thanks to a library of plans representing rhetorical relations.

In Figure 1, the intention acquisition phase is carried out basically by the domain and the interpersonal goal managers. The former decides which goals to adopt by means of some heuristics that consider the balance between user's and computer's goals. Currently the goal manager is not fully developed and it simply adopts the IS' most generic domain goal that doesn't conflict with an IP's one. The latter is realized by means of IF-THEN rules whose antecedent represents a generic situation and the consequent the interpersonal goal to be activated in that case[6].

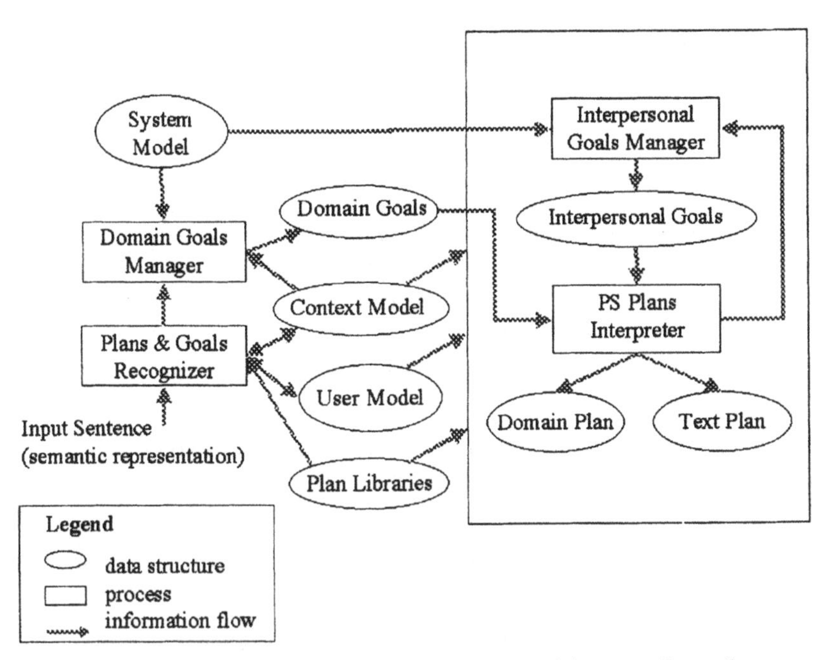

Figure 1. General architecture of the dialogue agent (pragmatic part)

The content-selection phase starts when the interpreter of the problem-solving plans is invoked for trying to satisfy the adopted goal. The interpreter is responsible for choosing and instantiating a problem-solving plan that, in turn, exploits knowledge expressed in the domain and linguistic plan libraries in order to find the best plan satisfying the current goal.

As we already mentioned, trying to satisfy a goal in a two-agents context may bring to the posting of communicative goals in order to obtain needed information, and keep the agents synchronized. When this situation arises the interpersonal goal manager is invoked to activate some further goals (the interpersonal ones) affecting the subsequent choice of the linguistic actions, hence the way the information will be conveyed to the IS (structuring). This process has two consequences:

- it allows to derive the first three factors related to content selection (discussed above) from the last three, i.e. from the structure of the problem-solving plans;
- it brings to the interleaved production of domain and linguistic plans, directed by the problem-solving library. This is a key point of the architecture, direct consequence of our view of the problem-solving plans, discussed above.

While the domain plan is ready to be exploited for determining the physical actions of the IP, the text plan needs some further processing in order to produce natural language text. In particular, the text plan describes the general organization of the material (structure and order of the propositional units), and some choices related to speech acts (direct and indirect forms). Hovy (1993) mentioned several uses of text structure: links between RST relations and discourse focus, choice of the syntactic roles, aggregation of the material in order to avoid redundancies and verbosity of text, text formatting. On the other hand, the speech acts library contains information needed to map the different forms on linguistic features like modality, tense, and aspect (Ardissono et al., 1995). These information should then be exploited in a phase normally referred to as *macro-planning*. The subsequent phases of *surface realization* and *lexical choice* should complete the process. These latter phases, and the issues concerning the possibilities for interaction among them, are not in the focus of this paper. Our output consists of an instantiated three-fold plan containing problem-solving, domain and linguistic actions.[7]

The system makes use of four problem solving libraries that contain, respectively, the knowledge about the problem solving plans, the actions of the domain, the speech-acts and the rhetorical relations. These libraries are written using a common formalism derived from (Kautz, 1990). It employs generalization and decomposition hierarchies to relate the actions and provides standard fields for specifying constraints, preconditions, effects, and optional steps.

While the decomposition hierarchy specifies the steps needed to perform an action, the generalization hierarchy allows to represent alternative ways to perform each of them, inheriting common parts (e.g. the *Exchange-message-with-prof* action may be specialized in *Meet* and *Send-e-mail*).

In our plans, standard epistemic operators like *Know-recipe*, *Knowif*, *Knowref*, and *Goal* are used to deal with user is and system is beliefs. An agent *Know-recipe* an action if he knows its constraints, preconditions, effects and decomposition. He *Knowif* a condition if he knows its truth value. *Knowref* denotes the agent knowing which values of a variable satisfy a description. Finally, *Goal* registers states of the world desired by the agents.

The problem-solving library describes the reasoning activity of an agent building a plan to reach a goal, and trying to perform it. In particular, our library models the interactions between agents produced by this activity. According to the principles of rational interaction (Cohen and Levesque, 1990), two agents acting in a common environment interact to notify to each other some conditions related to the planning process (e.g. unfeasibility of an action, satisfaction of a wanted goal) and ask some aspects of the actions they consider relevant in order to successfully perform them (e.g. constraints, preconditions).

The main action in the problem-solving library is the *Satisfy(a,s,g)* action, representing how an agent behaves when wanting to satisfy a goal, possibly interacting with another agent. It has three arguments specifying the agent that acts (*a*, for actor), the agent that made the request (*s*, for source), and the state of the world that the agents want to achieve (*g*).

Satisfy is concerned with finding the most generic action having the goal in its effect list, exploring the action in order to evaluate it and choose among alternative specializations (see description of *Explore*, below), and trying to perform the action, where four possibilities could arise:

1. The actor of the action is the agent *a* itself: it could then try to execute the action, making true the preconditions not yet satisfied, performing the actions in the decompositions, and possibly notifying to the other agent the unfeasibility of the action; when the action completes, in case it was done on behalf of another agent *s*, *a* will post a communicative goal to inform *s* of the fact.

2. The actor of the action is another agent *o*: then, *a* will post a goal causing a request to *o* being made; furthermore, *a* posts *a* communicative goal to know if the action was actually done by *o*.

3. The action *a* found on behalf of another agent *s* is different from the action that *a* inferred as *s*' immediate goal in *s*' plan: then, *a* notifies the fact that he believes a better action exists for achieving the adopted goal.

4. Looking for an action in order to achieve a goal on behalf of another agent *s*, *a* didn't find any: *a*, then, notifies *s* of the impossibility of reaching the goal.

When the agent wants to affect the mental state of the other one, or when the agent is willing to obtain an information, *Satisfy* invokes the interpersonal goal manager. The interpersonal goals generated will be used during the *Explore* step in order to choose among the linguistic strategies achieving the communicative goal.

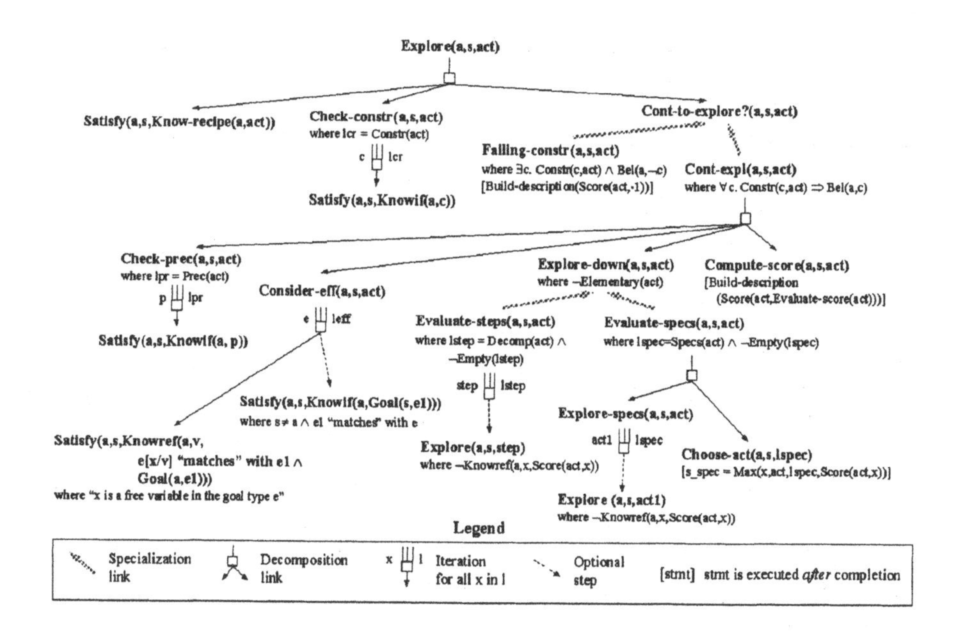

Figure 2. The Explore problem-solving plan

4 Choosing a response by evaluating alternative actions

A crucial part of the *Satisfy* problem-solving plan, hence, is the choice of the best action to perform among those having the goal in their effect list. This choice is performed by the *Explore* plan (see Figure 2) that evaluates the goodness of every candidate action by testing several of its features, like constraints, preconditions, steps, preferred effects for the system or the user. The evaluation proceeds in a hierarchic way: first the class of general actions reaching the given goal are considered, then each of them is refined by recursively evaluating its alternative specializations and choosing one of them. In this way, if an action has any specializations, the exploration phase is interleaved with the evaluation of the alternatives. The function Evaluate-score implements some heuristic criteria (described below) that score the action on the basis of the above-mentioned features. When there are no more specializations, either the action is an elementary one, or it has a decomposition; in the latter case, *Explore* is applied recursively to evaluate each single step. Note that the evaluation process is simplified if the system already knows the action score (see the *where* condition of the optional recursive steps).

In Figure 2 the *where* conditions, representing applicability restrictions for the action, are evaluated when an action is considered for execution. They are exploited either to establish bindings for the variables used to define the action (e.g. *lcr = Constr(act)* binds *lcr* to the list of constraints of *act*), or to determine if the action itself is appropriate to the current situation (allowing the interpreter of the problem-solving meta-plans to choose among alternative specializations, or to decide if an optional step has to be performed).

The evaluation of an action begins by ascertaining that the agent knows its relevant features, i.e. its constraints, preconditions, effects, and decompositions. Then all the features are considered with respect to their number, truth-value and relationship with the agents' goals. Constraints are checked; if just one of them is not satisfied, a negative score is associated to the action. This fact prevents from selecting the action because it is generally difficult or impossible to satisfy a constraint. The need for the agent to know these pieces of information in order to decide which action best further his goals is expressed by invoking the *Satisfy* action with the needed knowledge-related goal as argument; this accounts for the posting of new subgoals, that can lead the agent to initiate clarification dialogues. A situation where this occurs on the part of the system agent appears in Dialogue 2.

Clarification dialogues can start for knowing the various features of the action (as in first step of *Explore* in Figure 2[8]), the truth value of its constraints and preconditions (second and third steps), and to understand how the action effects impact on the agents' goals (see the *Consider-eff* step). In particular, the first step of the *Consider-eff* action states that a clarification dialogue can start when the actor has a goal involving a value, if he doesn't know whether it can fit in the action under analysis; in fact he needs this information to know if the action achieves something that he wants or not (e.g. one may have the goal: *at(agt,dest,t)* where $t \in (now, now+30')$, i.e. *agt* wants to be at *dest* in less than 30' from now. In this case he is interested in knowing what value takes t in the action *go-by-bus* in order to evaluate it with respect to *go-by-car)*. The second step states that if the considered action originated from a request made by some other agent, then it is important to know what are his attitudes toward the various effects.

The scoring criteria assign higher values to actions that better suit the current situation:

- *preconditions*: the score is negatively affected by the number of preconditions not yet satisfied.
- *effects*: they are evaluated according to how they match with the agents' goals, taking into account both user ID and system ID perspectives (as they are represented, respectively, in the user and system model). The general idea is that only effects for which the agents got a (positive or negative) preference should affect the action score.
- *steps*: they are taken into account by combining the score of each of them so that simpler actions could gain a higher score.
- *user's knowledge of the action*: when an action is known by the user, things are simpler because this prevents the system from planning a new explanation and the user hasn't to learn a new action; so, a known action is scored higher.

All these factors are combined in a weighted sum to obtain a value that is indicative of the action worth. Changing the weights it is possible to model different choice principles of the system: e.g. by weighting the effects more than the steps, it is possible to obtain a high score for an action preferred by both interlocutors even if its execution is complex. Another situation could be giving more importance to the system's goals with respect to the user's ones in case the system should fit a more prominent role with respect to the user. So the choice of the weights influences the degree of cooperativity of the system. Our scoring criteria, described in detail in (Sestero, 1998), proved useful to study how different factors affect the choice process.

5 Exploiting the linguistic libraries

The top-level actions of the linguistic library are the basic illocutionary acts needed for giving and obtaining information to (respectively from) another agent, and for making requests.

Each basic illocutionary act can be specialized in a simple (direct or indirect) linguistic act, or in a rhetorical structure achieving additional effects on the hearer. The more convenient specialization will be chosen by the problem-solving plans, according to what interpersonal goals are active.

The library of rhetorical relations, hence, can be seen as an extension of the basic speech act library in that, as the latter provides different ways (surface speech acts) to express a particular illocutionary act, the former supports more complex discourses by relating sequences of illocutionary acts according to their rhetorical achievements. For each basic illocutionary speech act the RST library provides different rhetorical means to realize them, exploiting additional information directly related to the content expressed by the illocutionary act. In Dialogue 2, below, two alternative ways are shown for asking a question adopting different realizations of the basic *Ask-info-if* illocutionary act.

IS: May I meet Professor Verdi?

IP': Have you a date with Professor Verdi? *(Ask-info-if-Direct)*

IP": Professors receive at office-hours time, or people with a date.
Have you a date with Professor Verdi? *(Ask-info-if-Background)*

Dialogue 2

IP" appears to be a more appropriate response than IP', because it gives more material and prevents a user clarification dialogue. But if a preference of the hearer was for simple discourse, IP'would be chosen.

Rhetorical plans are represented using the same formalism of domain and problem-solving plans. In particular, the problem-solving plans use all the scoring criteria described above for choosing a rhetorical action among the ones available for conveying the previously selected material. The effects of a rhetorical action are matched against the system interpersonal goals, while its applicability restrictions are checked to select an action appropriate to the contents of the knowledge base. In fact, the restrictions are used to specify the relationships occurring between the main content (nucleus; in our framework, typically a domain action) and some additional material related to it (satellites; e.g. the domain action's preconditions) that has to be mentioned in order to achieve the interpersonal goal. The decomposition field specifies how to link the whole material collected and may specify some linguistic features useful to connect the spans of text produced by the single statements.

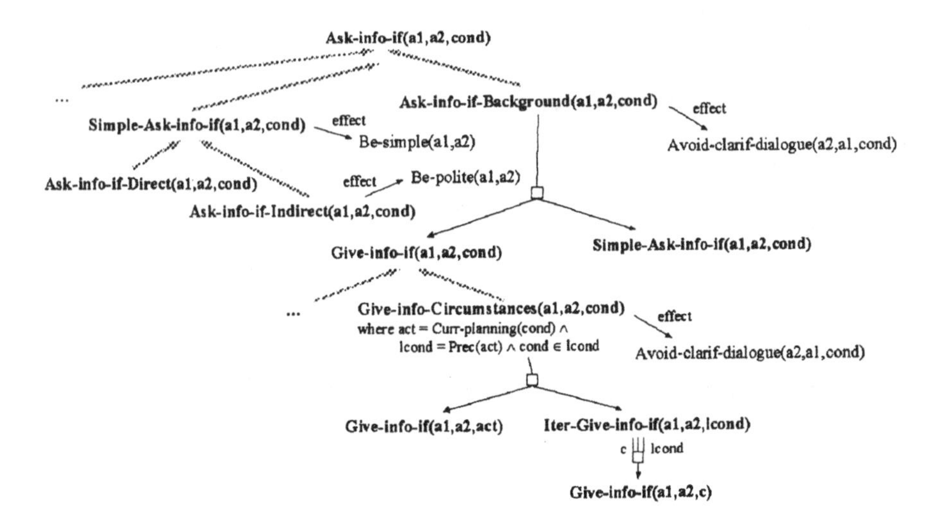

Figure 3. A portion of the linguistic libraries

A portion of the linguistic libraries, useful for producing the responses in Dialogue 2, is shown in Figure 3. Note that the function *Curr-planning(cond)* returns the action in which *cond* occurs and on which the agent is focused at the current stage of the plan-building process. In the figure, the effects of the basic illocutionary acts, inherited along the specialization hierarchy, are not shown; instead, the figure shows the *interpersonal effects* representing additional effects on the hearer produced by the adoption of the different linguistic means. From the shown portion of the library we see that a mean to avoid a clarification dialogue from the hearer when the speaker is asking the truth value of some condition *cond* is to provide some background first. Again, when informing somebody of a fact, a way to avoid a clarification dialogue about it is to provide some circumstantial information, like telling the context the fact is relevant for. e.g. for a precondition of an action, the context could be provided by mentioning the action and its precondition list.

6 An example

The structures described above can be used in producing responses like the system's one in Dialogue 3:

> U: I'm a computer science student. I would like to meet with Professor Verdi.
>
> S: Professors receive at office-hours time, or people with a date. Have you a date with Professor Verdi?
>
> U: No.
>
> S: Sending him an e-mail is better than meeting him, because he meets on Tuesday, from 9:00 to 12:00[9]. Verdi's e-mail address is: verdi@di.unito.it.

Dialogue 3

The interpretation of the first part of the user utterance lets the system activate the *computer-science-student* stereotype in the user model, while from the second part the system identifies the goal:

Goal(U, Perform(U, Meet(U, Verdi)))

The Meet action has the following effects:

Communication-took-place(person, professor)
Face-to-face(person, professor)
Loose-research-time(professor) (if ¬ Time=office-hours(professor))

Where the latter represents the fact that the professor will have less time left for research if this happens outside his office hours (note that to meet at office-hours is not a constraint of the action, so that in other situations, e.g. when the *graduating student* stereotype is active, the *Meet* action could be preferred over other actions). Since the latter effect conflicts with the system goal:

Goal(S, ¬ Loose-research-time(professor))

the goal manager adopts the most generic user's goal that doesn't conflict with the system's ones; this leads the *Explore* to evaluate the more generic action *Exchange-message-with-prof.* The *Explore* is then recursively applied to its alternative specializations, *Meet* and *Send-e-mail*; the latter having the following effects:

Communication-took-place(person, professor)
Quick-answer(professor, person),

that, according to the user model, are both desired by the user. Furthermore, a person needs an account to send an e-mail, and typically computer-science students have one. In order to evaluate the *Meet* action the system needs to know the truth value of its preconditions and, in particular, if the user has a date with the professor. A rule in the interpersonal goal manager infers that being the system cooperative on the linguistic level (Airenti et al., 1993), it should try to justify its question, in order to avoid a clarification dialogue from the user. The problem-solving process continues, then, trying to satisfy the communicative goal:

Goal(S, Knowif(S, ∃d.Date(U,Verdi,d)))

where the linguistic means *Ask-info-if-Background* and *Give-info-if-Circumstance* are selected by the *Explore* action due to the presence of the interpersonal goal *Avoid-clarif-dialogue*. After the user's reply, the problem-solving resumes on the domain level: skipping various details for simplicity of exposition, the *Explore* problem-solving plan balances the mentioned aspects of the current situation according to the chosen weights and eventually selects the *Send-e-mail* action.

Since the system believes a better action (with respect to the inferred one) exists for achieving the adopted goal, the system notifies the fact to the user. When trying to satisfy this communicative goal the interpersonal goal manager is invoked again and two rules fire, activating the goals *Justify-negative-cause* and *Increase-ability*. The latter is activated because the system is providing consulence, and from the user model it can be inferred that the user needs more information in order to execute the suggested action.

Hence, in the structuring phase, because the goal *Justify-negative-cause* is present, *Explore* selects from the linguistic library the *Give-info-if-Justification* plan. This plan links in its decomposition the main content (nucleus):

Better-plan(Send-e-mail(U,Verdi), Meet(U,Verdi))

with further information (satellite) providing a reason making the fact more acceptable by the user. Furthermore, the *Give-info-if-Enablement* plan adds Verdi's e-mail address, fulfilling the goal *Increase-ability*.

7 Conclusions and further work

In this paper we have been concerned with the production of a natural and cooperative response. We considered the crucial issues of choosing what information to provide and how to structure it, providing new insights on the two related problems of content selection and structuring in the framework of a rational agent involved in information-seeking dialogues.

We developed from the generation perspective a model of dialogue that was previously used to study the pragmatic interpretation activity of an agent. In such a model the underlying reasoning activity of the agent is explicitly represented by means of original problem-solving plans, that manage domain and linguistic actions.

An integrated plan-based architecture for a conversational agent has been described. The agent generates flexible answers, thanks to its ability to gather all information useful to evaluate alternative courses of action, and to exploit various linguistic means and knowledge to interact with the user.

Probably the main limitation of the model described is its initial degree of implementation. In particular, the model was developed considering hand-crafted examples and would need an extensive testing with real users.

The part that needs further development is that responsible for intention acquisition. It involves both the domain and the interpersonal goal managers. At the moment the decision to adopt another agent's domain goal is taken simply on the basis of lack of conflict with one of the planning agent's goals, and the rules implementing the interpersonal goals manager consider only a limited number of situations. We plan to encode some general criteria to relate the goals of two autonomous agents so that it would be possible to create and abandon goals coherently with their relative dependencies and the evolution of the problem-solving process. In addition, the goal managers should make use of a representation of the social relationships between the agents (see (Miceli, Cesta and Rizzo, 1995)) in that they provide the reasons for the interaction.

A related problem is an adequate treatment of failures in trying to execute an action. In our system they can be caused by a number of circumstances like: an unpredictable change in the state of the world (e.g. a selected-action's constraint becomes false), something going wrong during the action execution (e.g. some noise occurs in the communication channel obscuring the message), some wrong assumption made about the user's knowledge, user's lack of acceptance of a system's suggestion or request. At the moment, the problem-solving plans detect such anomalies and possibly notify them (in other words, possibilities for acknowledgements and negotiations are allowed), but a thorough treatment of the anomalous situation lacks. It would imply the agent ability to revise the overall plan, considering next-best possibilities, and setting up new goals appropriate to the changed situation.

We are also considering how it is possible to introduce some defaults in the action choice mechanism, in order to avoid producing too many clarification dialogues. At the moment, the only factors limiting system-initiated clarification dialogues are the absence of an explicit goal *Clarif-dialogues-allowed(S,U)*, and the information stored in the stereotypes. In general, the balance between the utility of a piece of information and the degree of user's annoyance should be considered (see (Raskutti and Zukerman, 1994)). One way to reduce the number of questions could be to produce extended responses with conditionals appropriate to different possible situations.

References

Airenti G., Bara B.G. and Colombetti M. 1993. Conversational and behavior games in the pragmatics of dialogue. Cognitive Science 17, 197-256.

Allen J. 1996. Natural Language Understanding. 2nd Edition. Benjamin Cummings, (540-576).

Appelt D.E. 1985. Planning English Sentences. Cambridge University Press, Cambridge, England.

Ardissono L., Lombardo A. and Sestero D. 1993. A flexible approach to cooperative response generation in information-seeking dialogues. In Proceedings of the 31st Annual Meeting of the ACL. 274-276. Columbus, OH.

Ardissono L., Boella G. and Lesmo L. 1995. Indirect speech-acts and politeness: A computational approach. In Proceedings of the 17th Annual Conference of the Cognitive Science Society. Pittsburgh, PA, 316-321.

Ardissono L., Boella G. and Sestero D. 1996. Uso di piani di problem-solving nel riconoscimento di piani e obiettivi. Interfacce Intelligenti. AI*IA Notizie. Periodico dell'Associazione Italiana per l'Intelligenza Artificiale. Supplemento Anno IX-3

Ardissono L. and Sestero D. 1996. Using dynamic user models in the recognition of the plans of the user. User Modeling and User-Adapted Interaction, 5(2):157-190

Bara B. G. 1990. Scienza cognitiva: un approccio evolutivo alla simulazione della mente. Bollati Boringhieri, Torino.

Belkin N. J., Cool C., Stein A. and Thiel U. 1995. Cases, Scripts, and Information-Seeking Strategies: On the Design of Interactive Information Retrieval Systems. Expert Systems with Applications, Volume 9(3), 379-395.

Brown P. and Levinson S.C. 1987. Politeness: some universals on language usage. Cambridge University Press, Cambridge, England.

Carberry S. 1988. Modeling the user's plans and goals. Computational Linguistics, 14, 23-37.

Carberry S., Kazi Z. and.Lambert L. 1992. Modeling discourse, problem-solving, and domain goals incrementally in task-oriented dialogue. Proceedings 3rd Int. Workshop on User Modeling. 192-201.

Carberry S., Chu-Carrol J., Green N. and Lambert L. 1993. Rhetorical Structure Theory: Necessary but not sufficient. Proceedings of the ACL Workshop on Intentionality and Structure in Discourse Relations.

Carberry S. and Chu-Carrol J. 1995. Response Generation in Collaborative Negotiation. In Proceedings of the 33rd Annual Meeting of the ACL, State University of New York, Buffalo, 136-143. Association for Computational Linguistics, Arlington, VA.

Castelfranchi C. and Parisi D. 1980. Linguaggio, conoscenze e scopi. Il Mulino. Bologna.

Cawsey A. 1993. Explanation and Interaction: The Computer Generation of Explanatory Dialogues. MIT Press, Cambridge, MA

Cohen P.R. and Levesque H.J. 1990. Rational interaction as the basis for communication. In Cohen, Morgan, and Pollack, editors, Intentions in communications, 221-255. MIT Press.

Fawcett R.P., van der Mije A. and van Wissen C. 1988. Towards a Systemic Flowchart Model for Discourse. In Fawcett R.P. and Young D. (eds.): New Developments in Systemic Linguistics. Vol.2: Theory and Application. London, Pinter, 116-143.

Hovy E. H. 1988a. Planning coherent multisentential text. In Proceedings 26th Annual Conference of the ACL, Buffalo, NY, 163-169.

Hovy E.H. 1988b. Generating Natural Language under Pragmatic Constraints. Lawrence Erlbaum, Hillsdale, NJ.

Hovy E.H. 1993. Automated discourse generation using discourse structure relations. Artificial Intelligence 63, 341-385.

Kautz H. 1990. A Circumscriptive Theory of Plan Recognition. In P.R. Cohen, J. Morgan, and M. E. Pollack, eds., Intentions in Communication, 105-133. MIT Press.

Lesmo L. and Lombardo V. 1993. Un approccio computazionale all'interpretazione del linguaggio. Epistemologia. Fascicolo speciale su Linguaggi e Macchine. 165-190.

Mann W.C. and Thompson S.A. 1988. Rhetorical Structure Theory: Towards a functions theory of text organization. TEXT 8(3):243-81.

McKeown K.R. 1985. Text Generation: Using Discourse Strategies and Focus Constraints to Generate Natural Language Text. Cambridge University Press, Cambridge, England.

Miceli M., Cesta A. and Rizzo P. 1995. Distributed artificial intelligence from a socio-cognitive standpoint: Looking at reasons for interaction. Acta Psychologica special issue on Cognitive Ergonomics.

Moore, R.C. 1985. A formal theory of knowledge and action. In J. R. Hobbs and R. C. Moore, editors, Formal Theories of the Commonsense World. Ablex Publishing Corp., Norwood, NJ, 319-358.

Moore J.D. and Pollack M.E. 1992. A problem for RST: The need for multi-level discourse analysis. Computational Linguistics 18(4):537-44

Moore J.D. 1995. Participating in Explanatory Dialogues. Interpreting and Responding to Questions in Context. MIT Press, Cambridge, MA.

Paris C.L. 1988. Tailoring Object Descriptions to a User's Level of Expertise. Computational Linguistics 14(3),64-78

Ramshaw L.A. 1989. A metaplan for problem-solving discourse. In Proceedings of the 29th Annual Meeting of ACL, 39-46, Berkeley, CA.

Raskutti B. and Zukerman I. 1994. Query and response generation during information-seeking interactions. In Proceedings of the 4th Conference on User Modeling. Hyannis, MA, 25-30.

Russell S. and Norvig P. 1995. Artificial Intelligence, A Modern Approach. Prentice Hall.

Sestero D. 1998. Producing Responses in Goal-Endowed Dialogue Systems. Doctorate thesis. University and Polytechnic of Torino.

Stein A. and Maier E. 1995. Structuring collaborative information-seeking dialogues. Knowledge-Based Systems, Volume 8, Numbers 2-3, Elsevier Science. 82-93.

Wilensky, R. 1981. Meta-planning: Representing and using knowledge about planning in problem-solving and natural language understanding. Cognitive Science 5, 197-233.

Winograd T. and Flores F. 1986. Understanding Computers and Cognition. Ablex.

Wooldridge M. and Jennings N. R. 1995. Intelligent Agents: Theory and Practice. Knowledge Engineering Review, Volume 10, Number 2.

Notes

[1] At the present time we are considering two-participants dialogues.

[2] We consider as related two goals having a common subgoal; in the example meeting Professor Verdi and sending him an e-mail are related because both include the more generic goal of communicating with him.

[3] The system should provide consultation about the services offered by a Computer Science Department.

[4] In pragmatics the concept of face was introduced by Brown and Levinson (1987) to characterize some wants that every participant to a dialogue normally has about freedom of action and self-image. They use this notion to explain why the interlocutors tend to smooth the interaction by exploiting indirect forms of communications.

[5] We follow the terminology introduced by (Castelfranchi and Parisi, 1980): adhesion concerns goals explicitly communicated by other agents, while adoption involves goals that have been inferred as belonging to other agents, hence are just plausible hypothesis on the other agents wants.

[6] E.g. IF S intends U to perform an action, S believes that U does not know the action decomposition, and S is providing consulence to U, THEN set up the goal to increase U's ability to perform the action.

[7] In the examples, though, we write the system's output in natural language for the sake of exposition.

[8] Since in our application the system plays the role of the domain expert, this step is specially important to recognize user's intentions underlying his questions during the

recognition phase. In general, however, an agent may be willing to reach a goal and perform the action himself but he may lack the knowledge about how to do it.

[9] We suppose that the present time is not Professor Verdi's office hours (because it is Wednesday). At the moment we do not consider the temporal evolution of the state of the world: we suppose that the world remains as it is when the system makes the plan. Furthermore, we suppose that some actions are to be performed immediately after the interaction (e.g. meeting a professor), while others could be planned for the future (e.g. giving an exam).

8 Deception and Suspicion in Medical Interactions

C. Castelfranchi, F. de Rosis and F. Grasso

1 Introduction

Some years ago, we started a research study devoted at investigating the reasoning processes involved in the dialogues between *agents with personality*; we focused, in particular, on conflict resolution dialogues. In choosing an application domain, we decided to exploit the medical literature, both for 'historical' reasons (our personal research interests) and because dialogues in this scenario are complex enough to provide interesting ideas without being trivial. In a previous work (de Rosis and Grasso, 1997; de Rosis et al., 1998b), we examined the styles of reasoning that guides such a dialogue and we formalized these styles in a dialogue simulation system, XANTHIPPE. The system, developed in Lisp, had a *believable* behaviour in most of the simpler situations. However, it was not able to deal with more sophisticated aspects of the reasoning process, such as elusion, reticence, omission and other stronger forms of deception.

This limit is not infrequent in human-computer interaction and, more in general, in multi-agent systems: as a matter of fact, the *sincere assertion* hypothesis is common to many systems simulating a dialogue between autonomous agents. It is generally agreed that sincerity is a necessary characteristic of cooperative interaction, in the sense that collaboration cannot exist without sincerity or when it is possible to withhold information. Moreover, in cooperative interactions, when an agent believes that a conflict exists, it always manifests it and adopts the goal of convincing the opponent to change its mind, if possible. One of the most sophisticated dialogue systems, due to Chu-Carrol and Carberry (1995) is based on this hypothesis, which also underlines the formalization of "rational agency" due to Van der Hoeck and colleagues (1997), as well as many other systems.

In our opinion, although the sincerity assertion hypothesis is justified in scenarios such as information seeking dialogues (see for instance ARTIMIS (Bretier and Sadek, 1997)), this does not apply to all types of conversations. "Lying is a fact of social life rather than an extraordinary or unusual event. People tell lies to accomplish the most basic social interaction goals, such as influencing others, managing impressions and providing reassurance and support" (DePaulo et al., 1996; Kashy and DePaulo, 1996). In cooperation, collaboration and dialogues, deception is present for at least two reasons:

a) there are forms of deception which are cooperative, in that they are aimed at helping the other: for instance, 'white lies'. Thus, a friend can deceive, a doctor can deceive and so on, for the benefit of the deceived person;

b) also within cooperation, collaboration or help, there may be conflicts; when a conflict exists, there is an inclination towards deceiving in order to better deal with possible obstacles or opposition. This is particularly true within collaborative relations, because people do not want to broken a collaboration but want to achieve, at the same time, their selfish or conflicting goals.

Moreover, in these situations (a deception for one's own benefit or for not brokening a collaborative situation) an agent may often decide not to communicate that it discovered a deception of the other; this agent will then deceive in its turn, by renouncing to the goal of forcing the opponent to tell the truth. Our claim is therefore that every system addressing conflict resolution dialogues in a realistic and believable way should take into account and be able to deal with deception and suspect. In particular, such a system needs to handle the subtle and implicit forms of deception, often based on implicatures, which are very common when the conflict among the agents is not open and is part of a collaborative attitude. It should consider that, to avoid compromising the collaboration, both conflict and deception are often extenuated and not made too manifest, and that the deceiving agent tends to give the opponent the opportunity to turn a blind eye, or even to be a party to it. For example, when a patient asks a doctor some advice about a delicate topic 'on behalf of a friend', the doctor may realize that this is a lie and that the patient is probably talking about himself; nevertheless, she may pretend to not notice it, and the patient is perhaps aware of that.

How is it possible to deceive without lying? How can an agent let the opponent to infer the false or ignore the truth, from a vague and incomplete message and without literally saying it? How can an agent be suspicious of the opponent and discover a deception? In this paper we try and give a preliminary answer to all these questions, by examining some conflicts between doctors and patients, their indirect and fuzzy deceptions and their principles of mistrusting. We do not intend to give here operational solutions, but rather to show guidelines that can lead to a solution, and principles on which, we believe, a formalization should be based.

2 State of the art

We can conclude, from previous considerations, that formalizing the reasoning processes leading both to deceive and to discover a deception is necessary, even in a cooperative dialogue. However, especially in cooperative dialogues, this formalization is particularly complex.

If deception is not allowed, it is relatively easy to define the conditions which have to hold for an agent A_i to come to believe in a proposition p which was communicated by another agent A_j. The first formal definition of Sincerity in an agents world is due to Cohen and Levesque (1995): "agent i is sincere to j about p if, whenever i wants j to come to believe p, i wants j to come to know p". In the same work, the two authors also give a semantic for the Inform speech act: "an inform is defined as an attempt in which to make an honest effort; the speaker is committed to making public that he is committed to the addressee's knowing that he knows p".

Subsequently, Van der Hoeck and colleagues (1997) have defined an operator establishing the conditions for the agent receiving the communication to revise its beliefs, according to the *credibility* of the source[1]. They, however, do not explicit the conditions for an agent to determine the trustworthiness or credibility level of another agent or of the piece of information received, nor how agents behave in cases in which they receive a *low credibility level* piece of information, and when more reliable information is missing.

This problem has inspired a few recent works. Demolombe (1997) focuses on the meaning of "reliability of an information source (or agent) i in regard to the validity of a sentence p", and addresses the problem of defining "reliability levels". Lelouche and Doublait (1992) define a *bluff* as a "false information deliberately introduced as true in somebody's knowledge base", in their application to military battlefields and strategy games. They define "deceiving behaviour generation rules", such as "IF William pretends to Mary that he loves her, THEN William kisses Mary". These rules are employed both to generate deceiving behaviours and to interpret them. The authors, however, admit that manipulating bluffs is very complex in nature, and that "it is impossible for an actor to transform a belief about a fact into a certainty, no matter the number of evidences that he may have to support his beliefs". Lee and Wilks (1997) make a further step in this direction, by examining a category of "conversational implicatures" which they call "residual", insofar as they hold when mistaken beliefs and deceptions can be excluded. They consider the cases in which, although a deceitful information is communicated, the aim of the communication is not to actually deceive the opponent (e.g. irony). In these situations it is clear that "the interacting agent j is trying to convince i about some proposition p that both of them may infer to be true".

Before passing to the main topic of this paper, that is the formalization of some significant examples of deception and suspect between doctors and patients, we try and describe the forms of deception and the techniques that may be applied to discover them, and we examine in more details the types of *conversational untrustworthy interchanges* on which we focus in this work.

3 Deception and suspicion

To deceive is not simply to lie, and to lie is not simply to say the false (Castelfranchi, Falcone and de Rosis, 1998; Castelfranchi and Poggi, 1998):

- first, both for deception and for lie (which is a particular form of deception), the 'subjective' truth, that is what the speaker believes, is more important than the 'objective' truth. A is deceiving B (or attempting to deceive B) when he is doing something in order to lead B to believe, either wrongly or incompletely, something that is true in A's beliefs. So, to accomplish a deceptive act, A should not necessarily say or let B to believe the false;
- secondly, deceiving does not necessarily require inducing B to believe something: concealing is a form of deception too, if the hidden information is relevant for B and is not a "secret";
- thirdly, communication is not necessary for deceiving (while it is necessary for lying).

In other words, there are several **facets of deception**:

- **passive** deception, when the deceiving agent simply lets the other agent ignore something that is crucial for him, or believe something that is wrong; and 'active' deception, when the deceiving agent does something in order to reach the same effect;
- deception **by ignorance**, when the effect of deception is that the deceived agent ignores something crucial for him (like in concealment, omission, etc.) and deception **by falsity**, when he believes something false (like in lies, bluff, etc.)
- deception **with communication** (like in lies and bluff) and **without any communication**. Not every social deception requires communication. It might be quite difficult, for instance, to call 'communication' the fact that A does nothing at all to obtain that B continues to ignore something or continues to believe something wrong. It is also difficult to extend the notion of communication to the case in which A does something to obtain that B does not know something else!
- deception by **implicit, behavioural communication** (e.g. bluff) and **by explicit** and **specialized communication acts**, like speech acts (e.g. lies).

Introducing these distinctions is important not only for conceptual reasons but also because in this paper we show cases of lie, cases of active concealment and cases where the patient or the doctor try to let the other believe something wrong or incomplete. We find, as well, cases of bluff, in which the agent attempts to let the other believe -from her/his behaviour- that s/he has not understood the request, or s/he is not aware of the other's deception. We will examine, finally, examples of subtle and indirect lie (Vincent and Castelfranchi, 1981) which are based on inferences: what the speaker literally says is not false but what s/he intends or hopes the other believes is false. In other words, while the goal of the information speech act is not deceptive, the super-goal (the effect the speaker intends to achieve, through the speech act, in the addressee's mind) is deceptive. This is what is usually called a 'half truth': what I say is true but I do not say all the truth, I conceal part of the truth in order for you to understand something wrong that I did not say. This is very important for several reasons, first of all to avoid responsibility. In indirect lies, the speaker exploits the hearer ignorance or wrong beliefs or weakness of rationality to induce him/her to believe something wrong: she plans the hearer to be deceived by her/himself.

3.1. Distrust principles

Many sorts of reasons exist to doubt or to know for sure that a source is saying something false, and maybe is lying, or to know exactly the object of its lie. Recognizing a false assertion is different from identifying a deception: the source saying the false may simply be making a mistake, or a misunderstanding might be present (for instance due to an ambiguity). The criteria for identifying falsity differ from those for identifying deception. They are, though, obviously related, insofar as it is possible to pass from one situation to the other and vice versa.

Two fundamental principles exist:

1. If x is saying something false, then x might be lying
2. If x is lying, then x meant to say something false (what x says might be false).

To evaluate a piece of information, then, two aspects need to be considered: the source and the communication content.

Criteria exist to evaluate a source (reliability) as well as the content of a piece of information (plausibility);from those criteria, one can derive the believability of the candidate, proposed belief and of the belief one was holding before, to decide which one to hold. Interactions exist between the two classes of criteria: for instance, the source competence is related to the content type. The criteria for suspecting of a deception concern the source, whereas the criteria for suspecting of a falsity concern the content. We trust a source by default (Grice, 1975) and we believe by default, unless we have specific reasons to distrust or to disbelieve. But, what sort of reasons? Let us first examine the process leading to believe that the communication is false and subsequently the process leading to believe that the source might be lying.

a. Implausible content

The basic principle to discover falsity is the *Law of Contradiction* (LoC), which concerns the content: "an agent cannot believe both P and not P; as one of them has to be false, it cannot be believed, it must be rejected". From a psychological point of view, however, the analysis of the content is much more complex, and concerns the "fuzzy" evaluation of its plausibility. A piece of information could be disbelieved though not being considered false, because it is not plausible, as:

- it contradicts another, more trustworthy source

- it contradicts other, personal information (what is known or can be inferred) which is more believable.

Let us now pass to the principles which lead to suspect of a source.

b. Contradictory source

A source contradicting itself is saying something false. In addition, if we suppose a perfect memory of what has been said, we can assume that a source cannot ignore to be contradictory, and therefore it is lying, that is it intends to tell the false. Knowing that a source is lying, though, is of no help to know which is the true, even if we are in the hypothesis of a two-valued world. If x says P, and P is false, then not P is true. But if x says both P and not P, we know that x is lying but we cannot identify whether P is true or not.

c. Opportunistic and tendentious source

Has the source a rationale for lying? Or, better, does the source benefit from the fact that I believe to what it says? The problem is then to recognize the source's plan, to understand whether the fact that I come to believe P is useful for its purposes (consider, for instance, the case of a salesman describing the qualities of the product he is trying to sell).

d. Flattering source

This situation is similar to the previous one, but in this case the source is concerned about the addressee's goals rather than about its own goals, and in particular about what the addressee may be pleased to believe.

e. Suspect source.

- the source has already lied (it is lying, it lied once);
- the source said it is lying;
- the source has a bad reputation (someone else, reliable, says it lied or it is lying);
- the source belongs to a class of liars.

We can then define the steps of a reasoning process to pass from falsity to lie:

1. as I do not believe to what the source says, what it says is not true;
2. if the source says something not true, it might lie (there are three possibilities: it made a mistake, there was a misunderstanding or it lied).

3. how can I be sure it lied?
   - could the source ignore the truth? to which information sources has it access? how competent is it?
   - is the source interested in telling the false?
   - is the source willing to please me?
   - is the source a liar?

4 Some examples of deception in the interaction between patients and medical staff

It is a common opinion that deception, if not lie, is applied by doctors in their interaction with patients, with a frequency which is related to the context (see, for instance, (Hope, 1995; Ryan, de Moore and Patfield, 1995; Teasdale and Kent, 1995). Though direct lie is recently thought to be incorrect, other forms of 'white deception' are considered as 'permissible', such as deliberate decision to withhold relevant information, half-truths, distortions of the truth, elusion. These forms of deception are justified, by people in charge for health care or by medical psychologists, with the aim of' promoting what is perceived as better care for the patient' and, more specifically, by principles of reassurance. Deception may help preventing the patients from becoming more anxious about their conditions, that might result in jeopardizing the goal to cure them. Deceptions are also used, especially by nurses, to help dealing with patients, or even to hide incompetence and avoid 'loosing face'.

Deception can concern several aspects of health care: non-disclosure of diagnosis in severe diseases, side-effects of drugs, prediction of prognosis, expected pain after operations, relationships with relatives. Arguments have also been raised against the traditional use of placebos, in which "the physician administers a treatment known to him or to her to be without pharmacologic potency and (...) either tells or allows the patients to believe that the treatment has such potency" (Brody, 1982).

A notable example of 'subtle lies' (Brody, 1982) in medical documents is given by explanations about side effects of drugs. After a linguistic analysis of the side effects descriptions in 25 medical package inserts, Glinert (1998) concludes that the necessity to pursue both the goal of warning of a hazard and the goal of reassuring the patient, may lead to downplay the warning, or to concentrate on the reassuring goal[2] or to hedge, by using generic concessions[3]. We drew a similar conclusion after an analysis of a corpus of transcripts of drug prescription explanations provided by English physicians (de Rosis, Grasso and Berry, 1998). Downplaying techniques were extensively used both when describing the patient health status and the therapy prescribed, and when warning about its possible side effects.

If deception by medical staff has been studied rather intensively, less has been said about deception by patients. We found two sets of examples in the literature, which seem to us a good source of reflection on this issue. The first one is concerned with some conversations between a doctor and a diabetic teenager, in UK; the second one with some conversations between a gynaecologist and a female patient about contraceptive prescriptions, in Italy. We'll try to make some reasonable interpretation of the reasoning process behind these dialogues which, however, we do not pretend to be the only one possible.

4.1 Dialogues with adolescent diabetics

Diabetes mellitus is a common metabolic problem in childhood, which requires a life-long regime of invasive, self-administered tests and injections and control of diet. Patients are therefore active decision-makers and are morally responsible for their actions. In describing the results of his observation of 47 consultations of adolescent diabetics in two clinics in the UK, Silverman (1987) reports several examples of young patients' deception, that he attributes to the production of feelings of guilt due to the patients' desire to be considered as 'reliable' in managing self-care. In the following examples, D stands for 'Doctor', P for 'Patient', A, S and G are young patient's names for 'Alan', 'Sylvia' and 'Gordon', whereas F stands for 'Alan's father' and M for 'Sylvia's mother'.

Example 1

The doctor has the prejudice of suspecting the young patient of lying, especially because the result of the self-test is "too good to be true".However, he does not manifest explicitly his distrust, nor does it accuse the patient to manipulate the results. His comment is implicit (in fact, the patient's father "translates" it). The boy is first silent; then, he seems to awkwardly try a false implicature.

D:	Alan, these figures look too good to be true. Is that right Alan?
A:	No
F:	What he means is have you been making them up?
	[no response]
	[...]
D:	Does anybody check them with you?
A:	Sometimes
D:	Well I think all we can say is that it's unlikely that the results really indicate your control.
	[Alan is fiddling with his sweater]

Figure 1: Example 1: dialogue with adolescent diabetics, from (Silverman, 1987)

Example 2

This is a situation of reticence and lie. The doctor starts by congratulating with the patient "if the results are real" (a case of irony?), but .. "are they real"? The boy seems to feel guilty, he is silent, does not respond to the congratulations, and then lies: he says he does not know whether the results are good, while he should have confessed that the results '"are good, BUT...". In effect, from the doctor's sentence he could have inferred the generalization "today things are OK", which the boy knows to be not true, and a sort of congratulating attitude, which he knows to be not justified. He should pronounce that "BUT" which could stop the doctor from making all those mistaken implicatures (the "BUT" is then said by the patient's mother). The boy, instead, expresses his puzzlement about the doctor's evaluation of the results. However, this puzzlement (which is genuine) is not actually related

D:	Well, you've got the record today, 22 percent
	.....
D:	Would you say the control's good?
S:	I don't know
D:	Come on!
M:	It was good but it's gone off lately
	.....
D:	Well, the control is a bit up and down, isn't it?
S:	Yes.

Figure 2: Example 2: dialogue with adolescent diabetics, from (Silverman, 1987)

to what the boy literally said (he perfectly knows that those results ARE good) but is related to what he thinks the doctor can infer (that he knows to be false).

Example 3

This is a case of deception by using a misleading inference, or "half truth". The boy tries to induce a false inference: from "two or three A day" he tries to induce the inference "two or three EVERY day".

D:	Okay (0.5) so what sort of results are you getting then?
G:	Well ( ) average between ten and six (1.0) not too bad
D:	Blood sugars you're talking about?
G:	Yeah blood sugars
D:	When are you doing them mostly?
G:	Well I'm doing them before my breakfast, before my tea and er ( ) now and again I'm doing them before bed and weekends. I'm doing them at dinner time and that
D:	Are you doing them one a day or are you doing them...
G:	Two or three a day
D:	Two or three every day?
G:	Well, not every day
D:	Hh hmm
G:	You know something like (2.0 second pause) one day, miss a day and then again (1 second pause)
D:	Uh I mean I'm impressed. I've not er been critical er been impressed if you've been doing these ( )

Figure 3: Example 3: dialogue with adolescent diabetics, from (Silverman, 1987)

4.2 Dialogues about contraceptives

The following conversations are English translations of dialogues which were recorded in a private family planning clinic (Petrillo, 1994).

Example 4

This is another case of reticence, with subsequent lie, with the aim of justifying a choice which is known to be not rational, and cannot be justified. The doctor pretends to believe what the patient says, but tries to lead the patient to communicate, as well, the real rationale for her choice. The patient keeps on lying, and attributes her own belief to her gynaecologist.

P: I would like you to prescribe me a contraceptive pill.
D: You would like to take the pill (2.0) and you already know other methods (.) why have you considered the pill?
[Ora vorresti prendere la pillola (2.0) e conosci gia' altri metodi (.) per quale motivo hai pensato alla pillola?]
P: Eh, I don't want to fit a coil!
[Eh, la spirale non la voglio mettere]
D: Why don't you feel like fitting a coil?
[Perche' non te la senti per la spirale?]
P: I don't know why... My gynaecologist advised me against it
[Non lo so (.) perche' il mio ginecologo me l'aveva sconsigliata]
D: Your gynaecologist advised you against it.. did he tell you why?
[Il ginecologo te l'ha sconsigliata non ti ha detto per quale motivo?]
P: He says it's a foreign body, after all...
[Dice che e' sempre un corpo estraneo (3.0)]
D: well, from a point of view...
[Va be' tu da un // punto di vista]
P: I'm definitely not inclined to fit it
[?Io non sono proprio propensa a metterla]
D: No, no I was saying that from a point of view, say, of contraceptive programme, it is correct that you now take the pill, it's a right period, you are young.
[No no io ti stavo dicendo che da un punto di vista (.) diciamo di programma di contraccezione e' giusto che tu adesso la prenda (la pillola) e' un periodo giusto, sei giovane.]

Figure 4: Example 4: dialogue about contraceptives, from (Petrillo, 1994)

Example 5

This is an example of reticence and elusion. The patient does not want to take the pill into consideration as an alternative contraceptive method. She then avoids an

D: OK? No, I was just thinking:: between coil and pill, which is the best thing to choose now (1.0)? You've come with a resolute position in favour of the coil
[Va bene? No pensavo appunto:: tra la spirale e la pillola quale fosse la cosa migliore da scegliere adesso(1.0)? tu sei gia' venuta decisa (.) per la spirale]
P: Hm I've come exhausted not resoluted, because I don't want another baby
[Eh sono venuta proprio esaurita non decisa perche' non lo voglio un altro figlio]
D: ?Yes I got it, but if you don't want other babies you could also...you don't necessarily have to use a coil
[?Si questo l'ho capito pero' per non volere un altro figlio no si puo' anche ... non necessariamente ti devi mettere la spirale]
P: What should I do, should I come to sleep at your home?
[E come faccio me ne vengo a dormire a casa tua?]

Figure 5: Example 5: dialogue about contraceptives, from (Petrillo, 1994)

indirect doctor's question, with the aims, at the same time, of both not taking the pill and not talking about her decision.

Example 6

If the patient's answer was deliberate, then this is a case of elusion of the question: the patient answers the question "why did you take the pill" instead of answering to

D: Did a doctor prescribe it or:: // did you just take it
[E ti era stata data da un medico o:://l'hai presa cosi']
P: No I just took it
[No l'ho presa cosi']
D: Ah why did you take it without...
[Ah come mai l'hai presa senza...]
P: Eh, in order to avoid another pregnancy
[Eh per non avere un'altra gravidanza]

Figure 6: Example 6: dialogue about contraceptives, from (Petrillo, 1994)

"why did you take the pill without prescription". Then, either she did not get the purpose of the doctor, or she just does not want to talk about that.

4.3. Comments on the examples.

A general observation about the previous dialogues concerns the conversants' behaviour. Both the patients and (especially) the doctors never lie "explicitly". They evade the question by making a joke (example 5), or use more subtle forms of deception, or omission, or reticence. Moreover, when realizing that the patient is lying, the doctors never reveal the deception, clearly preferring different aims. Rather, they try and stimulate the patients to tell the truth themselves, and if this does not happen, they just give up.

5 XANTHIPPE

XANTHIPPE is a dialogue simulation system, originally developed as part of a wider project: an advice-giving system in the medical domain. In the simulation, the system plays the role of the "expert", that is the doctor, whereas the user is the "patient". A more thorough description of the dialogue module can be found in (de Rosis et al., 1998b). Here, only its main characteristics are described.

The conversing agents in XANTHIPPE are *agents with personality*. Personality factors are close to representing the "aims" of an agent and the ways to pursue them (Carbonell, 1980; Castelfranchi et al., 1998). In conflict resolution conversations, personality traits can play various roles. They can influence the choice of the strategy to employ in a conflicting situation, the degree with which an agent is attached to its own goals or the reaction of an agent to the success or the failure of one of its strategies. If we assume that personality traits influence human communication, then also when conversing with a computer it has sense to consider these factors in the user model. There is by now agreement on the fact that a real "friendly" computer system has to be able to perceive the personality of its users to tailor its behaviour to them; it is admitted, as well, that an "intelligent" system has, more or less implicitly, its own behaviour and idiosyncrasy, which can be allegedly seen as a "personality" (Nass et al., 1995).

Each of XANTHIPPE's agent has a mental state formed by two, not totally symmetric components:

- one's own state, where own beliefs and goals are represented, together with the rules that link them (first order beliefs).
- other agent's default image, with a similar structure (second order beliefs).

Agents interact by exchanging communicative acts (Inform, Request, Ask-Whether, Ask-Why and so on) linked by rhetorical relations.

The conversation can be seen as the result of applying recursively several forms of reasoning, in a sequence that depends on the context, on the two agent's personalities and on the results of the previous reasoning step. The following forms of reasoning have been envisaged so far:

a. interpret the communication received

We do not consider the linguistic aspects of interpretation, and assume that a statement is always interpreted "correctly" as a standard communicative act. We classify communicative acts as *questions* or *proposals*, which activate different forms of reasoning and reaction.

b. discover a conflict between one's own beliefs and goals and the received proposal

After a proposal, the receiving agent has to decide whether it conflicts or not with its own belief and goal structure, by reasoning on its own mental state.

c. make hypotheses about the reasons supporting a proposal

The agent may decide whether to accept the proposal by reasoning only on its own mental state (as in the previous step) or also on the other agent's one; this decision is regulated, in the literature, by the agent's 'attitude', which is defined as cooperative or non-cooperative. In cooperative dialogues (Chu-Carrol and Carberry, 1995), the agent would accept a non-conflicting proposal without reasoning on the other agent's mental state: this form of reasoning would be activated only to discover weaknesses in the other agent's viewpoint, to be exploited in argumentation (Sycara, 1991). We maintain that believable agents (Reilly and Bates, 1995) show various levels of cooperativity as to specific goals, even within the same dialogue: cooperativity levels depend on the context, and therefore on the agent's higher order goals, but also on its personality. For example: an *altruistic* agent would behave in a *truly cooperative* way, by considering systematically the other agent's viewpoint, to verify whether the received proposal really matches this agent's presumed interests. In this context, it may consider the possibility that the other agent is insincere, to postulate whether to believe in the communication received or not: as we will see in next Section, this type of reasoning typically requires reflecting on the reasons why a proposal was made by the other agent.

d. decide when to make a question, and which question

In purely rational negotiation dialogues, information is requested only when the agent hasn't enough data to decide whether to accept the other agent's proposal. When believable agents are modelled, this decision is conditioned, as well, to *higher order goals*, which are essential in establishing when to make a question and which question. In our example dialogues, the doctor makes either 'open' or 'closed' questions. The first question type is not necessarily preferred when the doctor hasn't enough information to decide; it can be influenced, as well, from higher order goals, such as 'to encourage the patient to assume an active role', or to 'manifest an enlistening attitude'. In selecting a closed question, doctors might, on the contrary, be willing 'to show their competence', or 'to manifest their intention to place the patient on a parity position', and so on.

e. decide how to answer a question

After a question, the agent has to verify the truth value of its owns beliefs or goals (in case of true/false questions) or which data support a belief or a goal of its own (in case of why questions). When it is on the defensive (maybe because it is aware of its argumentation ability's weakness), it may be induced to select *elusion*, *reticence* or *lie* as an alternative to a completely *sincere* assertion. Agents can also ask to themselves why the other agent made the question (again, with an abduction process), especially if they are in a *defensive* or a *highly cooperative* attitude.

f. revise one's own or other's mental state

In the abduction process, personality factors play a role in selecting the 'most likely' cause of a conflict. Let us consider the case of an agent A_i which found two alternative explanations for a conflict with the agent A_j, both of them due to an error in one of the two agents mental state: in the first hypothesis, the conflict is ascribed to an error in A_i*'s* beliefs in the second one, it is ascribed to an error in A_j*'s* beliefs. If A_i is "self confident" then it will reject the first alternative and will consider the second one as more likely; an "insecure" agent will do the opposite.

g. examine the consequences of a change of mind

In this phase, consistency in one's own and other agent's image has to be insured by belief revision techniques.

h. decide how to react to a proposal or an answer.

After interpreting a proposal and discovering a conflict and the reasons behind it, the agent may react by declaring to accept it (by implicitly accepting to change of mind) or by making a counterproposal, and arguing for it. In purely rational dialogue simulation, argumentation is only a function of the strength of arguments available. In believable agents, strong or highly plausible arguments are not necessarily employed in answers. In the example dialogues about contraceptives, the doctor never argues "by discredit of a contraceptive", but prefers 'positive' arguments: even if she thinks that a contraceptive is preferable to another, for the particular patient examined, she never argues against it. The reason is probably that she doesn't want to encourage, in the patient, negative attitudes towards any contraceptive. In this phase, the agent will thus consider not only the subject of the proposal, but also whether other (higher order) goals exist, which deserve consideration; the agent's personality will play, as well, a role in this decision. Let us, for example, make the hypothesis that the agent concluded, in a previous step, that the conflict with the other agent is due to a divergence about a specific belief. It has thus to decide whether to change of advice about that belief or try to convince the other agent to do it: this decision will depend on how *persistent* the agent is. Another example: an *aggressive* agent might be willing to hold on a conflict even after the original causes have been -partially or totally- clarified. An *acquiescent* one might decide, on the contrary, to pass over the conflict even though it hasn't been solved. It is in this context that an agent has also to decide whether to manifest to its interlocutor that it discovered a deception: this decision is governed, too, by personality factors.

Our first prototype of XANTHIPPE does not include all the forms of reasoning that we mentioned, as agents consider one goal at a time, and act according to the common *sincere assertion* and *confidence* hypotheses. In other papers (de Rosis and Grasso 1997; de Rosis et al., 1998b), we showed examples of dialogues which can be simulated with the system. In these dialogues, agents show a 'personality-based' behaviour, but do not adopt any form of deception. To simulate the more complex and deceiving behaviours that we have exemplified in this paper, our conversing agents should be empowered with the following abilities:

a) ability to consider the possibility to avoid answering (also when the answer is known) or to answer insincerely if needed;

b) ability to reason about the other agent's communication (answer or proposal), by considering the possibility of 'insincerity';

c) ability to decide whether to disclose that insincerity has been discovered.

In the remaining of the paper we will examine how these situation may be faced.

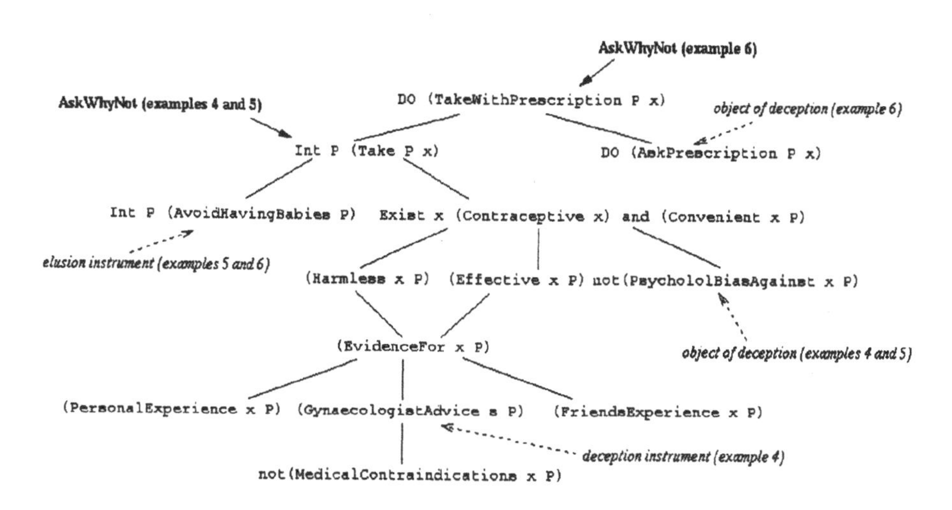

Figure 7: Beliefs state

6 Mental states and forms of reasoning to deceive and suspect

We will concentrate on the contraceptive prescription dialogues showed in Sect. 4.2. Let us suppose that the belief state of the patient (P) is as depicted in Fig. 7. The rules and beliefs showed in the picture are then first order beliefs: they all are connoted by the predicate **Bel P**. For the sake of simplicity, we assume that the doctor (D) has the same set of beliefs and rules about P, and that the beliefs in Fig. 7 are included in D's model as second order beliefs (that is, they are connoted by **Bel D Bel P**). Let us also assume that D thinks that both Pill and Coil are contraceptive methods which would be suitable to the patient, and that the patient wants to avoid having babies (as she came to the family planning service). D has therefore the following basic beliefs:

Bel D Bel P (Int P (AvoidHavingBabies P))
Bel D (Harmless COIL P)
Bel D (Effective COIL P)
Bel D (Harmless PILL P)
Bel D (Effective PILL P)

At the beginning of interaction in the three examples, D does not know the opinion of P about coil and pill being harmless and effective.

This background mental state of the two agents is common, we assume, to the three situations described in Sect. 4.2. As we anticipated, all the cases represent a deception that is activated by the doctor's request to the patient to justify her choice. In other words, in all the cases the patient deceives because she does not want to reveal and to discuss the reasons for her choice, nor she intends to change her mind about her choice. In the following subsections we will try and simulate the reasoning process that P and D might have used in the three situations.

6.1 Example 4

We start the analysis from the question which causes P's deception.

D: Why don't you feel like fitting a coil?
We can translate it as:

(Ask-why D (Bel P not (Int P (Take P COIL))))

P: I don't know why... My gynaecologist advised me against it.
By performing a backward reasoning, P finds a justification for her choice against the coil:

(Bel P (PsycholBiasAgainst COIL P))

Her problem now is to decide whether she really wants to communicate such a justification to P. She decides she rather not (we denote this belief as *object of deception*, in Figure 7). We can presume that P feels her position to be "weak": such a belief may be uneasy to justify, or it is something P does not want to think about, or P feels her reason is weaker than D's ones, or even ridiculous (in D's opinion). Another possible, less "irrational" interpretation is that P is simply not inclined to change her mind about the pill, as her belief is very strong:

(Bel P (Int P (Take P PILL)))

She then decides to adopt a reticence strategy. She looks for other plausible reasons against the Coil. Saying that she considers the Coil not effective for her:

(Bel P (not (Effective COIL P)))

would not be plausible enough, as D would easily find many counter-arguments, being stronger then she is on medical knowledge. She then chooses:

(Bel P (not (Harmless COIL P)))

and, making a further step on her backward reasoning, she chooses the motivation for this belief that she considers the strongest one, as it does not allow any argument:

(Bel P (not (GynaecologistAdviceFor COIL P)));

(we denote this belief as *deception instrument*, in Figure 7).

D: Your gynaecologist advised you against it.. did he tell you why?
D considers this communication with diffidence. She starts by examining the content:

a) is the *content plausible*?
   Let us suppose that D has a general (default) rule saying that a gynaecologist would advise any contraceptive method for which no contraindications exist, and the Coil in particular:

   (Bel D (not (MedicalContraindications COIL P)) → (GynaecologistsAdviceFor COIL P)))

   We also presume that D is not aware of any contraindication for that patient to use the Coil. From her point of view, then, the premise of the rule is (very likely) true, and the same for the conclusion. Therefore the communication is (very likely) false, not plausible.

b) is the *source tendentious*?
To establish this, D wonders whether P might have some good reasons for attempting to lead her to believe what she said, that is whether

Bel P Bel D not(GynaecologistAdviceFor COIL P)

has any convenient consequence for P. She then considers other possible alternative answers to her question. She realizes that if:

(Bel P (PsycholBiasAgainst COIL P))

then the communication about the gynaecologist would have the advantage, for P, to avoid explaining her psychological fears.

D then concludes that the source might be tendentious, and therefore the communication is very likely to be false. Now, D has to decide how to react. As she does not want to manifest her feelings, she pretends to accept P's explanation about the fictitious doctor. However, she still wants to know the real reasons of P's choice, she then asks further explanations:

(Ask-why P (Bel P not (GynaecologistAdviceFor COIL P)))

P: He says that it's a foreign body, after all.
P has no explanation for the communication she gave, as she was lying. But she has to answer something, if she wants to keep on with the story. She then chooses the simplest way, by ascribing to the doctor "her own" belief about the coil.

In the remaining of the conversation, D is even more suspicious about P: it is not plausible that a gynaecologist defines a coil as a"foreign body"; this is not a plausible contraindication. She, however, decides to forget about the deception: she clearly has some other goals with higher priority. Moreover, she in a sense obtained an answer to her question about P's reasons, even if indirectly.

6.2 Example 5

Again, we will concentrate on the sentences expressing the deception.

D: You've come with a resolute position in favour of the coil.
The doctor makes an assertion which is, in fact, a request for an elaboration about the patient's decision. We can presume that the question is:

(Ask-why D (Bel P (Int P (Take P COIL))))

or better, as D was considering the two alternatives "pill" and "coil", that the "real" question is:

(Ask-why D (Bel P not (Int P (Take P PILL))))

P: (...) I don't want another baby
We assume that P understands the real question (the doctor mentioned the pill in the same turn). She then, as in the previous example, wonders whether she wants to communicate the actual answer to D, and, again, she decides she rather not (this

is, again, the *object of deception*, as in the example 4). We do not enter into the detail of this decision. We can assume the same kind of reasons as in the previous example: a uneasy to justify belief, a psychological prevention, and so on. She then decides to stick with the literal question, pretending that she did not get the real one, and provides the 'easiest' explanation to that question:

Bel P (Int P (AvoidingBabies P)) (this is the deception instrument).

D: (...) you don't necessarily have to use a coil

D considers this communication with diffidence. She starts by examining the content:

a) is the content plausible?
   In this case the problem of plausibility does not apply: what the patient said is definitely true. The problem is that P did not actually answer D's question: her answer is not sufficient.

b) is the source tendentious?
   D does not think that P might have misunderstood the question, especially because of what has been said so far.

However, D does not enter into the details, and, either the misunderstanding was genuine or pretended, she decides to clarify her question:

(Ask-Whether D (Bel P (Exists x (Contraceptive x) and (Convenient x P) and (DiffersFrom x COIL)))

P: What should I do, should I come to sleep at your home?

P again refuses to talk about the pill as a possible alternative. She then manifests this by considering an alternative (we can translate it with "avoiding sex" for the sake of simplicity) that she knows cannot be considered as convenient:

Bel P ((Forall n (Contraceptive n) not (Do P (Take Pn))) $\rightarrow$not (MakeSex P)) and
Bel P (Int P (MakeSex P)) and
Bel P Bel D (Int P (MakeSex P))

It is remarkable that P decides to use irony to manifest this: it is a sort of "reductio ad absurdum" to prove that the coil is the only suitable technique.

6.3 Example 6

D: Why did you take it without (prescription)?

D's question is direct this time, even though the patient interrupts her before she can finish it:

(Ask-Why D (DO (TakeWithoutPrescription P PILL)))

P: In order to avoid another pregnancy.

The pattern is always the same: P wonders whether she wants to answer D's question and decides she rather not. She then decides to answer part of the question, pretending that she did not realize the whole one. In other words, she decides to answer the question:

(Ask-Why D (DO (Take P PILL)))

And an obvious reason for taking the pill is of course:

(Bel P Int P (AvoidHavingBabies P)))

7 Conclusions

The examples we have seen in the previous Section are all cases of a particular type of deception, arising after a Ask-why question and due to the answering agent's need to hide one of her beliefs. The adopted deception strategy consists of either (i) choosing an alternative and easier to justify answer (even though it is false and not completely plausible: see the example 4), or (ii) answering an alternative question after simulating a misunderstanding of the original one (like in examples 5 and 6).

Discovering a deception requires, to D, tracing P's decision process. This starts from evaluating the credibility of a communicated belief by examining, at the same time, its plausibility and the believability of the source; if the communication reveals to have a low credibility, the same kind of evaluation is repeated on some alternative hypotheses, so as to select the most credible of them as the true *object of the deception*.

All this suggests that modelling the reasoning process behind deception requires applying several techniques for 'ordering' beliefs and goals.

a) In deciding *whether* to deceive about an owned belief through reticence or elusion, the *strength* of beliefs is considered. This strength is a function of several factors: the 'difficulty to justify the belief', the 'difficulty to accept the risk of being obliged to abandon it' (for instance, after arguing with a stronger partner) or even the 'difficulty to reflect on the belief itself'.

b) In deciding *how* to deceive (which belief to select as an instrument to hide the real object of reticence), the plausibility of alternative hypotheses is evaluated, as a function of how likely it is that the alternative belief is considered as true by the interlocutor. This requires, again, considering the belief strength, though in a different sense (its plausibility) and by reasoning on second-order beliefs.

c) In *discovering a deception*, a symmetrical reasoning is made on the other agent: second-order beliefs are employed to discover whether the source might be tendentious, whether she might have reasons to hide some true beliefs. First, second (and maybe third)-order beliefs are employed to discover whether the data is plausible: is it plausible that I believe it? is it plausible that she believes it? Is it plausible that she believes I believe it?[4]

d) In deciding *whether to disclose* the discover of a deception, the strength of goals is considered. We can therefore say that simulating deceptive interchanges in conversations requires assigning two types of strengths to beliefs:

- a measure of *uncertainty* about their truth value, to evaluate their plusibility;
- a measure of *endorsement* or *epistemic entrenchment*, which Julia Gallier's claims to be linked to the belief *utility* (Gallier, 1992). This may have, however, at least two components: (i) the number of beliefs which are linked to the "to be revised" belief (something related to Gardenfors' *informational value* of beliefs (Gardenfors, 1992b)),and (ii) to what extent revising this belief would entail revising one's own goals.

If probability provides a well-grounded theory for treating belief uncertainty, the same is not true for belief utility and for the combination of the two types of weights into a overall measure of data plausibility. Similar problems exist, to set up how to combine data plausibility and source believabilty to provide a overall measure of belief credibility. In another work (de Rosis et al., 1998a) we describe a probabilistic way to deal with deceiving attitudes of agents under a *closed world* hypothesis, that is when all the world characteristics (agents' personalities, behavioural patterns, communicative acts etc) are known by all the participants to the dialogue. In this very strict hypothesis, we model the decision of deceiving 'at the right moment' and the progressive arising of suspect, in a playing agents world. The same model, however, does not work equally well in a more complex and open world such as XANTHIPPE's and does not allow treating all the types of belief strength that we examined in this paper. In addition, other deception forms that we showed in Sect. 5, both in the adolescent diabetics dialogues and in the medical package inserts, suggest that deception can be pursued not only by just telling the false or hiding the truth, but also by encouraging false implicatures or by softening the truth, through typically "fuzzy" techniques: something which requires applying still different uncertainty management methods.

A final, general consideration: examining real, sophisticated dialogues confirms our initial idea that there can be deception also in highly cooperative interactions, such as the relation between doctor and patient. If deceiving is so common in natural dialogues, and there exists a form of deception even in collaborative and help seeking situations, we cannot see why deception should be excluded when a user interacts with a computer, nor why a computer system should be trained to avoid deception in its responses. Politeness involves good manners, and good manners are a form of deception: it is then necessary even for a machine to be 'well-mannered'.

References

Bretier, P. and Sadek D. 1997. A rational agent as the kernel of a cooperative spoken dialogue system: implementing a logical theory of interaction. In LNAI 'Intelligent Agents III', J P Mueller, M J Woolridge and N R Jennings Eds.

Brody H. 1982. The lie that heals, the ethics of giving placebos. Annals of Internal Medicine. 97, 112-118.

Carbonell J. 1980. Towards a process model of human personality traits. Artificial Intelligence, 15.

Castelfranchi C., de Rosis F., Falcone R. and Pizzutilo S. 1998. Personality traits and social attitudes in Multi-Agent cooperation. Applied Artificial Intelligence, in press.

Castelfranchi C., Falcone R. and de Rosis, F. 1998. Deceiving in GOLEM, how to strategically pilfer help. AA98 Workshop on 'Deception, Fraud and Trust in Agent Societies'.

Castelfranchi C. and Poggi I. 1998. "La scienza dell'inganno" Roma, NIS.

Chu Carrol J. and Carberry S. 1995. Response generation in Collaborative Negotiation. ACL95.

Cohen P. R. and Levesque H. J. 1995. Communicative actions for artificial agents. Proceedings of ICMAS 95

Demolombe R. 1997. Formalizing the realiability of agent's information. 4th Model Age workshop on "Formal Models of Agents".

DePaulo B. M., Kashy, D. A., Kirkendol S. E. and Wyer M. M. 1996. Lying in everyday life. Journal of Personality and Social Psychology, 70, 5, 979-995.

de Rosis F. and Grasso F. 1997. Simulating plausible conflict-resolution dialogues. First International Workshop on Human-Computer Conversation. Bellagio.

de Rosis F., Grasso F. and Berry D. 1998. Refining instructional text generation after evaluation. Submitted to Computational Linguistics.

de Rosis F., Grasso F., Castelfranchi C. and Poggi I. 1998. Modeling Conflict Resolution Dialogs. In press on a book on 'Conflicts in AI', R Dieng and J Mueller Eds.

de Rosis F., Covino E., Castelfranchi C. and Falcone R. 1998. Bayesian cognitive diagnosis in believable multiagent systems. International Workshop on Belief Revision, Trento.

Galliers J. R. 1992. Autonomous belief revision and communication.In: Belief Revision, P Gardenfors (Ed), Cambridge Tracts in Theoretical Computer Science 29, Oxford.

Gardenfors P. 1992. Belief revision, an Introduction. In: Belief Revision, P Gardenfors (Ed), Cambridge Tracts in Theoretical Computer Science 29, Oxford.

Glinert L. H. Side effect warnings in British medical package inserts, a discourse analytical approach. To appear on the International Journal of Cognitive Ergonomics.

Hope T. 1995. Deception and lying. Journal of Medical Ethics. 21, 67-68.

Kashy D. A. and DePaulo B. M. 1996. Who lies? Journal of Personality and Social Psychology, 70,5,1037-1051.

Lee M. and Wilks Y. 1997. Eliminating deception and mistaken belief to infer conversational implicature. IJCAI97 Workshop on 'Collaboration Cooperation and Conflict in Dialogue Systems'.

Lelouche R. and Doublait S. 1992. Qualitative reasoning with bluff and beliefs in a multi-actor environment. Int J Man-Machine Studies, 36, 149-165.

Nass C., Moon Y., Fogg B .J., Reeves B, and Dryer C. D. 1995. Can computer personalities be human personalities? Int I Human-Computer Studies, 43, 223-239.

Petrillo G. 1994. Relazioni asimmetriche e strategie di influenza sociale: analisi di conversazioni medico-paziente. In F Orletti: Fra conversazione e discorso. La Nuova Italia Scientifica, Roma.

Quaresma P. and Lopez J. G. 1997. Modelling credulousness and cooperativeness in a Logic Programming framework. IJCAI97 Workshop on 'Collaboration Cooperation and Conflict in Dialogue Systems'.

Reilly W. S. and Bates J. 1995. Natural negotiation for believable agents. School of Computer Science, Carnegie Mellon University, CMU-CS-95-164.

Ryan C. J., de Moore G. and Patfield M. 1995. Becoming none but tradesmen, lies, deceptions and psychotic patients. Journal of Medical Ethics. 21, 72-76.

Silverman D. 1987. Communication and medical practice. Chapter 9: Policing the lying patient, surveillance and self-regulation in consultations with adolescent diabetics. SAGE Publications.

Sycara K. P. 1991. Pursuing persuasive argumentation. AAAI Spring Symposium on Argumentation and Belief, Stanford University.

Teasdale K. and Kent G. 1991. The use of deception in nursing. Journal of Medical Ethics. 21, 77-81.

VanDerHoek W., Van Linder B. and Meyer J. J. Ch. 1997. An integrated modal approach to rational agents. Utrecht University, Tech. Report UU-CS-1997-06.

Vincent J. and Castelfranchi, C. 1981. On the art of deception: How to lie while saying the truth. In H. Parret, M. Sbisa' and J. Verschueren (Eds.), Possibilities and Limitations of Pragmatics. Studies In Language Companion Series (Vol. 7). Amsterdam: John Benjamins, 1981.

Notes

[1] In Van Der Hoek et al's scale of credibility, (i) observation is the most trustworthy way of acquiring information, (ii) communication depends on the relation of trust, dependence or credibility between the sending and the receiving agents with respect to the formula, and on the credibility of the information itself, whereas (iii) default jumps (endogenous sources of information produced by default reasoning) are the less credible ones. However, their moral hypothesis of communication "partially contradicts the dependence of credibility attached to communication on the level of trust".

[2] "most people who are prescribed X will benefit from taking it, but some people can be upset from it", or even "along with its needed effects, a medicine may cause unwanted effects. Most people find it causes no problems"

[3] "just like all medicines"

[4] Many authors have defined the semantic of plausibility by improperly assimilating the concepts of possible and plausible. See, for instance, (Quaresma and Lopez, 1997): "A property P is possible if there is a hypothetical sequence of actions that leads to the state P. This process is verified by the construction of a hypothetical world where property P holds (...). If the hypothetical world is non-contradictory, then the property is plausible and it may be accepted". Such a non contradiction check is made on the hearer's belief set. On the contrary, in our opinion the discovering of deceptions should be evaluated, by the hearer, on the basis of the plausibility of the communication to the agent's which communicated it.

9 Parsing Utterances Including Self-Repairs

M. Nakano and A. Shimazu

1 Introduction

For a spoken dialog system to hold a natural conversation with humans, the parsing module has to be able to analyze a human utterance in real-time, obtain its semantic expression, and send it to the discourse-processing module. It is difficult to make such a parsing module because of the existence of phenomena that cannot be dealt with by the grammar for written sentences (Nakano, Shimazu and Kogure, 1994). Of those phenomena, this paper focuses on self-repairs and treats paraphrases and repetitions as kinds of self-repairs.

Previous methods for parsing utterances including self-repairs can be classified into four categories: namely, (i) those that detect self-repairs using lexical information before parsing (Heeman and Allen, 1994; Heeman, Lokem-Kim and Allen, 1996; Kikui and Morimoto, 1994; Tischer, 1996), (ii) those that detect self-repairs after failing to parse the utterance and parse it again (Sagawa, Ohnishi and Sugie, 1994), (iii) combinations of (i) and (ii) (Bear, Dowding and Shriberg, 1992; Shriberg, Bear and Dowding, 1992), and (iv) those that embed a mechanism for dealing with self-repairs (Den, 1996; Hindle, 1983).

As will be shown later, a dialog system holding a natural conversation with humans requires the incremental parsing of input utterances. Methods in categories (i) through (iii) cannot be used in an incremental parser, and those falling into (iv) depend on the parsing algorithms and cannot deal with some kinds of self-repairs.

This paper proposes a method in which utterances including self-repairs are parsed by using phrase structure rules for self-repairs with ordinary phrase structure rules for written sentences. It shows that such rules can be constructed based on the classification of self-repairs in dialog data. Since the method does not use a special mechanism but instead simply adds new phrase structure rules, it can be used with any parsing algorithms for phrase structure grammars. Therefore, utterances including self-repairs can be parsed incrementally using parsing algorithms such as the chart method (Kay, 1980).

This paper is organized as follows. Section 2 presents the results of our investigation and classification of self-repairs in dialog data. Section 3 discusses the role of the parser in a dialog system. Section 4 covers the above mentioned problems with the previous methods for dealing with self-repairs in a little more detail. Section 5 explains the phrase structure rules for dealing with self-repairs. Section 6 describes the implementation of the experimental system.

2 Investigation of self-repairs in dialogs

2.1 Dialog data

We investigated eighty dialogs recorded by NTT Basic Research Laboratories (Kawamori, Shimazu, Dohsaka, and Nakano, 1997). Ninety subjects participated. Each dialog was a telephone conversation in which a subject, E, explains a route to a location, L, to another subject, N. N did not know where L was before the dialog. In order to collect natural dialogs, N was instructed to go to L after the dialog. The dialogs comprise about 58,000 words and contain about 15,000 turns.

2.2 Self-repair model

Our investigation is based on a model in which a self-repair consists of three parts: *the reparandum part*, and *the editing expression*, and *the repair part* (Kawamori and Shimazu, 1996; Levelt, 1989; Otsuka and Okada, 1992; Sagawa et al., 1994). The point between the reparandum part and the editing expression is called the *interruption point.*

Removing the reparandum part and the editing expression makes the utterance syntactically and semantically analyzable. Editing expressions are fillers (*eeto, anoo*) interjections (a), phrases indicating denial (*janai*), paraphrase (*tteyuuka*), or apology (*gomennasai*), or sequences of these. Figure 1 shows an example of analysis with this model.

Atsugi kara	a	Machida kara	sarani 20-pun kurai saki ni itte
from	oh	from	more 20 minutes about forward to go
'from Atsugi	'Oh'	'from Machida'	'go ahead more about 20 minutes
reparandum part	**editing expression**	**repair part**	

Figure 1: An example of analysis of self-repairs

2.3 Classification of self-repairs in dialog data

We investigated self-repairs in the dialog data based on the above model and classified them from the viewpoints of (A) the phonological, syntactical, and semantic relationship between the reparandum part and the repair part, and (B) the content of the editing expression. Figure 2 shows the classification A[1] and Figure 3 shows the classification B. Table 1 shows some examples.

In the following, X, Y and Z represent the reparandum part, the editing expression, and the repair part, respectively.

(I) X and Z are phrases in the same syntactic category, and they satisfy one of the following conditions

- noun phrases
  - (I-1) They are identical noun phrases.
  - (I-2) They area noun phrases in the same semantic category.
- particle phrases (noun phrases followed by a case particle or a modal particle)
  - (I-3) The are identical particle phrases.
  - (I-4) They are particle phrases of the same case having noun phrases in the same semantic category.
  - (I-5) They are particle phrase having identical noun phrases.
  - (I-6) They are particle phrases having noun phrases in the same semantic category.
  - (I-7) They are particle phrases of the same case.
- particles (case particles or modal particles
  - (I-8) They are identical particles.
  - (I-9) They are different particles.
- verb phrases (or verb phrases followed by a conjunctive particle)
  - (I-10) They are identical verb phrases.
  - (I-11) They are verb phrases having identical main verbs followed by identical conjunctive particles.
  - (I-12) They are verb phrases followed by identical conjunctive particles.
  - (I-13) They are verb phrases having identical main verbs.
- adnominals
  - (I-14) They are identical adnominals.
- adverbs
  - (I-15) They are adverbs in the same semantic category.

(II) Both X and Z are well-formed substrings and X is a substring of Z.

(III) X is a word fragment and Z is a word.

- (III-1) X is a prefix of Z.
- (III-2) X is not a prefix of Z.

(IV) Self-repairs by stopping the utterance and restarting (fresh starts).

(V) Others.

Figure 2: Classification A

2.4 Frequency of self-repairs in each category

We investigated the frequency of self-repairs of each category of the above classifications in the dialog data. In the investigation, the following criteria were used.

- Analysis of combinations of multiple self-repairs

  How many self-repairs comprise one non-fluent part including self-repairs is ambiguous. For example, the disfluency in the utterance

(a) There is no editing expression.

(b) The editing expression includes fillers (*anoo, eeto*).

(c) The editing expression includes interjection (*hai*), phrases indicating denial (*janai*), paraphrase (*tteyuuka*), or apology (*gomennasai*).

(d) The editing expression is inaudible.

Figure 3: Classification B.

Utterance	A	B
[koko]$_X$ [a]$_Y$ [uketsuke]$_Z$ ni ori masu ga here oh reception LOC be POLITE CONJ 'I'm here----oh, at the reception'	(I-2)	(c)
[sore o]$_X$ [sono mae o]$_Z$ chokushinshite kudasai that OBJ its front OBJ go straight REQUEST 'please go straight at that--at its front'	(I-7)	(a)
[50-pun gurai kakaru]$_X$ [55-fun gurai kakaru]$_Z$ to omoi masu 50 minutes about take 55 minutes about take that think POLITE 'I think it takes about 50 minutes--takes about 55 minutes'	(I-13)	(a)
[20-pun]$_X$ [Aikoo-Ishida made 20-pun mo kakara nai]$_Z$ kara 20 minutes to 20 minutes take no because 'because, 20 minutes--it doesn't take 20 minutes to go to Aikoo-Ishida	(II)	(a)
[to]$_X$ [eeto]$_Y$ [Totsuka]$_Z$ ka Shoonandai desu FRAGMENT FILLER or COPULA 'it's To--Totsuka or Shoonandai	(III-1)	(b)
[sochira no moyori-eki]$_X$ [dochira kara irassyai masu ka]$_Z$ there of nearest station where from come POLITE INTERROGATIVE 'the nearest station--where are you coming from?'	(IV)	(a)
5-ban no hou no basunoriba [desu]$_X$, [kara]$_Z$ nori masu to No. 5 of direction of bus stop COPULA from get on POLITE CONJ 'it's bus stop No. 5--if you get on at'	(V)	(a)

Table 1: Examples of the classification of self-repairs.

basu-noriba ga, basu, basu no noriba ga ari mashite
bus stop subj bus bus pos stop subj exist POLITE
'there is a bus stop, bus, bus stop'

can be analyzed in the following two ways.

1. [basu-noriba ga]$_X$, [[basu]$_X$, [basu]$_Z$ no noriba ga]$_Z$ ari mashi te.
2. [basu-noriba ga, basu]$_X$, [basu no noriba ga ari mashi te]$_Z$

Analysis (1) has two self-repairs in categories (I-4) and (I-1), and analysis (2) has one (IV)-type self-repair. In our investigation, analyses resulting in self-repairs in categories (IV) and (V) were avoided if possible, and those resulting in self-repairs in categories (I), (II), and (III) were preferred. Of analyses giving self-repairs in categories (I), (II), and (III), the one providing the least number of self-repairs was chosen. For the above example, (1) was chosen. Twenty-five self-repairs satisfying conditions of both (I) and (II) were analyzed as type (I).

- Extent of self-repair

  Dialog participants sometimes negate what they said several turns ago. Therefore, the maximum extent of the self-repairs to be analyzed must be decided. Some previous analyses divide a dialog into sentences and analyze self-repairs within those sentences (Den, 1996; Sagawa et al., 1994). It is difficult, however, to divide natural dialogs like ours into sentences. Therefore, we decided to investigate only self-repairs in which no clauses are inserted between the reparandum part and the repair part. We found that the number of redundant expressions occurring across clauses is four percent of the number of the self-repairs.

We found 599 non-fluent parts with self-repairs in the dialog data, and our analysis revealed a total of 704 self-repairs in those parts. Table 2 is the frequency table for classification A and Table 3 is that for classification B. There was no double counting of self-repairs in each (I) category. For instance, a self-repair once counted as (I-1) was not counted as (I-2).

3 Utterance parsing module

Sentence boundaries are not clear in spoken language. In human-human conversation, back-channel utterances are inserted after case particles and conjunctive particles (Kawamori, Shimazu and Kogure, 1994). This means the hearer can react before the sentence finishes. In addition, the speaker seems to utter incrementally based on the hearer's reaction (Dohsaka and Shimazu, 1996). Therefore, the parsing module in a dialog system has to start parsing before the sentence finishes and output partial results. We call this *incremental parsing*.

Our parsing module works as follows (Shimazu, Kogure, Kawamori, Dohsaka and Nakano, 1996); when the speech recognition module outputs sequences of words and word fragments, the parsing module incrementally parses the sequences

category	frequency
(I-1)	52
(I-2)	90
(I-3)	8
(I-4)	32
(I-5)	7
(I-6)	2
(I-7)	10
(I-8)	8
(I-9)	15
(I-10)	6
(I-11)	5
(I-12)	4
(I-13)	28
(I-14)	2
(I-15)	1
(II)	12
(III-1)	153
(III-2)	226
(IV)	17
(V)	26
Total	704

Table 2: Frequency table for classification A.

category	frequency
(a)	537
(b)	114
(c)	51
(d)	2
Total	704

Table 3: Frequency table for the classification B.

and sends the semantic representations for well-formed substrings as soon as they are discovered (Shimazu, Kogure and Nakano, 1994). The discourse processing module then disambiguates the parsing results using contextual information.

4 Problems with previous methods

As mentioned earlier, the parsing of utterances including self-repairs is presently done in one of four ways: (i) by detecting self-repairs using lexical information before parsing (Heeman and Allen, 1994; Heeman et al., 1996; Kikui and Morimoto, 1994; Tischer, 1996), (ii) by detecting self-repairs after failing to parse the utterance and parsing it again (Sagawa et al., 1994), (iii) using combinations of (i) and (ii) (Bear et al., 1992; Shriberg et al., 1992), or (iv) by embedding a mechanism for dealing with self-repairs (Den, 1996; Hindle, 1983).

Methods (i) through (iii) above cannot be used in an incremental parser. Methods of type (iv) can be used in incremental parsing, but those proposed thus far cannot deal with the full range of self-repairs. Den's method (Den, 1996), for instance, deals with self-repairs with dependency analysis and is based on *bunsetsu* phrases[2]. Thus, it cannot deal with self-repairs within a *bunsetsu* phrase, such as (I-8). Moreover, it can deal with only self-repairs that appear in the corpus and ones similar to them and cannot use general rules. Hindle's method (Hindle, 1983), on the other hand, is an extension of deterministic parsing (Marcus, 1980), so it is not general; it cannot deal with self-repairs in category (II) of classification A.

Therefore, there is a need for a method that can deal with a large variety of self-repairs and that can be used in incremental utterance parsing.

5 Parsing with phrase structure rules for self-repairs

We introduce phrase structure rules in order to deal with self-repairs. Since this method does not use a special mechanism, but rather simply adds new phrase structure rules, it does not depend on parsing algorithms. This means adopting parsing algorithms that can handle incremental inputs, such as the chart method (Kay, 1980), can be used for the incremental parsing of utterances including self-repairs.

5.1 Unification-based grammar

Our method is based on the unification grammar framework (Shieber, 1986), in which the phonological, syntactic, and semantic information required to deal with self-repairs can be described uniformly. The grammar is Grass-J (Grammar for Spontaneous Spoken Utterances in Japanese) (Nakano et al., 1994), which is a grammar for Japanese utterances based on JPSG (Gunji, 1987). Grass-J features phrase structure rules for subcategorization construction, adjacent construction, modification construction, and relative clause construction. It covers such fundamental phenomena in written sentences as subcategorization, passivization, interrogation, coordination, and negation, in addition to copulas, relative clauses and conjunctions. Moreover it covers phenomena peculiar to spoken language such as case-particle omission, interjections and fillers. Figure 4 shows some of the phrase structure rules in Grass-J.

5.2 Phrase structure rules for self-repairs

Below we show the phrase structure rules for self-repairs constructed based on the analysis explained in Section 2. These are three rules (A, B, and C below) for grasping the relationship between the reparandum part and the repair part and one (D) for dealing with the editing expression. Rules A through C recognize two adjacent phrases satisfying conditions of (I), (II), or (III) as a phrase having the same syntactic and semantic information as the latter phrase.

- Rule A [for (I)]
  Z → X Z
  Condition: X and Z satisfy one of the following conditions.
  1. X and Z are noun phrases in the same semantic category. [for (I-1) and (I-2)]
  2. X and Z are case-particle phrases of the same case. [for (I-3), (I-4), and (I-7)]
  3. X and Z are case-particle phrases having the noun phrases in the same semantic category. [for (I-3), (I-4), (I-5), and (I-6))
  4. X and Z are case particles or modal particles. [for (I-8) and (I-9)]
  5. X and Z are verb phrases followed by identical conjunctive particles. [for (I-10), (I-11), and (I- 12)]
  6. X and Z are verb phrases (may be followed by conjunctive particle) having identical main verbs. [for (I-10), (I-11), and (I-13)]
  7. X and Z are identical adnominals. [for (I-14)]
  8. X and Z are adverbs in the same semantic category. [for (I-15)]
- Rule B [for (II)]
  Z → X Z
  Condition: The word sequence of X is a subsequence of that of Z.
- Rule C [for (III)]
  Z → X Z
  Condition: X is a word fragment and Z is a word.
- Rule D [for (c)]
  X' → X Y
  Condition: Y is an interjection, a phrase indicating denial, paraphrase, or apology, and X' is the same as X except that its reparandum feature value is yes.

These rules enables us to deal with self-repairs in categories (I), (II), and (III) and are in categories (a), (b), and (c).

Consider self-repairs in category (a). Rules A, B, and C can handle self-repairs in categories (I), (II) and (III), respectively. Self-repairs in category (b) can be dealt with like those in category (a), since, in Grass-J, a filler is defined as a word that modifies a subsequent word without changing that word's syntactic and semantic information.

Self-repairs in category (c) are dealt with by Rule D. The reparandum feature used in Rule D indicates whether the phrase has to be repaired or not. The value of this feature of ordinal phrases is *no*. Phrase structure rules not for self-repairs cannot be applied to feature structures whose reparandum feature value is *yes*. For example, the conditions below are added to Rule Subcategorize in Figure 4.

⟨M reparandum⟩ = no
⟨H reparandum⟩ = no
⟨C reparandum⟩ = no

Similar conditions are added to other rules. In Rules A, B, and C, the reparandum feature value of phrase Z is no while there is no constraint on that of X.

In Rule D, the reparandum feature value of X0 is yes while there is no constraint on that of X. The editing expression in self-repairs in category C is connected to the reparandum part with Rule D and forms a feature structure whose reparandum feature value is yes. Rules not for self-repairs cannot be applied to this feature structure, while Rules A, B, and C can connect it to a subsequent phrase. Figure 5 shows an example of the application of Rule D.

Figure 6 shows some parsing examples using these phrase structure rules. To simplify the tree, symbols NP, VP and so on are used in the figure instead of describing the complex feature structures. The rules used to construct the phrase are enclosed in the parentheses.

6 Implementation

We added Rules A through D to Grass-J. Conditions 1 through 8 in Rule A are described as disjunctions. Methods for handling feature structures with disjunctions efficiently (Eisele and Dörre, 1988; Hasida, 1986; Kasper, 1987) enable the efficient treatment of self-repairs satisfying multiple conditions. From the available methods, we chose constraint projection (Nakano, 1991). The condition in Rule B is difficult to encode in the unification grammar framework, so we attached a procedure to the phrase structure rule described in the declarative way.

We conducted a parsing experiment using a chart parser incorporating Grass-J with the above rules and confirmed successful parsing of thirty utterances in the dialog data. They include self-repairs in categories (I), (II), and (III) and in categories (a), (b), and (c).

1. Subcategorize

Rule for PP-VP contructions

M → C H
⟨M head⟩ = ⟨H head⟩
⟨H subcat⟩ = ⟨M subcat⟩ ∪ ⟨C⟩
⟨M adjacent⟩ = nil
⟨H adjacent⟩ = nil
⟨M adjunct⟩ = ⟨H adjunct⟩
⟨M lexical⟩ = no
⟨M sem index⟩ = ⟨H sem index⟩
⟨M sem restric⟩ = ⟨C sem restric⟩ ∪ ⟨H sem restric⟩

Symbols M, C and H are not names of categories but variables, or identifiers, of the root nodes in the graphs representing feature structures. M, C and H correspond to mother, complement daughter, and head daughter. The head daughter's subcat feature value is a set of feature structures.

2. Adjacent

Rule for VP-AUXV consturctions, NP-particle contgructions, etc.

M → A H
⟨M head⟩ = ⟨H head⟩
⟨M subcat⟩ = ⟨H subcat⟩
⟨H adjacent⟩ = ⟨A⟩
⟨M adjacent⟩ = nil
⟨M adjunct⟩ = ⟨H adjunct⟩
⟨M lexical⟩ = no
⟨M sem index⟩ = ⟨H sem index⟩
⟨M sem restric⟩ = ⟨A sem restirc⟩ ∪ ⟨H sem restric⟩

M, A and H correspond to mother, adjacent daughter, and head daughter. The head daughter's adjacent feature value is unified with the adjacent daughter's feature structure

Modify

M → A H
⟨M head⟩ = ⟨ H head⟩
⟨M subcat⟩ = ⟨H subcat⟩
⟨M adjacent⟩ = nil
⟨H adjacent⟩ = nil
⟨A adjunct⟩ = ⟨H⟩
⟨M adjunct⟩ = ⟨H adjunct⟩
⟨A adjacent⟩ = nil
⟨M lexical⟩ = no
⟨M sem index⟩ = ⟨H sem index⟩
⟨M sem restric⟩ = ⟨A sem restric⟩ ∪ ⟨H sem restric⟩

M, A and H correspond to mother, adjunct daughter (modifier) and head daughter (modifiee). The adjunct daughter's adjunct feature value is the feature structure for the head daughter.

Figure 4: Phrase structure rules in Grass-J

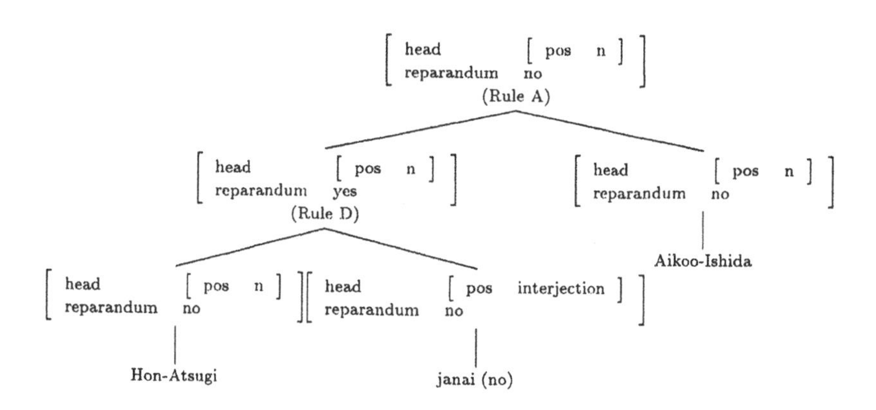

Figure 5: An example of the application of Rule D

7 Concluding Remarks

Based on an investigation of dialog data, we have developed a method for parsing utterances using new phrase structure rules for self-repairs. The phrase structure rules sometimes recognize phrases that are not self-repairs as self-repairs. For example, the utterance:

Hon-Atsugi, Aikoo-Ishida no futa-eki ni tomari masu
APPOSITION two stations at stop POLITE

(i.e. it stops at two stations), Hon-Atsugi and Aikoo-Ishida can be parsed as:

[Hon-Atsugi]$_X$, [Aikoo-ishida]$_Y$ no futa-eki ni tomari masu,

which includes a self-repair in category (I-2). To exclude erroneous parses, information other than syntactic and semantic information, such as context and prosody, should be used. How exactly to best utilize such information is a future problem. However, obtaining plausible results earlier (Shimazu, 1990) is effective from the viewpoint of the incremental parsing. For example, we could decrease the preference of the rules for self-repair, but how to decide the preference is yet to be studied.

How to deal with the fresh starts [self-repairs in category (IV)] is another challenge. They will be manageable if interruption points can be discerned in the real-time using acoustic information (Nakatani and Hirschberg, 1994).

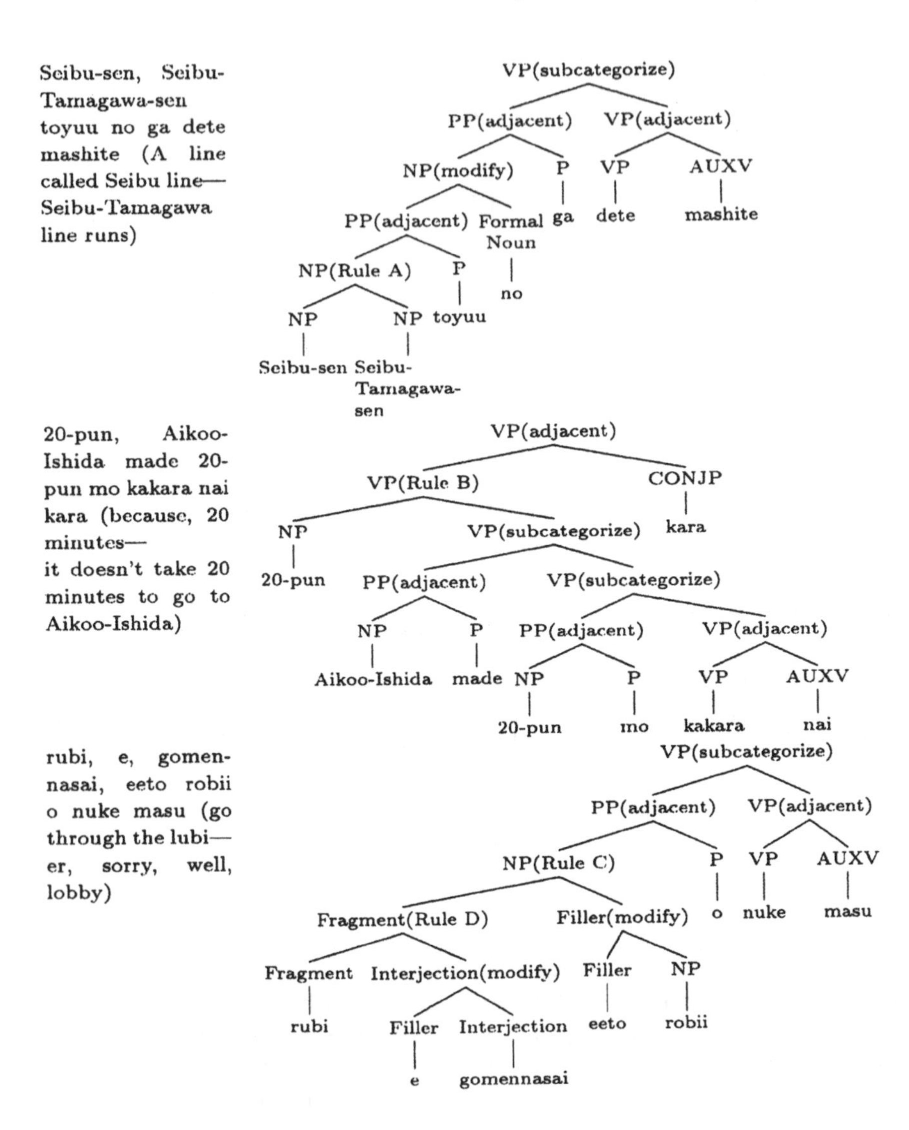

Figure 6: Parse trees for example utterances including self-repairs

Acknowledgments

We would like to thank Dr. Ken'ichiro Ishii, the executive manager of the Information Science Research Laboratory for his encouragements and comments. We had precious discussions with the members of Dialogue Understanding Research Group and Dr. Yasuharu Den of Nara Advanced Institue of Science and Technology. Thanks also go to Mizuho Inoue and Yutaka Imai who helped us to analyze the dialog data.

References

Bear, J., Dowding, J. and Shriberg, E. 1992. Integrating Multiple Knowledge Sources for the Detection and Correction of Repairs in Human-Computer Dialog. In ACL-92, pp. 56-63.

Den, Y. (1996). A Uniform Approach to Spoken Language Analysis. Ph.D. thesis, Kyoto University.

Dohsaka, K. and Shimazu, A. 1996. A Computational Model of Incremental Utterance Production in Task-Oriented Dialogues. In COLING-96, pp. 304-309.

Eisele, A. and Dörre, J. 1988. Unification of Disjunctive Feature Descriptions. In ACL-88, pp. 286-294.

Gunji, T. 1987. Japanese Phrase Structure Grammar. Reidel, Dordrecht.

Hasida, K. 1986. Conditioned Unification for Natural Language Processing. In COLING-86, pp. 85-87.

Heeman, P. and Allen, J. 1994. Detecting and Correcting Speech Repairs. In ACL-94, pp. 295-302.

Heeman, P., Lokem-Kim, K. and Allen, J. F. 1996. Combining the Detection and Correction of Speech Repairs. In ICSLP-96, pp. 358-361.

Hindle, D. 1983. Deterministic Parsing of Syntactic Non-fluencies. In ACL-83, pp. 123-128.

Kasper, R. T. 1987. A Unification Method for Disjunctive Feature Descriptions. In ACL-87, pp. 235-242.

Kawamori, M. and Shimazu, A. 1996. On the Interpretation of Redundant Expressions in Spoken Language. In SIG-NLC92-41, Institute of Electronics, Informa- tion and Communication Engineers, pp. 31-38. (in Japanese).

Kawamori, M., Shimazu, A., Dohsaka, K. and Nakano, M. 1997. Construction of Corpora for Dialogue Processing. In SIG-NLC97-5, Institute of Electronics, Information and Communication Engineers, pp. 31-36. (in Japanese).

Kawamori, M., Shimazu, A. and Kogure, K. 1994. Roles in Interjectory Utterances in Spoken Discourse. In ICSLP-94, pp. 955-958.

Kay, M. 1980. Algorithm Schemata and Data Structures in Syntactic Processing. Tech. rep. CSL-80-12, Xerox PARC. (Reprinted in B. J. Grosz, K. S. Johns, and B. L. Webber (eds.) Readings in Natural Language Processing, Morgan Kaufmann 1986).

Kikui, G. and Morimoto, T. 1994. Similarity-Based Identification of Repairs in Japanese Spoken Language. In ICSLP-94, pp. 915-918.

Levelt, W. J. M. 1989. Speaking. MIT Press.

Marcus, M. P. 1980. A Theory of Syntactic Recognition for Natural Language. MIT Press.

Nakano, M. 1991. Constraint Projection: An Efficient Treatment of Disjunctive Feature Descriptions. In ACL-91, pp. 307-314.

Nakano, M., Shimazu, A. and Kogure, K. 1994. A Grammar and a Parser for Spontaneous Speech. In COLING-94, pp. 1014-1020.

Nakatani, C. H. and Hirschberg, J. 1994. A Corpus-Based Study of Repair Cues in Spontaneous Speech. Journal of Acoustic Soceity of America, 95 (3), 1603-1616.

Otsuka, H. and Okada, M. 1992. Incremental Elaboration in Generating Spontaneous Speech. In SIG-NLC92-41, Institute of Electronics, Information and Communication Engineers. (in Japanese).

Sagawa, Y., Ohnishi, N. and Sugie, N. 1994. A Parser Coping with Self-Repaired Japanese Utterances and Large Corpus-Based Evaluation. In COLING-94, pp. 593-597.

Shieber, S. M. 1986. An Introduction to Unification-Based Approaches to Grammar. CSLI.

Shimazu, A. 1990. Japanese Sentence Analysis as Argumentation. In COLING-90.
Shimazu, A., Kogure, K., Kawamori, M., Dohsaka, K. and Nakano, M. 1996. Internal Communication in Dialogue Processing Systems. In Proceedings of the Second Annual Meeting of the Association for Natural Language Processing, pp. 333-336. (in Japanese).
Shimazu, A., Kogure, K. and Nakano, M. 1994. Cooperative Distributed Processing for Understanding Dialogue Utterances. In ICSLP-94, pp. 99-102.
Shriberg, E., Bear, J. and Dowding, J. 1992. Automatic Detection and Correction of Repairs in Human-Computer Dialog. In Proceedings of the DARPA Speech and Natural Language Workshop, pp. 419-424.
Tischer, B. 1996. The Syntax of Self-Corrections in Dialogues. In Proceedings of ECAI-96 Workshop on Dialogue Processing in Spoken Language Systems, pp. 79-83.

Notes

[1] In this paper, we do not distinguish nouns from noun phrases, and neither do we distinguish verbs from verb phrases.
[2] A *bunsetsu* phrase consists of a content word and some (possibly zero) function words.

10 A Synthetic Evaluation of Dialogue Systems

K. Hasida and Y. Den

1 Introduction

It is relatively easy to evaluate technologies such as morphological analysis and information retrieval in objecive and empirical terms, because unique solutions can be defined for such tasks. There has been no established method for evaluating natural language dialogue systems, however, because dialogue is a very complex task involving massive interaction and it is impossible to define unique solutions for dialogues. In order to advance researches on dialogue systems, there should be some empirical method for evaluating them. For instance, whether the theory of plan inference (Cohen and Perrault, 1979; Allen and Perrault, 1980; Perrault and Allen, 1980; Allen 1983) is really useful in the design of a dialogue system should be evaluated by an empirical measure.

Generally speaking, an evaluation had better be objective and quantitative. First of all, as a matter of course, objective evaluation is preferable for the sake of fairness. Secondly, an artifact made for some purpose should eventually be evaluated in terms of the quantitative degree to which that purpose is fulfilled. Such an evaluation will be almost necessarily a blackbox evaluation, such as in ATIS (Boisen and Bates, 1992), TREC (Harman, 1995), MUC (MUC, 1991), and so forth. However, blackbox evaluations are often inappropriate for immature technologies like dialogue systems. For example, the Loebner Prize Competition (Epstein, 1992), which is essentially Turing test, requires dialogue systems to talk like people. Since there is currently no systematic method to meet this requirement, ad hoc techniques abound and are successful in the contest. It will have little contribution to advancing the dialogue technology.

The rest of the paper discusses *DiaLeague*, a framework to evaluate natural-language dialogue systems on a blackbox, synthetic, objective, and quantitative basis. *DiaLeague* is an attempt to establish an evaluation method which should promote productive research on dialogue systems. Machine-machine dialogues and human-machine dialogues are compared in the context of evaluation of dialogue systems.

2 *DiaLeague*

Objective and quantitative evaluation should concern the degree to which the goal of the system in question is fulfilled. Given the goal of a dialogue system to perform some task which requires an interactive communication, it would be sensible to evaluate the system in terms of the degree of fulfillment of that task, which also reflects the efficiency of communication. In the Loebner Prize, the definition of human-like conversation is too vague to objectively evaluate the performance. Such a problem will not arise when an objectively defined task is used whose achievement depends upon the communication efficiency.

The authors, in cooperation with other colleagues, have conducted a series of contests to evaluate natural-language dialogue systems along this line. The evaluation framework is called *DiaLeague*. For each pair of dialogue systems participating in a *DiaLeague* contest, the two systems are required to jointly fulfill a task by talking to each other, and they get the same score according to the degree of achievement of the task. Each system is evaluated in terms of the average or total score over all the dialogues it participates in.

This round-robin format was adopted for the sake of openness, which means that the range of information each system should deal with be unrestricted and open. The openness in this case corresponds to an ability of diverse conversation required in order to mark a high score through conversations with various different partners.

Openness may be better implemented in an evaluation by making the machines talk with humans, because humans tend to display much more diverse patterns of discourse than machines do. Since the major engineering goal of dialogue systems is human-machine communication in natural language, dialogue systems should be evaluated with respect to their ability to communicate with people. However, many human subjects are necessary for the sake of fairness of the evaluation, because humans can memorize previous tasks, get tired, and so on. The round-robin format is to avoid the cost of involving many humans, though we will later discuss how to involve many human subjects without too much cost.

Since the two systems earn the same score in each dialogue, the systems should cooperate with each other to obtain higher scores. This is considered sensible, because the primarily expected ability of dialogue systems should be that of cooperative communication, and also because cooperativity holds of the most basic level of communication — nonnatural meaning (Grice, 1969).

3 The Route Task

The following requirements were considered in designing the task for *DiaLeague*.

- The task should be realistic in the sense that it makes intuitive sense in our daily, real world. It should also be interaction-inducing in the sense that interactive communication mostly accounts for its fulfillment.
- The evaluation should be intuitively understandable in order to gain a wide social recognition. The task should be realistic for this sake. The intent of the interaction inductance is that the task should not be performed mainly by individual problem solving but be more efficiently done by incremental dialogue.

DiaLeague has used the *route task*, which meets these requirements. It is an adaptation of the map task used in the dialogue corpus projects at Edinburgh University (Anderson et al., 1992) and Chiba University (Aono et al., 1994). The most essential difference between the two types of tasks is that the roles of information giver and receiver are fixed in the map task but not in the route task. In the route task, neither of the dialogue participants knows the solution and they jointly try to find it by mutually giving information. Also, the map task presupposes a very high ability of pattern recognition far beyond the current state of the art, whereas the route task does not involve such an aspect. The moderate difficulty of the task is essential for the evaluation to be productive.

In a route task, the two dialogue participants are given two railway route maps which are similar but involve subtle differences. The maps are not visual data but encoded symbolically. The task is to find the path from the start station to the goal station. This path must be contained in both the maps. These maps share the same start and the goal stations. Shown in Figure 1 is an example task. The color (indicated by the texture in this figure) of the links represent lines. The stations connected by consecutive links of one color are reached from each other without transferring trains. For instance, [Setagaya, Kagosima, Abiko, Neyagawa] is a line in the first speaker's map. The maps are different in two respects. First, some links are present in one map but absent in the other. Second, the names of some stations are known in one map but not in the other. Each unknown name is indicated by a '?' followed by a number. In the current example, 'Higasiosaka -> Nagoya -> Huzimi -> Kakogawa -> Dazaihu -> Kagosima -> Setagaya' is the only one solution. Shown in Figure 2 is a sample dialogue in which this solution is reached. In the parentheses are English translations of the utterances, which are currently assumed to be in Japanese. This is a dialogue between two dialogue systems.

In the route task, the speakers must communicate with each other in order to figure out the intersection of the two maps. In this type of task which motivates communication by distributing the relevant information to the participants, it is always possible that the first speaker initially gives all its information to the second, who then solves the problem by itself and tells the solution back to the

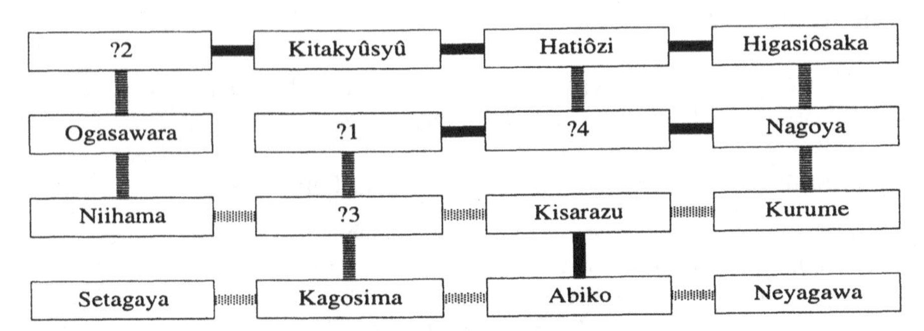

First speaker's map

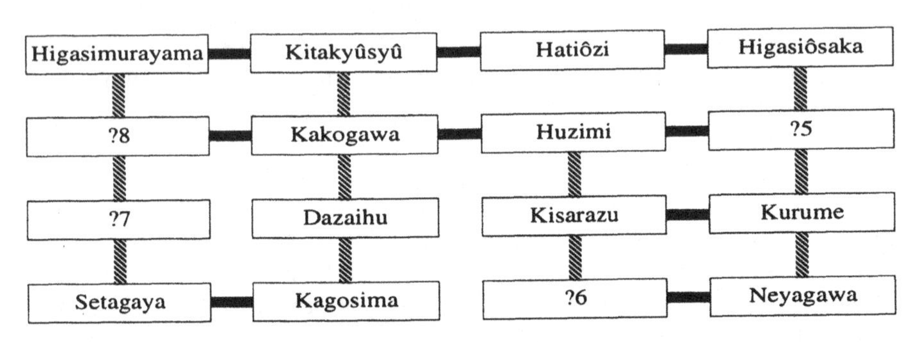

Second speaker's map

Figure 1: An example route task: Start = Higasiôsaka, Goal = Setagaya

first. When the difference between their information is small enough, however, it is more efficient to try to communicate the difference only than all of your information. So the route task is an interaction-inducing task, whose achievement is mostly accounted for by incremental communication.

The score is higher when the dialogue is shorter. The length of a dialogue was defined to be the number of characters in the first *DiaLeague* in 1995, but later it has been revised to be the number of segments (content words) for the reason discussed later. There is an upper bound on the length of the dialogue, which has been 300 segments so far. A positive score is given to the participants of a successful dialogue.

A dialogue is successful when

- it is over in a finite period of time,
- it is not longer than the upper bound,
- the two dialogue participants answer the same path as a solution,
- both of them know the names of all the stations on that path, and
- the path is in the intersection of the two route maps.

A few different ways of calculating the scores have been used in different *DiaLeague* events. Below is an early example.

D when the dialogue is successful
0 when the dialogue length exceeds the upper bound
-D when one dialog participant stops responding

D is the upper bound on the dialogue length minus the actual dialogue length. In recent contests, the score is zero when one dialogue participant stops responding, because it is often easy to make systems avoid stopping and continue a nonsense dialogue.

The openness of the route task is low in two respects, in particular under evaluation of machine-machine dialogues. First, solution strategies are easy to share among dialogue participants. Apparently the simplest strategy is to incrementally (step by step, stationwise) propose the candidate paths and check if they are included in the partner's route map. Dialogues are very probably restricted along this line, because most of the designers of dialogue systems are expected to be aware of this strategy. Second, the diversity of linguistic expressions tend to be limited, because they have only to refer directly to the same level of information as the data structure of the task --- the symbolic representation of maps. For instance, utterance to the effect 'Can we go to Niihama?' will concern if there is a link from the current station to Niihama. The complexity of human dialogue mainly comes from the complexity of the world to talk about which necessitate linguistic expressions at various levels of abstraction, but machine-machine dialogue concerning the route task will not so much induce such complexity.

A desirable task is one for which there is no apparent strategy that machines easily converge to and in which there is no apparent direct correspondence between the abstraction levels of linguistic expressions and the semantics of the task. A task involving some pattern recognition may meet these desiderata, but such a task tends to be too hard for the current technology. So *DiaLeague* is tentatively using the route task, in a hope that more insight about better tasks could be gained through actual experiences with the route task.

4 Machine-Machine Dialogue

DiaLeague began with *DiaLeague*'95, an exhibition match in July 1995 which demonstrated machine-machine dialogues. After that, there have been two contests, *DiaLeague* '96 Spring Session and *DiaLeague* '96 Summer Session, in March 1996 and July 1996, respectively. They feature machine-machine dialogues, too.

DiaLeague '95 was neither a contest nor a round-robin series, but apparently the best performing participant system was Akane95 (Sato, 1996). This system regarded the route task as knowledge acquisition from dialogue, and was designed with a particular emphasis on gaining high scores in *DiaLeague*. Many tactics

	naist	csl1	csl2	atr2	ntt	tut	atr1	total
naist	—	-282/ 0	-282/ 0	189/ 204	-294/ 0	0/-297	0/-293	-1055
csl1	-282/ 0	—	158/ 135	-283/-294	129/-202	-92/-174	-297/-297	-1499
csl2	-282/ 0	158/-135	—	-283/-294	131/-202	-199/-116	-297/-297	-1546
atr2	189/ 204	-283/-294	-283/-294	—	-297/-290	-264/ 105	183/-241	-1565
ntt	-294/ 0	129/-202	131/-202	-297/-290	—	-146/-166	-297/-297	-1931
tut	0/-297	-92/-174	-199/-116	-264/ 105	-146/-166	—	-297/-292	-1938
atr1	0/-293	-297/-297	183/-241	-297/-297	-297/-297	-297/-292	—	-2722

Table 1: Machine-Machine Dialogues in March 1996

were employed, such as saying 'north, 6' instead of 'Let's go as far as the 6th station to the north.' This is because in *DiaLeague* '95, the length of a discourse was defined in terms of the number of characters. The discourse length is now the number of segments, in order to discourage such a trick.

DiaLeague '96 Spring Session involved seven systems. **atr1** and **atr2** were developed at ATR Interpreting Telecommunications Research Labs, **csl1** at Sony Computer Science Laboratory and Tokyo Institute of Technology, **csl2** at Sony CSL, TIT and Electrotechnical Laboratory, **naist** at Nara Institute of Science and Technology, and **tut** at Technical University of Toyohasi. Two tasks were used and a round-robin series of 42 dialogues were conducted. Table 1 shows the result. The two figures in each inner slot of the table are the scores of two dialogues using the two tasks. The right-hand figure is a score of a dialogue using the task shown in Figure 1. The systems in the leftmost column are the first speakers in the left dialogues, whereas the systems in the top row are the first speakers in the right dialogues. The champion was **naist**, which suppressed the losses better than the others.

	naist-ob	atr	tut	crl	naist	Total
naist-ob	—	1/1	1/			7
atr	1/1	—	1/1			6
tut	1/1		—			5
crl				—		0
naist1					—	0

Table 2: Machine-Machine Dialoges in *DiaLeague '96* Summer Session, 1996.

DiaLeague '96 Summer Session involved **atr** (same as **atr2**), **crl** (developed at Communication Research Laboratory), **naist1** (different from the previous **naist**), **naist-ob** (same as the previous **naist**), and **tut**. In this session, the scores were calculated simply by giving 1 point to a successful dialogue and 0 point to an unsuccessful one. The result is shown in Table 2.

The organization of this table is the same as Table 1, except that blank indicates a zero point.

A: Hatiôzi-e ike -masu -ka. (Can we go to Hatiôzi?)
DIR can-go POLITE INTERR

B: Hai (Yes.)

A: Hatiôzi-no sita -e ike -masu -ka. (Can we go below Hatiôza?)
GEN below DIR can-go POLITE INTERR

B: Ike -mase -n (We can't go there.)
can-go POLITE NEG

A: Higasiôsaka-kara Nagoya-made ike -masu -ka. (Can we go from Higasiôsaka to Nagoya?)
SRC DEST can-go POLITE INTERR

B: Nagoya-wa doko -desu -ka (Where is Nagoya?)
TOPIC where COPLA-POLITE INTERR

A: Higasiôsaka-no sita -desu. (it is under Higasiôsaka.)
gen below COPULA-POLITE

B: Hai (Yes.)

A: Nagoya-no hidari-e ike -masu -ka. (Can we go to the left of Nagoya?)
GEN left DIR can-go POLITE INTERR

B: Hai, Huzimi-made iki-masu (Yes, we go to Huzimi.)
yes DEST go POLITE

A: Huzimi-no hidari-e ike -masu -ka. (Can we go to the left of Huzimi?)
GEN left DIR can-go POLITE INTERR

B: Hai, Kakogawa-made ike -masu (Yes, we can go to Kakogawa.)
yes DEST can-go POLITE

A: Kakogawa-no sita -e ike -masu -ka (Can we go below Kakogawa?)
GEN below DIR can-go POLITE INTERR

B: Hai, Dazaihu-made iki-masu (Yes, we go to Dazaihu.)
yes DEST go POLITE

A: Kagosima-e ike -masu -ka. (Can we go to Kagosima?)
DIR can-go POLITE INTERR

B: Hai (Yes.)

A: Setagaya-e ike -masu -ka. (Can we go to Setagaya?)
DIR can-go POLITE INTERR

B: Hai (Yes.)

Figure 2: Sample dialogue concerning the task in Figure 1

5 Human-Machine Dialogue

DiaLeague had so far employed the round-robin format in order to avoid the cost of preparing many human subjects for the sake of fairness of the evaluation. Rapidly increasing number of people being involved in the Internet, however, it may be possible to invite many human talkers through the WWW and evaluate dialogue systems with respect to the ability of communication with people. The authors have developed a 'dialogue server' which mediates keyboard-based conversation between dialogue systems and humans, and have used it in collecting data of human-machine dialogues.

For the sake of evaluation of dialogue systems, dialogues with humans are apparently more desirable in various respects than dialogues among machines. First of all, a great deal of openness can be introduced in the evaluation by involving humans, because human dialogues tend to be very diverse even under such a simple setting as the route task. Dialogue systems will hence be required to understand diverse human utterances. They may use high-level tactics, such as asking 'Can we go to Tokyo by transferring at Nagoya?' for instance, because such tactics would work with humans. Second, evaluation of dialogues with humans will take into consideration naturalness, comfortability, and so on, for humans. In order to converse efficiently with people, a dialogue system should not just understand their utterances but also make itself easily understood by them. It should not bore or irritate people, or they might quit talking before the task is fulfilled. Third, a round-robin evaluation by dialogues among dialogue systems provides just a relative evaluation among the systems but not an absolute evaluation of each system. On the other hand, we can evaluate each system on an absolute basis by looking at how it talks with people.

However, the fairness of evaluation might be as hard to guarantee with dialogues with humans as with dialogues among machines. For instance, one could employ many people to talk seriously when they recognize their conversation partner as a certain system but quit talking otherwise. The only way to block such a dirty trick would be to involve many human talkers. To do so, some setting attractive for general users may be necessary, such as making humans compete with each other with respect to their abilitites to talk with machines.

The dialogue server has been used to collect data on human-machine dialogues. Table 3 summarizes the dialogues thereby done in three months from December 1996 to March 1997. The four dialogue systems involved here are the same ones

	first		second		total	
system	#dialogs	score	#dialogs	score	#dialogs	score
tut	78	4464	47	2189	125	3608
naist-db	45	5066	49	1734	94	3329
crl	81	1254	50	756	131	1064
atr	45	468	68	127	113	263

Table 3: Human-Machine Dialogues from Dec. 6, 1996 to Mar. 6, 1997

	first		second		total	
system	#dialogs	score	#dialogs	score	#dialogs	score
`naist-ob`	43	12653	41	5934	84	9373
`tut`	38	9644	34	4773	72	7344
`crl`	35	811	34	3982	69	2373
`atr`	39	1776	40	1970	79	1874

Table 4: Result of Human-Machine Dialogues from March 6 to 13, 1997

in *DiaLeague* '96 summer session, except that `atr` had been revised to `atr'`. For each system, the two entries under 'first' and 'second' indicate the number of dialogues and the overall score for those dialogues where the system was the first and the second speakers, respectively. The entries under 'both' indicate the total number of dialogues and the overall score. The overall scores in the table are 100 times the average scores for the relevant dialogues. The authors first ascribed the apparently worse performance of `atr'` than `atr` to the revision, but this turns out implausible as mentioned later.

A special contest session of human-machine dialogues was conducted for the following one week, from noon of the 3rd to noon of the 13th, in March 1997. This event had been announced as 'The First Dialogue Contest,' a competition among humans concerning their ability to talk with machines. But the main intent was to motivate more people towards more serious conversation and thereby obtain more and better data for evaluating dialogue systems. Table 4 summarizes the result. Note that, as expected, more dialogues per unit time are done during a contest than in usual occasions shown in Table 3. Also as expected, humans talk more seriously in a contest, which should account for the better overall scores in Table 4 than in Table 3.

The collected dialogues may reveal or clarify some characteristics of human-machine dialogue. For instance, as expected again, humans tend to adapt to machines more than vice versa, as suggested by the fragment dialogue in Figure 3. H is a human and M is a machine. Human adaptability is also indicated by the tendency of increasing ratio of successful dialogues with people who did many dialogues.

A set of round-robin matches among the dialogue systems was conducted after the contest session of March 1997. Table 5 summarizes the result. Each inner slot

	`naist-ob`	`atr`	`tut`	`crl`	total	score
`naist-ob`	2539	1736	555	0	5274	6278
`atr`	0	1541	180	0	4015	4779
`tut`	444	558	1180	0	2917	3472
`crl`	0	0	0	403	403	479

Table 5: Result of League Matches in Spring 1997

of the table represents the total scores obtained from twelve dialogues. The set of tasks used for the dialogues is the same for all the slots. The system in the leftmost column are the first speaker in the dialogues, whereas those in the top row are the second speaker. The ranking in Table 4 is essentially the same as in Table 2 except for the bad scores of `atr'`. This suggests that `atr'` overfits to dialogues with machines, and probably so does `atr`. It is hence further suggested that machine-machine dialogues fail to capture some essential aspects of human-machine dialogues.

H: Nisiyosino-kara Niihama-ni ike -masu -ka (Can we go from Nisiyosino to Niihama?)
SRC DEST can-go POLITE INTERR

M: Niihama-wa doko -ni arum-desu -ka. (Where is Niihama located?)
TOPIC where LOC exist COPULA-POLITE INTERR

H: Nisiyosino-no minami. (South of Nisiyosino.)
GEN south

M: Niihama-wa doko-ni arun-desu-ka. (Where is Niihama located)

H: Nisiyosino-no minami-desu. (It's to the south of Nisiyosino.)
GEN south COPULA-POLITE

M: Niihama-wa doko-ni arun-desu-ka. (Where is Niihama located?)

H: Gotenab-no higasi-desu. (It's to the East of Gotenba.)
GEN east COPULA-POLITE

M: Niihama-wa doko-ni arun-desu-ka. (Where is Niiham located?)

H: Nisiyosino-no minami-ni ari -masu. (It's to the south of Nisiyosino.)
LOC exist POLITE

M: Hai. (I see.)

Figure 3: Part of Human-Machine Dialogue in the First Dialogue Contest

There are eleven people who had ten or more dialogues with the dialogue systems during the contest period, and six of them outperformed `naist-ob`. The human champion's overall score was 11328, versus 6278 of `naist-ob`. In this connection, the overall scores in Table 4 are better than those in Table 5, except that `atr` performs better with machines than with people.

Another contest was held for one week from September 25 to October 2, 1997. The result is surveyed in Table 6. `naist1'` (a revision of `naist1`) participated

	first		second		both	
system	#dialogs	score	#dialogs	score	#dialogs	score
crl'	86	14405	55	9083	141	12329
tut'	98	11852	87	8829	185	10430
naist-ob	106	11546	69	7215	175	9838
atr'	87	5066	80	2318	167	3750
naist1'	34	3029	26	823	60	2073

Table 6: Human-Machine Dialogues for one week (The Second Dialogue Contest) through September ~ October 1997.

from the middle of the contest, which accounts for the small number of its dialogues. `crl'` and `tut'` are revisions of `crl` and `tut`, respectively. These two revisions appear successful because these two systems outperform the others systems in terms of dialogues with people.

However, machine-machine dialogues among the same set of systems lead to a rather different comparison, as shown in Table 7. This table is organized in the

	naist-ob	crl'	atr'	tut'	naistl'	total=score
nasit-ob	2093	260	1316	256	0	6413
crl'	0	1784	644	1125	0	5739
atr'	0	0	1293	0	0	5140
tut'	164/395	142	694	451	0	2539
naistl'	0	0	0	0	0	0

Table 7: Machine-Machine Dialogues in October 1997

same way as Table 5. Since a common set of ten tasks is used for each pair of dialogue systems (that is, each slot of the table), each system is involved in 100 dialogues, where a dialogue in which the system talks to itself is counted twice. So the total point is equal to the overall score, which is 100 times the average point. Here a system wins a positive number of points in a dialogue when its partner obtains the right path --- the same way of grading as for people. Two systems won different points only when `tut'` is the first speaker and `naist-ob` is the second, as indicated by the two figures in the corresponding slot: they won 164 points and 395 points in total there, respectively.

Note that the difference in ranking between human-machine dialogues and machine-machine dialogues is much greater between Table 6 and 7 than between Table 4 and 5. This suggests that machine-machine dialogues cannot be an appropriate basis on which to evaluate dialogue systems. In contrast, human-machine dialogues appear to be a stable basis for evaluation, because the ranking among dialogue systems is nearly equal among Table 3, 4 and 6. Table 3 and 4 show almost the same ranking. `tut` and `naist-ob` are exchanged between the two sessions, but the differences between the two systems are small in both cases, and the overall better scores in the latter session in Table 4 may be because it is a contest. Similarly, the ranking between `atr'` and `naist-ob` is preserved in Table 6. Still better performance of the systems here is probably accounted for by higher incentives of the human talkers involved. In fact, the First Dialogue Contest (Table 4) included 463 dialogues, whereas the Second (Table 6), 728. A major cause of this increase may be the greater amount of award in the Second Dialogue Contest. In the First Dialogue Contest, it was announced that the best three human talkers would win 15,000, 10,000, and 5,000 yen, whereas in the Second, the awards were 30,000, 20,000 and 10,000 yen. Moreover, none of the best three talkers contacted the organizers to actually get their awards in the First Dialogue Contest, whereas the best three talkers all received their awards in the second contest. This suggests that the participants in the latter contest had stronger overall incentives than in the former.

The data obtained through the *DiaLeague* events are currently under investigation. The developers of `crl'` (Kumamoto and Ito, 1998) have analyzed 141 dialogues involving `crl` and observe:

- users tend to talk politely to machines, and
- expressions used by humans are not influenced by those used by machines,

among other things. Further examination of the data, including comparisons of different dialogue systems, is necessary to find out more lessons for designing dialogue systems.

6 Final Remarks

An attempt, called *DiaLeague*, to evaluate dialogue systems has been reported. The data obtained through *DiaLeague* events show that machine-machine dialogues cannot very well approximate human-machine dialogues as a basis for evaluating dialogue systems. The same data appear informative also on how to design dialogue systems.

DiaLeague will continue mainly as an evaluation of human-machine dialogues, while using machine-machine dialogues as a complementary source of data. The route task will be used for the time being, but some more open tasks should be considered when the participating dialogue systems become so smart that the route task is trivial for them. An extreme generalization of the route task is the theorem-proving task, which is to give the two dialogue participants two very similar but slightly different axiom sets of the first-order predicatelogic and require them to prove a theorem using only axioms in the intersection of the two sets. Since this is a very general task subsuming many concrete ones, it could introduce plenty of openness into the domain of dialogues, but it might exceed the current state of the art. Like the Loebner Prize task, it may be too hard to evaluate dialogue systems based on this task in a productive manner. It may be more realistic to try to evaluate customizability with respect to the domain of dialogues, as is the case with MUC.

The dialogue server and records of past dialogues can be reached from the following WWW page, http://www.etl.go.jp/etl/nl/dialeague/

The current dialogue server is Japanese-based and also the current dialogue systems talk Japanese only, but an English version of the dialogue contest is also planned to launch. Such a setting in which humans and machines can talk to each other over the WWW is useful not only for evaluating dialogue systems but also for collecting data about various types of conversation between people and machines. The Internet is not just a subject of research on information retrieval and so forth, but also a very rich resource for basic research.

Acknowledgments

The authors would like to thank the other members of *DiaLeague* execution committee (Katashi Nagao, Hideki Kashioka, Keiichi Sakai, Akira Shimazu, Mikio Nakano and Kentaro Inui) and contributors of dialogue systems (Kiyotaka Atsumi, Masato, Ishizaki, Akira Ito, Tadahiko Kumamoto, Takashi Miyata, Satoshi sato, Atsushi Yamada, and Yuuki Watanabe) for their cooperation in conducting various *DiaLeague*-related events.

References

Allen J. F. 1983. Recognizing Intentions from Natural Language Utterances, In Brady M. and Berwick R. C. Computational Models of Discourse, pp. 107-166. MIT Press, Cambridge MA.

Allen J. F. and Perrault C. R. 1980. Analyzing Intention in Utterances. Artificial Intelligence, 15, pp. 143-178.

Anderson A. H., Bader M., Bard E. G., Doherty G., Garrod S., Isard S., Kowtko J., McAlister J., Miller J., Sotillo C., Thompson H. and Weinert R. 1992. The HCRC Map Task Corpus. Language and Speech, 34(4), pp. 351-366.

Aono M., Ichikawa A., Koiso H., Sato S., Naka M., Tutiya S., Yagi K., Watanabe N., Ishizaki, M., Okada M., Suzuki H., Nakano Y. and Nonaka K. 1994. Tizukadai Kopasu: Tyukanhokoku (Map Task Corpus: An Interim Report, in Japanese). In JSAI SIG-SLUD-9402, pp. 25-30.

Boisen S. and Bates M. 1992. A Practical Methodology for the Evaluation of Spoken Language Systems In Proceedings of the Third Conference on Applied Natural Language Processing, Trento, Italy, pp. 162-169.

Cohen P. R. and Perrault C. R. 1979. Elements of a Plan Based Theory of Speech Acts. Cognitive Science, 3(3), pp. 177-212.

Epstein R. 1992. Can machines think? The quest for the thinking computer. AI Magazine, 13(2), pp. 80-95.

Grice H. P. 1969. Utterer's Meaning and Intentions. Philosophical Review, 68(2), pp. 147-177.

Harman D. 1995. The First Text Retrieval Conference (TREC1). TR 500-207, National Institute of Standards and Technology Special Publication, Gaitherberg, MD,

Kumamoto T. and Ito A. 1998. Taiwa Sisutemu tono Taiwa niokeru Yuza no Hurumai ni Tuite (An Analysis of User Input Sentences in Dialogues with Our Dialogue System, in Japanese)' JSAI SIG-SLUD-9703, 21-26.

[MUC-3]. Proceedings of the Third Message Understanding Conference. Morgan Kaufmann, 1991.San Mateo, CA,

Perrault C. R. and Allen J. F. 1980. A Plan-Based Analysis of Indirect Speech Act American Journal of Computational Linguistics, 6(3-4), pp. 167-182.

Sato S. 1995. Taiwariigusen '95 ni taisuru Kihonsenryaku (Basic Strategies for DiaLeague '95, in Japanese) In IPSJ SIGAI 96-AI-103, 1996, pp. 13-18.

11 Designing for Naturalness in Automated Dialogues

C. Cheepen and J. Monaghan

1 Introduction

Many of the automated telephone dialogue systems currently in commercial operation are intended to be used by the general public. This means that the typical human callers who use the system/s are essentially novice users who do not build up expertise over a period of time. To cater for such a user group, designers strive to make their dialogues as 'natural' as possible. In this paper we discuss and illustrate what 'naturalness' means in the context of the kind of automated dialogues which are at present in operation. We present some examples from automated dialogues, focusing particularly on openings, closings, confirmations and repairs, and compare these with the way similar operations are carried out in human-human dialogues. We summarise a set of experiments carried out recently to investigate how callers respond to supposed 'naturalness' in automated dialogue systems, and we conclude with some comments which challenge current ideas about what really is 'natural' for an automated dialogue.

2 Dialogue types

From a top-down perspective, a very important distinction to make at the highest level of the analysis of dialogic discourse is the one between the transactional and interactional poles of discourse meaning (Brown and Yule, 1983; Cheepen, 1988). At the whole text level this concerns the orientation of the participants towards the field of discourse. Thus, the goal of the speech event may be either external (i.e. an observable and obvious goal in the world outside the conversation - a transactional goal) or internal (i.e. a goal which has its main relevance within the conversation, in terms of the effect of the conversation on the relationship of the speakers - an interactional goal). As our subsequent discussion will indicate, however, all but the briefest texts combine aspects of both types of behaviour.

From the point of view of the present discussion, interaction is more usefully viewed as a strand of communication which focuses primarily on the participants and the relationship between them, although it can have a knock-on effect on the ongoing transactional goal.

The kind of dialogue which is a suitable candidate for automation is one in which the overall goal of the speech event is a primarily transactional one, for example, telephone banking, travel enquiries, ticket booking and the like. Even in these dialogues, however, there will inevitably be some interactional content, and this cannot be regarded simply as 'window dressing', as in some cases it may function to promote (perhaps even permit) the attainment of the transactional goal. Our previous research work on the various functions of spoken language in the office context has underlined the transactional importance of linguistic activity beyond the solely goal- or transaction-oriented. In an efficient office, business tasks are not accomplished by simply 'getting down to business' - this is even true of relatively low-level tasks like dictation (Monaghan, 1992). It is usual, for instance, to find discoursal items such as greetings included in a dictation tape. At first glance it may appear that an opening utterance on a dictation tape such as "hi Susan" is simply an interactional 'optional extra', but in practice this serves as a clear signal of 'beginning of dictation session', and is therefore functioning to promote the transactional goal of successful dictation/transcription.

As we will see, transactional telephone dialogues between humans contain a substantial sprinkling of such interactional material, and again it appears that much of this is functioning towards the achievement of the transactional goal. In automated dialogues currently in use there is also (usually) some interactional content, but, as our examples will show, it tends to be restricted to particular areas of the dialogue.

3 Interactional material and naturalness in dialogue

An important feature of transactional dialogue is the degree of formality. This is largely a matter of linguistic style, which is observable in the vocabulary, grammar, and turn taking mechanisms of the dialogue. All these elements are, of course, closely related to the relationship of the co-conversationalists within the speech encounter - i.e. are the speakers equals or non-equals? This is a question which is essentially domain-specific - that is to say, the topical domain and the overall transactional goal of the dialogue set up a set of expectations about what is appropriate - or we can say 'natural' - for that particular speech encounter.

Stylistic features of this kind may (and do) vary from one dialogue to another in human-human discourse, even though the speakers may be the same, and clearly the degree of formality is an important consideration for designers of automated dialogues. Dialogue designers will, for example, provide different styles of system prompts for a telephone banking service and an entertainment information service - e.g. they will use different vocabulary and grammar for the different applications. Other factors also play a part in this kind of design decision, however. In the case of a telephone banking service, for example, the service provider is dealing with regular customers who have some kind of ongoing relationship with the bank and its staff. On the basis of this, they request from the dialogue designer a system with a degree of informality, in an attempt to convey to the caller that s/he is receiving a similar service to that otherwise provided by a human being who is a member of the bank staff.

This kind of catering for the 'human-ness' of callers (i.e. adding a friendly, 'conversational' flavour to the discourse) can be generally categorised as interactional rather than transactional language, and designing dialogues with interactional content which is appropriate to both the kind of application and the particular implementation is an integral part of producing 'natural' systems - i.e. those which behave in accordance with the callers' expectations. In the following sections of this paper we will examine some examples of automated dialogues, consider how interactional material is used, and compare this with the ways such signalling is accomplished in transactional telephone dialogues where the caller is interacting not with an automated system but with a human agent.

We will focus on four particular areas of discourse - openings, closings, confirmations and repairs. Finally, we will refer to our experiment on how 'naturalness' functions in automated, transactional dialogues, and make some observations about what is, and is not, appropriate for a dialogue between a human being and a machine.

4 Openings in dialogue

In all the automated systems currently in commercial use in Britain there is great consistency in the way the dialogue opens. A telephone banking system illustrates a typical opening:

Welcome to the XXX Telephone Banking Service

Example 1

The inclusion of "welcome" (an item found at the beginning of most automated dialogues) functions transactionally as the first signal that the caller is connected to the system. It is also clearly intended as some kind of interactional signal - a marker of politeness, designed to provide some degree of naturalness in the system. Note that the overall pattern of the utterance is <interactional signal> <announce the name of the service>. If we consider the way a non-automated service dialogue opens, we can see that this naturalness signal is not an attempt to emulate human dialogic talk - the item "welcome" in initial position is not normally found in human utterances except, perhaps, in a formal, monologic speech. An example from a call to an Electricity Call Centre staffed by human agents will illustrate how a human agent typically opens a service dialogue:

Blankshire Electricity - how may I help you?

Example 2

This opening formula is typical of transactional telephone dialogues where members of the public ring in for a particular service or set of services.

Rather like the "welcome" item in Example 1, this opener also contains a section which functions both transactionally and interactionally - "how may I help you". Clearly the formulaic structure of this section signals politeness, and some directly interpersonal material is also included in the form of the personal pronouns "I" and "you", but the transactional function (i.e. you may ask me questions) is also evident, along with the purely discoursal message of the question form, which both requires an answer and hands the next conversational turn to the caller.

Note that the pattern here is <announce the name of the service> <interactional signal>, which is the reverse of the order found in automated dialogues. Let us consider this in more detail, and develop some ideas about how this operates in terms of perceived naturalness for the callers.

As we have pointed out, the item "welcome" is not normally found in initial position in human utterances. We have mentioned that it may occur in the context of a formal speech, but even then it will, in the majority of cases, be prefaced by other introductory material such as "I'd like to welcome you all....." In automated dialogues, however, this is the normal opening item in the system's first utterance, and this has great significance for the caller.

When dialling a telephone service, a caller often does not know in advance whether the call will be answered by a human agent or an automated system.

Indeed, in many cases the caller may well be expecting to talk to another human being and be unaware that the service has been automated. If that is the case, then s/he will expect to hear the pattern illustrated in Example 2 above - an announcement of the name of the service followed by some kind of invitation to ask a question. For current automated systems, particularly those of any complexity, this is not a practical design, because the range of possible responses the caller might make is too large (and too uncertain) for the underlying speech recognition technology to cope with. Designers cannot, then, simply allow callers to ask questions in 'free format', but must guide the callers to respond with items which the system can recognise and deal with. In our telephone banking example, this is done after the opening announcement (and, in fact, after an embedded subdialogue which obtains security information such as the caller's PIN) by giving the caller a restricted set of choices of what to say next:

For an account balance, say one.
To order a statement, say two. (etc.)

Example 3

Clearly, for a caller who is expecting to deal with a human agent, this does not match with the expectations s/he has about how the dialogue is likely to proceed.

On the contrary, such a caller will expect, after an agent's offer of "how may I help you", to take over the control of the dialogue by introducing the next topic of conversation, whether that is getting an account balance, ordering a statement, or some other business s/he wishes to conduct. The caller must, then, revise those expectations considerably on encountering an automated system.

The use of "welcome" in initial position is extremely useful here, because it signals to the caller from the very outset of the dialogue that the system is an automated one - it is an opening which only a machine would deliver, so all expectations about how the dialogue can proceed must be revised to accommodate this. It appears, then, that designing dialogues to open in this way is an unambiguous signal of automation, which, appearing first in the talk, allows the caller the maximum possible time to adjust to this provision, and to adopt expectations about the future structure of the dialogue which are appropriate for talking with a machine. In most cases, callers respond reasonably well to such a cue, and the overwhelming majority are successful in completing their transaction, so the signalling is obviously effective and appropriate. In terms of what works (dialogically) and how system utterances fit with callers' expectations about what should happen next in the discourse, we can, then, regard such an opening as 'natural' - *given that one participant to the dialogue is a machine.*

5 Closings in dialogue

Closings in automated systems differ substantially from closings in human-human dialogues. Human interactants move slowly towards the final closing via a set of closely collaborative turns in which they repeatedly deliver closing signals such as "right", "OK" and the like, which function both to negotiate and agree the eventual closing and to provide a series of opportunities for both parties to open a new topic of conversation if required (Schegloff and Sacks 1973). Automated dialogues do not provide such flexible functionality - instead they typically allow the human caller one opportunity to raise a new topic, and then close without further delay.

Consider the following example from our telephone banking service:

If you require further assistance please hold on.
Otherwise please replace your receiver now.
Thank you for calling XXX Telephone Banking Service. Goodbye.

Example 4

Compare this with a typical closing in a human-human dialogue:

Agent	**right right that's fine then**
Caller	**is that alright (inaud)**
Agent	**OK**
Caller	**tomorrow then**
Agent	**tomorrow yeah I'll ring the showroom anyway today to let them know and then there won't be any problem when you go in**
Caller	**OK then thanks a lot**
Agent	**OK can you just take some ID with you and everything**
Caller	**OK then (inaud)**
Agent	**alright**
Caller	**bye**
Agent	**bye**

Example 5

Note here the high incidence of repetition of closing signals, coupled with the explicit references back to (and reinforcement of) topics which have clearly already been dealt with earlier in the dialogue (the sequence beginning "tomorrow then...").

Clearly, this kind of closing sequence (which is very typical of human telephone transactions) owes much to the patternings which characterise unscripted casual conversation - the kind of speech event in which the speakers are concerned primarily with interaction rather than transaction.

It illustrates, perhaps, the tendency of human beings to express solidarity with one another through the exchange of language more or less regardless of the actual purpose of the talk.

This is an example which underlines the essential difference between friendliness and user-friendliness. The linguistic expression of personal solidarity may well be (and certainly appears to be) appropriate for inclusion in what is a highly transactional dialogue when the dialogue participants are both human beings; undoubtedly it makes carrying out the transactional business which is the goal of the encounter more pleasant for both speakers. In cases where one dialogue participant is a machine, however, this would be extremely inappropriate - so much so that a human caller encountering such a sequence in an automated dialogue would be at a loss how to respond. It would not match with the caller's expectations about how machines behave. We can, then, regard the extremely minimal closing illustrated by Example 4 as 'natural' for automated dialogues.

We should note here that some transactional functionality which is present in human-human dialogues is inevitably lost when the closing sequence is so short. As we have indicated, a caller using an automated system gets only one opportunity to raise a new topic during the closing sequence. If the caller then remembers that s/he does want to access another part of the service there is no option to do this in the current encounter - the only possibility is to let the system disconnect and to ring again. We suggest that some increased potential for reopening could profitably be built into the dialogue systems of the future by, perhaps, providing a 'talk-over' facility to pick up any input from the caller which occurs up to the final disconnection.

6 Confirmations

Confirmation is an essential component of transactional dialogues of any complexity, to ensure that the transactional goal is properly understood by both participants and the actions which are taken as a consequence of the dialogue (e.g. transferring money from one bank account to another) are accurate. Furthermore, human beings, in their dialogues with other human beings (whether those dialogues are primarily transactional - i.e. business-oriented, or primarily interactional - i.e. social), are accustomed to exchanging confirmation sequences with great frequency. The familiarity - one might say omnipresence - of confirmation is such that the linguistic constructs which humans use to signal it are very deeply ingrained in their dialogic behaviour, so that changing that behaviour radically in order to fit in with the requirements of an automated system is potentially very problematical, and may lead directly to dialogic breakdown.

As our examples will illustrate, the confirmation structures which are built into many current commercial automated systems bear very little resemblance to those which speakers naturally produce (and appear to expect) when engaged in dialogue with other human beings. In subsequent sections of this paper, we will present some examples of confirmation in transactional telephone dialogues between human speakers, outline some of the problems these indicate for the design of automated dialogues, and compare them with some confirmation sequences currently being used in automated systems. We will also make some recommendations about how a consideration of the human-human mechanisms for confirmation could profitably inform the design of the automated dialogue systems of the future.

6.1 Information verification

In dialogues where names and addresses must be taken, there is an obvious need for confirmation, to ensure that the details are correctly understood.

Research carried out at BT Research Laboratories, as background to the development of an experimental speech-based in-house directory enquiries system, has explored a number of different ways of doing confirmation. The following fragment illustrates one mechanism:

System	**And now say the surname**
Caller	**Foster**
System	**And now spell the surname**
Caller	**F-O-S-T-E-R**
System	**Is the surname Foster?**
Caller	**Yes**

(Attwater et al., 1996)

Example 6

This practice of asking for a spelling to confirm recognition of the name before problems arise is clearly designed to ensure that the caller is made aware of the system's procedures to achieve accurate recognition. It is not, however, how humans naturally do confirmation. Consider the following example, which is an extract from a human-human transactional dialogue, where a similar detail is being confirmed:

([ ] indicates simultaneous speech)

Agent	**what's the address then please you're moving out of**
Caller	**I'm moving out of six Bullerforte Road**
Agent	**Buller[forte]**
Caller	**[yeah]**
Agent	**how do [you]**
Caller	**[B]**
Agent	**spell that**
Caller	**B-U-double L**
Agent	**yes**
Caller	**E-R**
Agent	**yes**
Caller	**F-O-R-T-E - Bullerforte [Road]**
Agent	**[Road] where's that please**
Caller	**Cole Green Hatf[ield]**
Agent	**[Hat]field just bear with me a moment please**

(Call Centre Corpus, University of Surrey)

Example 7

Confirmation in this fragment is carried out over a much wider section of the dialogue, and participants collaborate closely to construct the sequence as a joint production. Note the characteristic overlapping of turns at talk, which is so pronounced that the sequence resembles, in many respects, a round song. Close matching is evident even in the talk which is not directly focused on the detail being confirmed - note the opening two utterances of the fragment, where "moving out of", first uttered by the agent, is echoed by the caller in response.

The 'spread out' and 'turn sharing' nature of confirmation in Example 7 clearly illustrates that when the dialogue is between a human caller and a human agent, the linguistic behaviour of the participants is very different from what happens between a human caller and an automated system. It is doubtful whether such elaborate (and yet so gracefully managed) patterning could be built into an automated dialogue to allow callers to communicate in what is obviously their preferred 'natural' manner. We would also argue that, even if this could be implemented, it would not be welcomed by the human caller, who is more likely to reserve that preferred 'natural' manner for occasions of talk with a 'natural' co-conversationalist - a human being, and to avoid such dialogue patternings when talking with a machine (see section 7 below).

Other characteristics of the dialogue, are, however, more suitable candidates for inclusion in the design of future automated systems. One particular feature, clearly observable in the examples, is the tendency of speakers to confirm points throughout the sequence by echoing linguistic items in one another's utterances. This is very important for dialogue design, particularly as so many commercial systems are designed to require only yes/no responses to confirmation requests. We will return to this point later.

6.2 Channel checking

Telephone dialogue participants typically check (and confirm) that the communication channel is open at the beginning of the discourse, with the matched openers hello/hello. They also carry out the same procedure when there has been some break in the talk, as in the following extract:

Agent **just bear with me a moment please**
Caller **yes**
AGENT CONSULTS RECORDS
Agent **hello**
Caller **hello**

(Call Centre Corpus)

Example 8

Automated dialogues do not provide for this. Instead, when the system is retrieving information from elsewhere, it is usual for music to be played, and when the dialogue resumes there is no opportunity for the caller to contribute a confirmation to the talk.

6.3 Discourse monitoring

There are clearly observable areas of human-human dialogue where participants are involved in agreeing that they are at the same structural place in the discourse. For instance in the closing sequence (which, as Schegloff and Sacks (1973) point out, is also the "preclosing" sequence which may lead to the reopening of a topic) - they produce and repeat confirmation signals over a very long series of turns.

Consider the following:

Agent	**and you get you know it goes on towards all your[(inaudible)]**
Caller	**[(inaudible)] the quarterly bill every other three months**
Agent	**yes you will [yeah]**
Caller	**[yeah]**
Agent	**for information**
Caller	**yeah OK then**
Agent	**OK**
Caller	**alright thanks a [lot then]**
Agent	**[thanks for] ringing then bye.[bye]**
Caller	**[right] bye**

(Call Centre Corpus)

Example 9

As in the other examples from human-human dialogue, confirmation in this extract is characterised by an overwhelming tendency for the speakers to repeat one another's utterances. This is done by sequential echoing, as in "yeah OK then", followed by "OK", and often involves overlaps, such as "alright thanks a lot then", overlapped by "thanks for ringing then".

This patterning is never found in automated dialogue systems. A sophisticated telephone banking system currently in use in Britain illustrates how the preclosing/closing sequence is usually managed:

System	**Would you like another service, yes or no?**
Caller	**No.**
System	**Thank you for using XXX Telephone Banking Service. Goodbye.**

Example 10

The only option offered to the caller in this kind of dialogue is to open a new topic (i.e. ask for another service), by answering "yes" to the first question - s/he has no opportunity to join in with the winding down of the dialogue. x

6.4 The problem of yes and no

As our examples show, confirmation in human-human dialogue is overwhelmingly carried out by speakers repeating (either as an echo or in duet) one another's utterances, or sections of those utterances. In automated dialogues, however, the human callers are directed to confirm points raised by the system by answering either "yes" or "no". This is a serious problem for dialogue design, both from the point of view of naturalness, and, more seriously, from the point of view of transactional usability. If a system is designed to accept only yes/no responses at particular points in the dialogue, and if this does not fit with the callers' expectations, then serious trouble may arise when what the caller does say is misunderstood. This in turn will lead to further confirmation requests and an extension of the trouble. Designers, as we have seen, attempt to avoid this problem by explicitly instructing the callers to use yes/no responses, but, particularly in a very complex dialogue, this can result in considerable user frustration, and, even at this cost, may not prove fully effective, as other research work has illustrated.

Reporting on "unexpected responses" by callers to experimental dialogue systems, Foster et al., (1992) describe the difficulties which arose from callers answering system prompts with a range of different tokens, when the currently active recognition vocabulary was restricted to "yes" and "no".

The users' 'error rate' in this respect was so high, and the 'mistake' so persistent, that the research team found it necessary to include in the system a prompt to callers to use only yes/no answers. This alone did not solve the problem, as, even after hearing (and obeying) the prompt on the occasion of the first confirmation, callers did not restrict themselves to yes/no responses on later occasions even within the same dialogue. The research team in this case resorted to inserting the prompt on every occasion when a confirmation was requested, which resulted in a dialogue which was both unduly lengthy and increasingly lacking in naturalness.

Similar difficulties were encountered during work on the Intelligent Speech Driven Interface Project (ISDIP). The research team here found that users typically responded to confirmation requests arising out of imperfect recognition of an item by repeating the item, rather than using a yes/no response. The system prompt in this case appeared on the screen. The team experimented with different screen positions for the prompt, but found that even when the prompt was placed immediately adjacent to the confirmation request, many users still repeated the misrecognised item, often following their repetition with utterances such as "oh I mean 'yes'". This of course was disastrous for recognition of the item, which greatly reduced the confidence of the users in the system's overall capability (Cheepen, 1994).

Given these research findings, and taking into account the illustrations in the extracts given above, it is clear that human callers do not naturally use yes/no answers as a preferred response to confirmation requests.

7 Repairs

All automated dialogues of any complexity provide for repairs which come into operation when things go wrong in the discourse. However strictly the menu structure is controlled to avoid what can be regarded as navigational problems (where the caller is unable to move from one section of the service to another), unavoidable difficulties with speech recognition occur in any kind of public access system, and system utterances are built in to signal this to the caller and to ask for a repetition of the problematical item.

Typically, these utterances take the following form:

I'm sorry, I didn't catch what you said. Please speak just after the tone.
I'm sorry, I didn't hear you say anything.
I'm sorry, I didn't understand that.

Example 11

Problems of misrecognition also occur in human-human dialogue, but they are dealt with differently, and the difference is, we suggest, a rather surprising one:

Agent	**have you rung up with your reading**
Caller	**pardon**
Agent	**have you rung with your reading**

Example 12

Note here that the caller's misrecognition of the agent's first utterance is signalled by the single item "pardon", in contrast to the rather elongated "I'm sorry, I didn't understand that" in Example 12 above. We do not consider this to be an idiosyncratic response - similarly brief signalling of misrecognition is the norm in many telephone transactions between human dialogue participants. It is common, for example, to hear the single response of "sorry" when a piece of information has been misheard. More usually, of course, human interactants avoid occasions of misrecognition by collaborating to produce often lengthy sequences of checking and confirmation while particularly crucial pieces of information are being exchanged (see section 5.1, Example 7).

8 Less is more

As we have seen in the preceding sections, dialogue in automated systems is managed very differently from dialogues between human beings where the overall transactional goal is similar. The interactional component - i.e. that which in human-human dialogue provides the natural style so characteristic of human talk - is still present, but in a greatly truncated form. Natural-seeming tokens such as "goodbye", "please" and "I'm sorry" are used, but the long subdialogues which provide their immediate context in human-human dialogue are not permitted in automated systems.

We propose that, whereas such strongly 'conversational' characteristics are often appropriate to a transactional dialogue when both participants are human beings, they are most certainly not appropriate - indeed, not natural - when one dialogic participant is a machine. It is clear that designers are to some extent aware of this, because they do not build into their dialogue systems 'full' versions of interactional segments of talk - as our examples illustrate, they include only the most minimal representations.

The question which now arises is why do they even go this far? If lengthy stretches of interactional language are inappropriate for human-machine dialogue, why is any interactional content considered appropriate? As our examples indicate, there are some instances where a token may be functioning interactionally and transactionally. This is, as we have suggested, the case with an item like "welcome", which occurs at the beginning of the first system utterance. Although, at first glance, this appears to have a primarily interactional function, it also serves to signal to the caller "you are now talking to a machine". This alerts the caller to the fact that the dialogic patterns which might be expected when the call is to a human agent are not now on the menu, and a new set of rules and expectations must now be put in place.

Other items usually found in automated dialogues are not, however, serving any observable transactional function. "I'm sorry I didn't understand that" and similar system utterances are an example of this. While it is clearly transactionally very important for the system to signal to the caller that a particular input has not been understood, we would argue that the inclusion of "I'm sorry" here is inappropriate for an automated system, and the same is true of standard politeness signals such as "please" and "thank you".

In other words, we take the view that a 'natural' dialogue between a human being and a machine should not, as in the many automated systems currently in commercial use, attempt to mimic human dialogue, but should take full account of the non-human 'nature' of the machine. Automated dialogues are overwhelmingly transactional speech events - not opportunities for the pleasurable give-and-take of essentially human interactional talk.

8.1 Naturalness in automated dialogues - an experiment

To test this hypothesis, the research team at Surrey, working on the development of design guidelines for automated dialogues, carried out a set of experiments using two stylistically different dialogues for a telephone banking application. The original version of the dialogue was based on a system currently in operation in the commercial sector. The system prompts contained a wealth of interactional linguistic tokens, such as:

Welcome to the XXX
I'm sorry I didn't understand that
Please say the number you want after the tone

We then stripped all interactional material out of the prompts (replacing person-oriented items with impersonal equivalents when necessary for coherence), and used the resulting, pared-down dialogue as our alternative version, which we called the 'denatured' version. Both versions of the dialogue were interfaced with the same underlying dummy database of banking information.

We devised a set of banking tasks to be carried out:

get account balance
order statement
transfer funds
pay bill

and prepared a set of scenarios which provided a contextual rationale for the tasks. We carried out two phases of the experiment, with 12 users for the initial, pilot phase, and a further 22 for the main phase. These subjects were asked to call both versions of the system and carry out the tasks. The dialogues between system and caller were taped, and after completion of the task set with both versions, callers were asked to evaluate the dialogues. Specifically, this involved filling out a questionnaire which simply asked which version they preferred and why.

8.2 Experimental results

We used both objective and subjective measures to analyse the results of our experiments. Our objective measures involved counting transactional errors (i.e. breakdown of dialogue, inability to carry out particular tasks), and timing the task-based dialogues for the different versions. We found that the denatured version was as efficient as the original version in terms of transactional success - i.e. callers encountered no particular difficulties in carrying out their tasks. We also found that the denatured version resulted in a slightly shorter transaction time (though this was not statistically significant), due to the removal of some of the linguistic content in the system prompts.

The subjective measure was the sum of the callers' evaluations. The overwhelming majority of callers in both the pilot and the main phase of the experiment preferred the denatured version to the original. No subjects preferred the original to the denatured. The reasons given for preferring the denatured version were consistent across the evaluation questionnaires. Although, as we have said, the denatured version did, in fact, result in slightly shorter dialogue times, callers perceived them as considerably shorter. This response was reinforced by many subjects, who commented on their evaluation forms that the denatured version (they knew it simply as the 'second version') was "not so long winded", "more to the point", even (in one case) "more user friendly". (For a more detailed account of the experiments, see Williams and Cheepen, 1998.)

Clearly, then, the absence of interactional language - or 'naturalness tokens' - in automated system prompts does not lead to transactional difficulties for human callers, and nor does it lead to user dissatisfaction. On the contrary, our experimental subjects indicated a clear preference for talking to a machine which did not - even to a minimal extent - emulate the interactional behaviour of a human agent.

9 Conclusions

The experiments described in the previous section have indicated that the use of interactional language tokens in heavily transactional dialogues offers none of the advantages designers aim for, and that equivalent denatured prompt sets perform equally well in terms of overall transactional success. Using interactional linguistic material provides no advantage in transaction times, and results in negative evaluations in terms of perceived speed and general preference for users.

The experiments represented a situation where there was a failure of appropriate naturalness, due to an incongruence between the dialogic context - i.e. a highly business-oriented transactional domain - and the prompting strategy. The human-like tokens represent a component of the dialogue which is unnecessary and, in fact, inappropriate, in the transactional domain. These additional tokens serve only to irritate users since they are unsuitable for the business-oriented, human-machine context where relationship building between participants is irrelevant.

While the experiment demonstrates the context-dependent nature of naturalness in one domain only, the study gains strength from its pertinence to current spoken interface implementation and design practice.

All too often dialogues are sprinkled with human-like tokens because of the naive and, as we have illustrated, ill-founded assumption that these will make the dialogue more natural and usable for the novice caller. In this paper we have proposed a more circumspect approach to dialogue design which is focused on the goals of the caller, and the goal of the dialogue that will be undertaken. Naturalness does not exist as an absolute, rather it is an emergent property of a well-matched prompt set and dialogic context.

Acknowledgements

This paper has arisen partly out of ongoing research on an ESRC-funded project Guidelines for the Design of Advanced Voice Dialogues, under the Cognitive Engineering Programme, project number L127251012. Partners in the project are the University of Surrey, UK and Vocalis Ltd., Cambridge, UK.

References

Attwater, D.J. et al., 1996. Dialogue design in advanced speech applications BTRL Research publications

Aust, H. 1996. Dialogue Modelling. In Proceedings of The Fourth European Summer School on Language and Speech Communication, Budapest

Brown, G. and Yule G. 1983. Teaching the Spoken Language. Cambridge University Press, Cambridge.

Cheepen, C. 1988. The Predictability of Informal Conversation, Frances Pinter.

Cheepen, C. 1994. Friendliness and user friendliness in speech-driven interface design, Pragmatics, 4:1.

Foster, J.C., Dutton, R., Jack M.A., Love, S., Nairn, I.A., Vergeynest, N. and Stentiford, F. 1992. Design and evaluation of dialogues for automated telephone services, Proceedings of the Institute of Acoustics Autumn Conference, Speech and Hearing, Windermere.

Monaghan, J. 1992. Fundamental research underlying the design of an automated dictation system, Proceedings of Institute of Acoustics Autumn Conference, Speech and Hearing.

Schegloff, E.A. and Sacks, H. 1974. Opening up closings. 1973, in Turner, R. (ed). Ethnomethodology, Penguin.

Williams, D. and Cheepen, C. 1998 (in press) "Just speak naturally": designing for naturalness in automated spoken dialogues', Proceedings of CHI '98.

12 Turn Taking versus Discourse Structure

J. Cassell, O. E. Torres and S. Prevost

1 Introduction

The Turing test has always been conceived of as a test of the *content* of a computer's contribution to a conversation. That is, from typed output, we are supposed to try to tell whether text was generated by a human or a computer. Recent advances in speech technology have led us to conceive of a Turing test taken over the phone. What about a face-to-face Turing test? What kinds of behaviors would a computer have to exhibit to convince us that it was not a grey box but a living, breathing body? We are perhaps not ready today for such a competition, but7 we may be one day. This paper attempts to move the field of human-computer conversation in that direction—in the direction of *embodied* dialogue with computers. In other work (Cassell et al., 1994; Cassell and Thórisson, in press), we have concentrated on hand gestures, intonation, head movement, and gaze. The current work revisits the question of gaze and attempts to reconcile two competing approaches to the general question of generating nonverbal behaviors.

Although there has been substantial research dedicated to the study of nonverbal communicative behaviors (including gaze behavior), such research has focused *either* on the interaction between conversational regulation (e.g. turn-taking) and nonverbal behaviors *or* the interaction between discourse structure and nonverbal behaviors. That is, there has been little research on the interaction between turn-taking and discourse structure, and even less research that takes both types of linguistic structures into account in investigating nonverbal behaviors. This lacuna is due to historical accidents of disciplinary boundaries rather than any lack of inherent theoretical interest. The current paper addresses the problem of designing conversational agents that exhibit appropriate gaze behavior through an approach that ties information structure to turn-taking. In this new approach, the exchange of looks between participants is related to both information threads and the exchange of turns during the flow of conversation. We turn to this new approach because current approaches have failed to capture the relationship of gaze behavior to contextual boundaries in the incremental exchange of information. In order to account for this aspect of turn-taking, we employ information structure distinctions as a representation of coherence in the accumulation of information within and across turns in dyadic conversations. We examine gaze behavior in relation to propositional content. Semantic content is divided into thematic and rhematic constituents that allow propositions to be presented in a way that highlights the shared content between utterances.

After conducting an empirical analysis on experimental data, we propose these heuristics: the beginning of the thematic part of an utterance is frequently accompanied by gaze behavior that looks away from the hearer, while the beginning of the rhematic part is usually accompanied by gaze behavior that looks toward the hearer. In cases where the beginning of the theme coincides with the beginning of a turn, the speaker always looks away from the hearer. In cases where the beginning of the rheme coincides with the end of the turn, the speaker always looks toward the listener. A simple algorithm for assigning gaze behavior is proposed on the basis of these heuristics. We describe work in progress to implement a conversational agent with capabilities for generating gaze behavior related to propositional content in order to illustrate the application of this research to human-computer conversation.

2 Background

2.1 Gaze and Turn-Taking

When people engage in conversation, they take turns speaking. Turns almost always begin and end smoothly, with short lapses of time between them. Taking into account the dynamic and fast paced nature of conversations, it is remarkable that there are so few occasions when conversation breaks down through simultaneous speech or interruption.

In fact, the time between the exchange of turns is often too short to be explained as the result of the hearer's waiting for the speaker to finish before the hearer starts to speak. This is even more significant if one considers that pauses across turns are sometimes even shorter than pauses within a turn itself. Duncan (1972; 1974) suggests several cues that the speaker employs to indicate the end of a turn or invite the hearer to take a turn. These cues include falling pitch at the end of a sentence, the drawl of a syllable at the end of sentence, the termination of a gesture, specific phrases at the end of syntactic units, and changes in gaze direction, such as the speaker's looking away from the hearer as an utterance begins and toward the hearer as the utterance ends. Goodwin (1981) elaborates on the role of gaze in turn-taking by also considering the gaze of the hearer and the coordination of the gaze of conversational participants. He claims that the speaker's look away at the beginning of turns occurs to avoid overloading information in the planning of an utterance. Because of research by Duncan,

Goodwin and others, gaze behavior has come to be seen as the only cue to turn-organization and has been used as such in the design of embodied conversational agents.

2.2 Gaze Behavior of Conversational Agents

Takeuchi and Nagao (1993) and others have illustrated the communicative value of the face in human-computer conversation. Research by Cassell et al., (1994) and Pelachaud et al., (1996) on the design and implementation of autonomous human-like conversational agents incorporate some of the findings of Duncan and Goodwin to simulate the role of gaze and backchannel feedback in turn-taking. They generated gaze behaviors of the sort correlated with the beginnings and ends of turns. For long turns, the speaker (an animated human-like conversational agent) looks away from the hearer at the beginning of a turn and looks toward the hearer at the end of a turn. For short turns, the speaker looks toward the hearer from the beginning to the end of the turn. They also modeled rules and functions for the diverse types of feedback that take place within a turn. In their model of turn-taking behavior within a turn, the speaker looks at the hearer during grammatical pauses to obtain feedback. Then the hearer looks at the speaker and nods; this backchannel communication is followed by a speaker continuation signal consisting of a look away from the hearer, if the speaker intends to hold the turn.

Thórisson's research (1997) on interactive communicative humanoids uses a situated model of turn-taking based on Sacks et al., (1992; 1974). According to Sacks et al., turn-taking is a phenomenon in which rules are subject to the control of the participants and emergent patterns arising from the interaction of the rules. Thórisson built an interactive communicative humanoid with turn-taking as one of its most relevant and robust features. He addresses the problem of real-time turn-taking by integrating turn-taking with a model of conversants' actions. In his model of conversant actions there are two roles: speaker and hearer. For each role, he defines different classes of behaviors, including perceptual, decision, and motor tasks. His efforts are mainly focused on defining the nature of the underlying perceptual mechanisms. User testing of Thórisson's conversational agent showed that presence of these nonverbal feedback behaviors (gaze, nods, beat gestures) diminished disfluency on the part of users and increased perceived efficiency of the humanoid agent. (Cassell and Thórisson, in press)

2.3 Information Structure

Whittaker et al., (1988) addresses how speakers signal information about discourse structure, beyond the level of the individual utterance, to hearers looking at the mechanism for shifts of control in conversations. The present research follows this discourse-related approach by concentrating on the flow of information between conversants and the informational threads that affect gaze behavior. One way of modeling such discourse phenomena is through information structure (Halliday, 1967), which describes the relationship between the content of utterances (or clauses) and the emerging discourse context. Information structure allows the representation of information within an utterance to be connected with the knowledge of the speaker and hearer and the structure of their discourse. By employing such a model, we are attempting to formalize Goodwin's suggestion that gaze behaviors (and the consequent restarts, pauses, and hesitations) are indicative of "the speaker's attention to the construction of coherent sentences for his recipient" (Goodwin, 1981).

We follow Halliday (1967) in using the terms "theme" and "rheme" to describe information structural components of an utterance. Other terms, such as "link" and "focus", have been widely used in the literature and are roughly synonymous (cf. Vallduvi, 1990). The theme represents the part of the utterance that links it to the previous discourse and specifies what the utterance is about. The rheme, on the other hand, specifies what is contributed to the discourse with respect to the theme. That is, the rheme specifies what is new or interesting about the theme, and generally contains the information that the hearer could not have predicted from context. The linking of thematic threads in a discourse is part of what makes it coherent. In the sections below, we provide evidence, through the use of these information structural categories, that gaze behavior is directly related to discourse coherence.

3 Motivation

Research approaches to the study of conversational gaze behavior concentrate on providing descriptive models of the sentence planning and surface generation aspects of this phenomenon. Although the models proposed by Duncan and Sacks et al., served as the basis for the computational prototypes of Cassell et al., and Thórisson, they do not adequately address other issues involved in the predictive modeling and simulation of gaze behavior generation. First of all, Duncan's signaling approach examines surface linguistic phenomena to investigate what cues signal the end of a turn. None of the phenomena investigated actually correlate highly or predictably with turn-taking. That is, although looking toward the hearer is taken to be a reliable signal of giving over the turn, the majority of glances toward the listener are not found in the context of ends of turns. The employment of "turn constructional units" by Sacks et al., is useful for describing the fundamental units in the exchange of turns, but it does not adequately address how conversants recognize these units. A general theory of turn-taking should account for a consistent range of indicators that serve the very specific function of signaling the end or the beginning of a turn. A different approach for an empirical analysis could entail identifying first the boundaries of a turn and then attempting to explain how the turn exchange is signaled.

We chose to look at the distribution of gaze behavior for clues. That is, rather than looking at turns and all of the nonverbal behaviors that correlate with them, we chose to investigate the nonverbal behavior most popularly assumed to be indicative of turn-taking. In doing so, we wished to also begin to repair a rift between two fields of study. The study of turn-taking has been the purview of conversational analysis (inter alia (Duncan, 1972; Goodwin, 1981; Sacks, 1992), a field derived from sociology. The study of discourse structure (inter alia, Halliday, 1967) has been the domain of linguists, who often neglect to talk to sociologists. And computational work that models language use perpetuates a similar divide (compare Luff et al., 1990, with Prevost, 1996). But theme and rheme (information structure) are, like turn-constructional-units, an account of the accumulation of information. The exchange of turns is related to information threads in the flow of the conversation. This can be intuitively validated if one thinks of a chain of utterances in which new utterances are interpreted in the context of previous utterances. Current approaches to the study of turn-taking have failed to capture the relationship of turn-taking behavior to contextual boundaries in the incremental exchange of information. In order to examine this relationship, the research approach presented in this paper included conducting an empirical analysis that uses information structure distinctions as a representation of coherence in the accumulation of information within and across turns in dyadic conversations. Prevost's work (1996) toward more natural spoken language generation demonstrates the benefits of using a representation of information structure to capture focal distinctions of importance in assigning intonational patterns to an utterance.

Concretely, in terms of implementation goals, if information structure can be shown to predict gaze behavior, then all paraverbal behavior in autonomous humanoid conversational agents (intonation, hand gestures, and gaze) can be driven by a single underlying information structure representation. This is an extension of our earlier work (Cassell and Prevost, in preparation) employing the relationship between information structure and nonverbal behaviors to predict when intonation and gestures will occur in the stream of speech. Such an implementation will facilitate investigating and modeling the interaction among these phenomena.

4 Experimental Data and Empirical Methodology

In order to examine the contribution of turn-taking and information structure to gaze behavior, we collected data from subjects carrying on conversations, and analyzed the distribution of gaze behavior with respect to the two variables of interest, and their interaction. In particular, we transcribed speech, gaze behavior, and head movements which occurred during the first three and a half minutes of three dyadic conversations recorded on videotape. Participants in each conversation were strangers to one another. All participants in the three different two-person conversations were given the same instructions: they were told to sustain a conversation on whatever topics they liked for at least 20 minutes. All of them were native speakers of North American English. They were informed that the purpose of the data collection was to study several aspects of face-to-face interaction. All of them consented to be videotaped.

The conversations were videotaped using two cameras and a microphone placed so that the upper-body space of all participants was completely visible and their voices could be comfortably heard. The interaction was videotaped without altering the focus, zooming in or out, or increasing or decreasing the level of sound. The cameras and the microphone were set up in full view of the participants. The video camera, the microphone, and the video tape were running before participants started their conversations and were not stopped until the conversations ended. The positioning of the video cameras allowed a view of details in the process of interaction, particularly head movements and gaze behavior.

The data presented below are based on 100 turns taken from the three conversations examined. For each turn there were four steps in the transcription process, in order to ensure independence and consistency in transcribing verbal and nonverbal behaviors of the speaker and the hearer during and between gaze behaviors. In the first pass, we transcribed the verbal behavior of the speaker, mainly words and pauses. In the second pass, we transcribed the nonverbal behavior of the speaker, basically gaze behavior. In the third pass, we transcribed the verbal and paraverbal behaviors of the listener, mainly "hmm" and "uh-huh," in alignment with the transcription of the speaker's utterances. In the fourth pass, we transcribed the nonverbal behaviors of the listener, mainly head nods, also in alignment with the transcription of the speaker's utterances.

An attempt was made to include only some types of nonverbal and verbal behavior and two different types of pauses: filled and unfilled. Nonverbal behaviors were mainly of three types: beginning of a look away from the hearer, beginning of a look toward the hearer, and the head nods of the hearer. Unfilled pauses were considered to be noticeable lapses of silence in the talk of speakers.

Three main units of empirical analysis were employed: turns, themes, and rhemes. A "turn" is the talk of the speaker delimited by the talk of the hearer, with the exception of ongoing communicative behavior by the hearer that lacks propositional content. The "beginning of a turn" was defined as the first word of a new turn. The "end of a turn" was defined as the last word +/- one word. The "theme" represents what the utterance is about—what links it to previous utterances The "rheme" represents the contribution to the pool of knowledge in the conversation. The example below illustrates the theme/rheme annotations for the text of utterances, using BTh (beginning of theme) , ETh (end of theme), BRh (beginning of rheme) and ERh (end of rheme):

Q: What do you do?
A: BTh (I work with) ETh BRh (Mike B.) ERh

5 Results

Two patterns previously investigated in the research literature are the occurrence of a look away from the hearer at the beginning of a turn and a look toward the hearer by the end of a turn. We verified these claims and, in addition, found the occurrence of a look away from the hearer at the beginning of a theme and a look toward the hearer at the beginning of a rheme. Most interestingly, however, we found a pattern correlating gaze behavior with the conjunction of information structure and turn-taking. Tables 1-4 display these results.

	BT	BTh	BTh at BT
LA	44%	70%	100%
No LA	56%	30%	0%

Table 1: Look-Away (LA), Beginning of Turn (BT) and Beginning of Theme (Bth)

	LA when BT, not BTh	LA when BTh, not BT	LA when BTh and BT	Other LA
All of LA	28%	22%	10%	40%

Table 2: Distribution of Look-Away (LA)

	ET	BRh	BRh at ET
LT	16%	73%	100%
No LT	84%	27%	0%

Table 3: Look-Toward (LT), End of Turn(ET), Beginning of Rheme (BRh)

	LT when ET, not BRh	LT when BRh, not ET	LT when ET and BRh	Other LT
All of LT	12%	40%	3%	45%

Table 4: Distribution of Look-Toward (LT)

As described in the literature, the speaker does look away from the hearer at the beginning of a turn, although we found this pattern to occur around half of the time. Of all the turn beginnings in our data, 44% were accompanied by look-aways. In terms of how much gaze behavior is accounted for by turn-taking, these look-aways constituted 38% of all the look-aways in our data (see columns 2 and 4 in Table 2). On the other hand, as we hypothesized, a stronger pattern is found if we look at the interaction between information structure and gaze behavior. 70% of the parts of utterances that were identified as thematic were accompanied by the speaker initially looking away from the hearer. These look-aways account for 32% of all the look-aways in the data (see columns 3 and 4 in Table 2). 40% of all the look-aways from the hearer were not associated with either the beginning of a turn or the beginning of thematic material. Most strikingly, however, when the beginning of a theme coincided with the beginning of a turn, speakers always looked away. Thus, our results suggest that the information structural category of themes accounts for some gaze behavior, and that a cotemporaneous beginning of a theme and beginning of a turn always elicits a look-away.

According to the literature, the speaker looks toward the hearer at the end of a turn or at least is already looking toward the hearer by the end of a turn. This pattern is observable in the data, but leaves open the question of how close to the end of the turn this behavior occurs. In Tables 3 and 4, we counted look-towards that occurred within one word of the actual end of an utterance. Of all these ends of turns (given the one word window), 16% included a look-toward. These look-towards represented only 15% of all the look-towards in our data. A look-toward at the beginning of rhematic material occurred in 73% of the instances. These look-towards account for 43% of all the look-towards in our data. 45% of all the look-towards were not associated with either the end of a turn or the beginning rhematic material. Most strikingly, however, when the beginning of a rheme occurred within one word of the end of a turn, the speaker always looked at the listener. Thus, our results suggest that the information structural category of rhemes accounts for some gaze behavior, and that a cotemporaneous rheme and end of turn always elicits a look-toward.

It is clear that the association of turn-initial and turn-final units with information structure units is *very* predictive of gaze behavior. It is also clear that we still cannot account for the majority of gaze behavior (look-towards in particular) with the association of information structure and turn-taking. Additional analyses of the data (not reported here) suggest that backchannel and other kinds of utterance-medial feedback may be accounting for look-towards.

6 Multimodal Dialogue Generation for a Conversational Agent

The results described above are interesting from an ethnomethodological and linguistic point of view, but also for their utility in designing autonomous conversational agents—embodied dialogue systems. Simple "discourse envelope" behaviors of the sort described here—feedback nods, gaze behavior, beat gestures—have been shown to have a powerful effect on how efficient, smooth, and human-like people's interactions with machines can be (Cassell and Thórisson, in press). And yet, rote application of the same nonverbal behaviors can make the computer agent seem overly mechanical, unengaged, and not trustworthy. In our earlier work, we implemented a simple turn-taking strategy for gaze assignment in an autonomous conversational agent (Thórisson, 1997). This agent, Gandalf, interpreted the user's speech, gaze, and gestures (by having the user wear cybergloves and an eyetracker), and in return produced appropriate facial expressions, gestures, and spoken responses. Specifically, some of Gandalf's communicative behaviors included blinking, raising the eyebrows, turning to and gazing at either a graphical model of the solar system or the user, offering nonverbal cues to show when it decided to take a turn, and producing beat and pointing gestures when appropriate. In our current work, we are modifying the conversational agent's capabilities in order to take into account the results presented here, as well as other results in our laboratory on the interplay between interactional (such as turn-taking) and propositional (such as theme/rheme) conversational content.

These advances are only possible by increasing the generativity and autonomy of the system. Currently, Gandalf produces short, canned responses with embedded intonational markings also defined in advance. Its turns are always coextensive with a single utterance. We are currently enhancing the system by adding multimodal dialogue generation capabilities (speech, intonation, turn-taking) from the knowledge base and a discourse model. A consequence of these extensions is that utterances can be longer and contain more information. Additional work in our lab on intonation and turn-taking supports the existence of nonverbal behavior within utterances and, as such, is compatible with Gandalf's present nonverbal behavior generation capabilities across utterances. The work includes implementing the automatic assignment of suitable gaze behavior and generating intonational markings for the thematic (with a look-away and a rise-fall-rise tune respectively) and the rhematic (with a look-toward and rise-fall tune respectively) constituents of an utterance. Our goal is an architecture that will integrate all aspects of conversation, from planning discourse moves to reacting to interactional cues. Augmenting Gandalf's turn-construction algorithm with an information structure algorithm is a first step toward such an architecture.

7 Conclusions and Future Work

Previous research on gaze behavior has focused primarily on its role in turn-taking. However, as our data shows, turn-taking only partially accounts for the gaze behavior in discourse. Although our preliminary findings are consistent with the conclusions drawn in turn-taking research, our data suggests that a better explanation for gaze behavior integrates turn-taking with the information structure of the propositional content of an utterance. Specifically, the beginning of themes are frequently accompanied by a look away from the hearer, and the beginning of rhemes are frequently accompanied by a look toward the hearer. When these categories are cotemporaneous with turn-construction, then they are strongly—in fact, absolutely—predictive of gaze behavior.

Why might there be such a link between gaze and information structure? The literature on gaze behavior and turn-taking suggests that speakers look toward hearers at the ends of turns to signal that the floor is "available"—that hearers may take the turn. Our findings suggest that speakers look toward hearers at the beginning of the rheme—that is, when new information or the key point of the contribution is being conveyed. Gaze here may focus the attention of speaker and hearer on this key part of the utterance. And, of course, signaling the new contribution of the utterance and signaling that one is finished speaking are not entirely independent. Speakers may be more likely to give up the turn once they have conveyed the rhematic material of their contribution to the dialogue. In this case, gaze behavior is signaling a particular kind of relationship between information structure and turn-taking.

We are currently implementing the algorithm proposed here in an autonomous communicative humanoid agent, to provide it with capabilities for more natural gaze behavior related to propositional content and turn-taking. We would like to use a similar algorithm, along with information about intonation, to predict when rhematic units occur in *input*—that is, when users have uttered the key contribution of their utterance. This would allow us to focus speech understanding efforts on this part of the utterance. The symmetry between input and output reflects our belief that it is not the integration of modalities per se that is the interesting problem in embodied dialogue systems, but how to exploit the function of those modalities in the intelligence of the system. Ultimately we hope that this research and other research along these lines will allow the Turing test to be taken face-to-face.

References

Cassell, J., Pelachaud, C., Badler, N.I., Steedman, M., Achorn, B., Beckett, T., Douville, B., Prevost, S. and Stone, M. 1994. "Animated Conversation: Rule-Based Generation of Facial Expression, Gesture and Spoken Intonation for Multiple Conversational Agents." Computer Graphics 94.

Cassell, J. and S. Prevost. (in preparation). "Embodied Natural Language Generation: A Framework for Generating Speech and Gesture."

Cassell, J. and Thórisson, K. (in press). "The Power of a Nod and a Glance: Envelope vs. Emotional Feedback in Animated Conversation Agents." Journal of Applied Artificial Intelligence.

Duncan, S. Jr. 1972. "Some Signals and Rules for Taking Speaking Turns in Conversations." Journal of Personality and Social Psychology, 23(2), 283-292.

Duncan, S. Jr. 1974. "On the Structure of Speaker-Auditor Interaction during Speaking Turns." Language in Society, 3(2), 161-180.

Goodwin, C. 1981. Conversational Organization: Interaction between Hearers and Speakers. Academic Press. New York, NY.

Halliday, M. 1967. Intonation and Grammar in British English. Mouton: The Hague.

Luff, P., Gilbert N., Frohlich, D., eds. 1990. Computers and Conversation.: Academic Press. New York, NY.

Pelachaud, C., Badler N. and Steedman, M. 1996. "Generating Facial Expressions for Speech." Cognitive Science, 20(1).

Prevost, S. 1996. "An Information Structural Approach to Spoken Language Generation." Proceedings of the 34th Annual Meeting of the Association for Computational Linguistics.

Sacks, H. 1992. Lectures on Conversation, Vol. I and II.: Blackwell. Cambridge, MA.

Sacks, H., Schegloff, E.A. and Jefferson, G.A. 1974. "A Simplest Systematics for the Organization of Turn-Taking in Conversation." Language, 50, 696-735.

Takeuchi, A. and Nagao, K. 1993. "Communicative Facial Displays as a New Conversational Modality." Proceedings of InterCHI 93.

Thórisson, K.R. 1997. "Gandalf: An Embodied Humanoid Capable of Real-Time Multimodal Dialogue with People." Autonomous Agents 97.

Whittaker, S. and Stenton, P. 1988. "Cues and Control in Expert-Client Dialogues." Proceedings of the 26th Annual Meeting of the Association for Computational Linguistics.

Vallduvi, E. 1990. "The Informational Component." PhD thesis, University of Pennsylvania, Philadelphia, PA.

13 The BABY Project

P.A.P. Rogers and M. Lefley

1 Introduction

Language plays a central role in human communication. The benefits gained by building machines having the ability to perform natural language processing (NLP), "cannot be underestimated" (Joshi, 1991). Since this publication, those words relate to much wider language domains in light of the explosion of electronic textual information. Consider the benefits to humanity if machines existed which were able to assimilate knowledge by reading large volumes of text, précising, prioritorizing and presenting it from the perspective of particular contexts or different languages.

Natural language is complex and diverse, and processing it by machine remains a hard problem to solve. Specific challenges include the large number of exceptions which exist (e.g. Collier, 1994), and that its acquisition is predominantly by positive example, (e.g. Crain, 1991; Meier, 1991). In addition NLP applications must deal with added complexities of language such as inaccuracy, incompleteness, imprecision and ambiguity (e.g. Manaris and Slator, 1996).

There are two methodologies used to process natural language by machine; devising and employing a set of rules which underlie the nature of language, and designing machines to acquire language. The latter methodology can be split into symbolic and subsymbolic (connectionist) approaches. For wide domain applications, all three of these approaches suffer from severe limitations as itemised below:

1. The overriding problem with rule based theories of wide domain language modelling, is that no theory has so far formulated which specifies the structure of such environments. This state of affairs is implicit in Collier's (1994) reflection that "a large proportion of the NLP community do not believe that general principle rules will provide a solution to the language problem".

2. Designers of machines which acquire language rules of wide domain environments via exposure, are faced with some especially difficult AI problems. Two prominent examples being that language contains many exceptions to the rules being acquired and that the language domain to which the machine is exposed consists predominantly of correct examples. Indeed Gold (1967) demonstrated that a set of rules for any non-trivial language could not be learned from positive examples alone.

3. Though *human* language processing suggests that connectionist approaches may eventually provide a solution to wide domain language processing, machines implementing this methodology which are large and complex enough to process such an environment are currently impossible on both theoretical and technical grounds.

This research proposes a new, wide domain solution related to the third category listed above. The difference between this research and others in this category, is that it models neural networks from a higher abstraction than the currently popular biological level. This is achieved by modelling the *behaviour* rather than the *mechanism* of brain-like architectures. The method of language processing being investigated in this research is at an early stage of development and is therefore not yet intended to compete with other, more established approaches. Research is currently confined to investigating how far the idea can be pursued using empirical results as the metric to continue.

Motivated by the notion that cognition (particularly at low levels) is a pattern association process, a machine is being developed that detects commonalities in the language to which it is exposed and processes them so as to produce natural language interaction with people. The project is called **Baby**. Following a description of the Baby approach, results are presented which show dialogues between its implementation and a linguistically competent human which demonstrate Baby's:

- ability to acquire regularisations and exception in language, by exposure to positive example only;
- ability to use this knowledge to hypothesise grammatically correct, novel linguistic constructs;
- correspondence to human language acquisition behaviour.

2 Baby

Baby is part of a research programme that is not yet complete. A sub-set model interface (**Babette**), has been constructed, which shares sufficient of Baby's design criteria such that it can provide supporting evidence for the approach in general. Mechanism and results shown later in this paper were based upon and generated by Babette.

2.1 Theoretical underpinning

NLP systems employ either symbolic and/or subsymbolic solutions. Symbolic systems are based upon the physical symbol hypothesis first proposed in 1976 by Newell and Simon (Rich and Knight, 1991). Here, theories of the nature of language are modelled in a computing machine by the creation, modification, manipulation copying and deletion of symbols which represent that language. Although Newell and Simons' stated hypothesis that *"A physical symbol system has the necessary means for general intelligent action."* (Newell and Simon, 1976) remains largely intact; implementations are intrinsically linked to explanative powers of theory being modelled. Wide domain natural language implementations employing this approach have achieved relatively limited success because theories which specify the structure of, or the ability to acquire such environments, have so far proved illusive.

Artificial neural networks (ANNs) copy some aspects of the mechanism used in animal nervous systems. They employ nodal summing units, interconnected by weighted connections. The nodes are arranged in layers with input units corresponding to problem start variables, output units corresponding to problem solution states and an indeterminate number of hidden units. Implementations of this approach to language solutions have shown promising results, (e.g. Rumelhart and McClelland, 1986a; Sejnowsky and Rosenberg, 1987; Elman, 1990; Pollack, 1990; Cottrell, 1989; Waltz and Pollack, 1985), but lack theoretical underpinning and suffer from design difficulties such as the scaling effect, choice of appropriate teaching strategies, choice of topology or the local/global minima effect.

A currently popular approach uses hybrid systems. Here, either different types of connectionist networks, or more commonly, the combination of connectionist networks and conventional symbolic systems are employed (see Wermter, 1995). This is a *'horses for courses'* strategy where symbolic and subsymbolic implementations are mixed and matched, each contributing in areas where their computational power are best suited. Although such systems have shown interesting behaviour, very little impact has been made into the domain width problem. Such applications continue to deal with specific aspects of language processing, such as parsing or semantic elicitation (see Wermter and Weber, 1996).

Rather than employing pure symbolic, subsymbolic or hybrid strategies, Baby uses a different approach by modelling neural architectures at a higher level of abstraction than the biological level. This is achieved by modelling the behaviour of, *rather than the mechanism of*, neural networks. Baby does not model a theory of the nature of language and therefore uses no artefacts such as a lexicon or grammar rules set; nor does it use any of the devices contained in neural models such as summing nodes or weighted connections. Instead, Baby models some aspects of neural network behaviour.

For example Baby:

- uses raw (i.e. un-symbolized) data throughout all processing stages;

- detects and manipulates patterns in such data;
- associates patterns in new inputs with previously experienced patterns;
- allows patterns which contribute to processing to survive and those that do not, the possibility to die;
- produces solutions derived from interaction between patterns derived from new input and stored patterns;
- undergoes learning strategies;
- contextually hypothesises solutions to novel problems.

2.2 Constraints, Assumptions and Heuristics

This work is underpinned by a number of constraints, assumptions and heuristics. In order to simplify the problem domain, a self-imposed constraint is applied which restricts the language domain to text. This is a surprisingly, if not uniquely, small constraint for an NLP system. No consideration need be given to the style of language used, the kinds of topics discussed or indeed the native language employed.

A central assumption of this work is that for a given user of a language, the response state engendered from reading a textual stimulus, can be simulated by detecting previously experienced stimuli which share the greatest commonality with the current stimulus and synthesising a response state from patterns associated with the experienced stimuli's contemporaneously, acceptable response.

The number of possible patterns between strings (particularly those with similar structure), is very large. To overcome the problem of having to process the large amounts of data thus produced, a small sub-set of patterns are selected which is likely to include the ones that will contribute to further language interaction with people. The particular sub-set of all patterns are selected by the application of a set of heuristics. The heuristics used are listed below; *chunks* refer to elements of candidate patterns:

1. only concatenated chunks are considered;
2. larger chunks are selected in preference to smaller chunks;
3. selected chunks cannot exist within, or overlap, others;
4. chunks have to be at least two characters in length;
5. the order of selected chunks and non-selected chunks is preserved.

Individuals of the subset produced which can be used by Baby to process further language interface with people are considered valid, those which do not are eventually allowed to die. This allows Baby to use the complexities of the problem domain to select winning solutions, obviating the need to define what it is that constitutes a successful pattern.

2.3 *Implementation*

This section describes the way in which Babette is implemented. To aid comprehension, the following list of terms have specific meanings in this paper:

2.3.1 Definitions

1. **Character**: any ANSI character except 47 (/), 126 (~), 91([) and 93(]) [1]
2. **String:** any combination of characters.
3. **Common** (element of a string): any coincidence of one or more characters that occur between two strings.
4. **Constant** (element of a string): common element that is hypothesised can be used by Babette to process language interaction with people.
5. **Variable** (element of a string): an element which is not a constant.
6. **Signature**: a string with its constants identified.
7. **Target signature**: a signature which Babette can use to process natural language interaction with people.
8. **Similarity**: a string identified with a set of its commonalities.

2.3.2 Feature detector

The feature detector is an important subsystem of Babette. Its purpose is to detect patterns between strings of characters which comply with the heuristic set, i.e signatures.

2.3.2.1 Feature detector specification. Consider the general case of any two strings, amongst all strings of a given alphabet.
Let: **X**, **S(0)**, **S(1)** and **S(2)** be sets on the infinite universe of all strings, **Z**
and: $a \in \mathbf{Z}$, $b \in \mathbf{X}$, $c \in \mathbf{S(0)}$, $d \in \mathbf{S(1)}$ and $e \in \mathbf{S(2)}$

where: a = any character string,
b = an a which represents an utterance of a language,
c = matching concatenated characters between two b, i.e. **common** elements,
d = a c whose match complies with a set of heuristics, i.e. **constant** elements,
e = those d which can be processed to perform natural language interaction with humans.

and: $\mathbf{X} \subset \mathbf{Z}$, $\mathbf{S(0)} \subset \mathbf{Z}$, $\mathbf{S(1)} \subset \mathbf{S(0)}$, $\mathbf{S(2)} \subseteq \mathbf{S(1)}$

i.e.

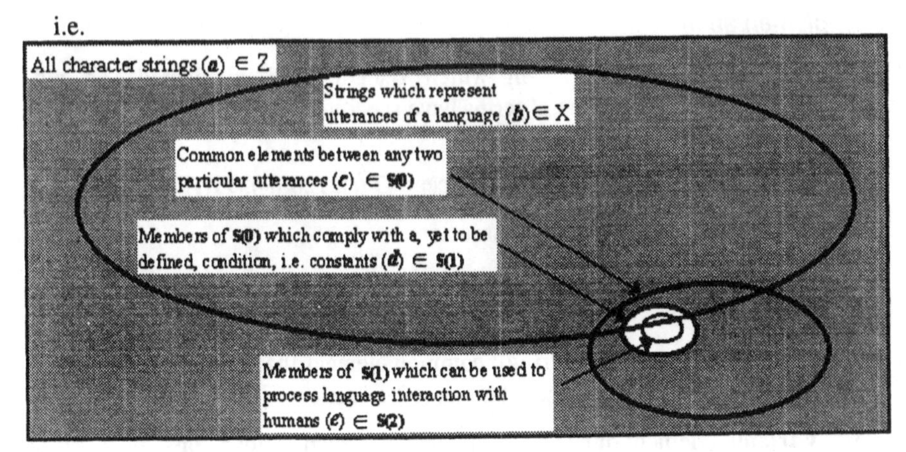

Figure 1.

Also let: **S(3)**, **S(4)** be sets on the finite universe of **similarities** between a given ***b*** pair, **S(5)**.

and: $x \in$ **S(3)**, $y \in$ **S(4)** and $z \in$ **S(5)**.

where: z = a ***b*** pair identified with a particular set of their ***c*** = **similarity**,
x = a ***b*** pair identified with a particular set of their ***d*** = **signature**,
y = a ***b*** pair identified with a particular set of their ***e*** = **target signature**,
v = non-***d*** elements of a ***b*** pair, (shaded in fig.1) = **variables**,

and: $S(4) \subseteq S(3) \subset S(5)$ and $v \in$ the relative complement **Z | S(1)**

Given this domain and some minor restrictions imposed by the software environment (Visual Basic), the feature detector's input and output can be defined as:

> **Input**: any two strings with lengths between 1 and 65,535 characters[2].
> **Output:** the set **S(3)** which is equal to (or a manageably small superset of) **S(4)**, whilst remaining contained by **S(5)**.

2.3.2.2 Feature detector implementation. Heuristics 1, 2 and 4 are modelled by arranging the order in which sub-strings of the two input strings are selected and compared. The process is similar to that used to present serially ordered input to parallel processors, e.g. in the case of ANNs, NETTALK (Sejnowski and Rosenburg, 1987) or PARSNIP (Hanson and Kegl, 1987). In common with both of these example applications, a 'sliding window' is employed.

For a given input string, various window lengths are selected and slid from left to right thus traversing it. Starting with a window of length equal to the length of the input string, the process is repeated with successively shorter window lengths (one character at a time), down to a two character length. This ensures that every sub-string of two or more characters is selected only once. For each different sub-string of the input string, a window of the length of that sub-string is slid a character at a time across the comparison string, to determine whether the comparison string contains the current sub-string of the input string. Heuristic 3 is modelled by the application of a set of conditions. Heuristic 5 is modelled by number labelling each variable in an ascending, sequential series, from left to right in both strings. Only variables of the same label number are analysed for further constants. In the case that a match between two sub-strings complies with all heuristics, then it is afforded constant status. The process iterates until no more constants can be formed. The resulting string(s), identified with their constants, are considered to be signatures of the input strings.

2.4 General operation.

Babette's operation can be crudely divided into on-line and background processing, though they are in fact inter-related processes. On-line processing occurs interactively with reception of input stimuli, storing or matching them with pattern analyses produced during background processing. Background processing may occur at any time after Babette receives two or more input stimuli; its purpose is to detect patterns between data stored as a result of on-line processing.

2.4.1 On-line processing.

As Babette receives separate textual stimuli, they are segregated into pairs. The first of each pair is labelled as a stimulus and the second as that stimulus' response. These stimulus/response pairs are stored in raw character form as *textual couplets*, (see sections 2.4.3 and 2.4.4 for further on-line processing).

2.4.2 Background processing.

At some time following the reception of at least two textual couplets, background processing can be invoked. Its purpose is to detect patterns between textual couplets and store them as *feature couplets* along with their variables in an associated table. Each time that background processing is invoked, every permutation of textual couplet stimulus elements and their corresponding response elements undergoes feature detection. The metric used to determine which textual couplet(s) are to be paired as feature couplets, is the length of the constants which they share. Once converted to feature couplets, the textual couplets which created them are deleted. The process iterates for the textual couplets which remain until no more can be converted into feature couplets. Variables are detected by exposing each feature couplet to each of the original textual couplets that were used to create the feature couplet(s). If the stimulus and response elements of a given feature couplet can be subtracted from (respectively) the stimulus and response element of a textual couplet, then this action is performed. The strings which lay in between the subtracted patterns of the textual couplet strings, are stored as variable elements for the feature couplet. The position(s) where the variable(s) occurred in the feature couplet are numbered sequentially, such that each number refers to a different variable, positions where the variable is the same possess the same number, e.g. for the textual couplet:

What is cat?
A cat is a feline.
and the feature couplet:
[What is a][?]
[A][is a][.]

the resulting analysis is:

[What is a]1[?] with variables: **cat**
[A]1[is a]2[.] with variables: **cat/feline**

2.4.3 Factual responses.

There are two methods by which a factual reply can be formed. Firstly, if a new stimulus corresponds exactly with the stimulus element of a textual couplet then the textual couplet's response element is returned. Secondly, if the stimulus element of a feature couplet, can be subtracted from a new stimulus and the remaining variables correspond to the variables stored in the table associated with the stimulus element of the feature couplet, then the response element of that feature couplet with its appropriate variables are returned.

2.4.4 Hypothesised responses.

If a new stimulus contains patterns which correspond to the patterns stored as the stimulus element of a feature couplet, but after pattern subtraction the resulting variables are not stored in the feature couplet's corresponding variable table, then Babette hypothesises a reply. This is formed by subtracting the pattern of the stimulus element of the target feature couplet from the new stimulus, leaving variables. Hypothesised replies are formed by inserting those variables into appropriate slots in the response element of the target feature couplet.

2.4.5 No response.

If neither a factual nor hypothesised response can be made from a new input stimulus, then Babette prompts for an appropriate response using the words "How should I reply?". The input stimulus and the human response to Babette's prompt are stored as a new textual couplet.

3 Results

Tables I and II show conversations between a linguistically competent human and Babette. In each case, Babette begins with no linguistic knowledge, i.e. no textual or feature couplets. To show the results in an easy to comprehend format, background processing is invoked after the reception of each two stimulus response pairs. A double question mark "??" is used to indicate a Babette hypothesis.

3.1 Acquisition by positive exposure.

The test chosen to illustrate Babette's ability to acquire language behaviour through positive exposure involves the learning of plural inflections.

No.	Human utterance	Babette's reply
1	What is the plural of snake?	How should I reply?
2	The plural of snake is snakes.	OK
3	What is the plural of ant?	How should I reply?
4	The plural of ant is ants.	OK
5	What is the plural of datum?	The plural of datum is datums??
6	The plural of datum is data.	OK
7	What is the plural of agendum?	The plural of agendum is agendums??
8	The plural of agendum is agenda.	OK
9	What is the plural of deer?	The plural of deer is deers??
10	The plural of deer is deer.	OK
11	What is the plural of window?	The plural of window is windows??
12	The plural of window is windows.	OK
13	What is the plural of septum?	The plural of septum is septa??
14	The plural of septum is septa.	OK
15	What is the plural of deer?	The plural of deer is deer.
16	What is the plural of window?	The plural of window is windows.

Table I

Utterances 1 - 4 enable the system to learn one type of regular plural formation. This is evidenced in the incorrect hypothesised plural formations to utterances 5 and 7. Utterances 5 - 8 expose the system to another form of regular plural formation. Utterances 9 and 10 provide an exception to either of the regularities previously experienced. Utterance 11 is a novel stimulus and produces a correct hypothesis learned from utterances 1 - 4. Utterance 13 is again novel and produces a correct hypothesis learned from 5 - 8. Utterance 15 shows that Babette has learned a fact from one of its generalisation hypotheses. Utterance 16 shows the retention of an, as yet, exception to all generalisation exposures as a fact.

3.2 Correspondence with human language acquisition.

The manner in which past tense formations are learned, illustrates how Babette can be considered to exhibit human-like behaviour in its language acquisition.

Much psycholinguistic research has concentrated upon past tense learning (e.g. Brown, 1973; Ervin, 1964; Kuczaj, 1977). This work suggests that children acquire the ability to form the past tense of verbs in a three-stage process. In summary:

Stage 1. Small vocabulary of verbs in the past tense, predominantly irregular, e.g. take/took and come/came. No generalisation of the small set of regular past tenses that *are* known. Past tenses appear to be learned by rote rather than by rule.

Stage 2. Much larger vocabulary of regular past tense formations. Generalisation of regular inflections observed with new verbs and non-words. Generalisation overrides rote learning, causing previously known irregular past tenses to be incorrectly formed e.g. "taked" or "comed".
Stage 3. Greatly expanding vocabulary. Maintaining generalised inflection behaviour re-acquiring correct exception past tensing. Later forming minor regular clusters, e.g. "ow" to "own" or "ing to "ang ").

To compare the enormous exposure experienced during human language acquisition to the 30 utterances shown in table II is asking rather a lot. However, a correspondence between Babette's language learning behaviour and human acquisition is observable.

No.	Human utterance	Babette's reply
1	What is the past tense of have?	How should I reply?
2	The past tense of have is had.	OK
3	What is the past tense of go?	How should I reply?
4	The past tense of go is gone.	OK
5	What is the past tense of give?	How should I reply?
6	The past tense of give is gave.	OK
7	What is the past tense of get?	How should I reply?
8	The past tense of get is got.	OK
9	What is the past tense of take?	How should I reply?
10	The past tense of take is took.	OK
11	What is the past tense of is?	How should I reply?
12	The past tense of is is was.	OK
13	What is the past tense of give?	The past tense of give is got.
14	What is he past tense of is?	The past tense of is is was.
15	What is the past tense of start?	How should I reply?
16	The past tense of start is started.	OK
17	What is the past tense of jump?	How should I reply?
18	The past tense of jump is jumped.	OK
19	What is the past tense of sweep?	The past tense of sweep is sweeped??
20	The past tense of sweep is swept.	OK
21	What is the past tense of keep?	The past tense of keep is keeped??
22	The past tense of keep is kept.	OK
23	What is the past tense of run?	The past tense of ran is runed??
24	The past tense of run is ran.	OK
25	What is the past tense of part?	The past tense of part is parted??
26	The past tense of part is parted.	OK
27	What is the past tense of creep?	The past tense of creep is crept??
28	The past tense of creep is crept.	OK
29	What is the past tense of have?	The past tense of have is had.
30	What is the past tense of keep.	The past tense of keep is kept.

Table II

Stage 1. Utterances 1 - 12 show Babette's exposure to a series of irregular past tense verb formations. By definition, such formations share little commonality between their verb inflections. Babette's replies reflect this by producing no hypotheses, though each past tense formation has been remembered by rote as exampled in utterances 13 and 14.

Utterances 15 and 16 represent the first example of a regular past tense cluster, because only one example exists at this point, Babette considers it to be another irregularity as evidenced by its reply.

Stage 2. Utterances 17 and 18 are considered to represent the greater vocabulary of regular verbs learned by children in this stage. Although Babette remembers previously learned exceptions and thus does not incorrectly hypothesise them with regular past tense inflections, it does now begin to hypothesise new verbs using its majority regularity, e.g. "sweeped" and "keeped" in utterances 19 and 21 respectively.

Stage 3. As exposure to new stimuli continues, Babette begins to learn more exceptions, e.g. "run"/"ran" in utterances 23 and 24, and assigns new verbs with their appropriate inflections according to their similarity to the various regular clusters learned, e.g. "part"/"parted", "creep"/"crept" in utterances 25 - 28. Utterances 29 and 30 show Babettes's ability to learn facts from rote learning and confirmed hypotheses, i.e. in this case from utterances 2 and 22.

4 Conclusions

This research is motivated by the relatively modest success achieved in developing wide domain natural language processing machines over the last 40 years or so. For this type of application, it is assumed that rule based approaches are wrong-headed and that pure connectionist models are likely to be prohibitively complex for today's technology and theoretical underpinning. This approach utilizes a more abstract perspective than the currently popular biological level. Here the behaviour rather than the mechanism of neural networks is modelled.

Even given the crude nature of Babette, we have shown its language behaviour exhibits some interesting, human-like performance,
i.e. it

- learns regular grammatical structures;
- learns exceptions to those regularities;
- learns by exposure to only positive examples;
- generalises regular grammatical structures in its experience to hypothesise response to novel input;
- simulates aspects of child language acquisition.

This performance to the extent that it is illustrated in the tests could be easily reproduced using a relatively simple rule based system. A crucial aspect of this approach is that the language behaviour exhibited here is achieved without the use of conventional theories about the nature of language, i.e. no lexicon, no grammar, or any other hand-crafted language modelling device. A machine has been presented that automatically acquires some important aspects of language as a result of exposure to it. All of the rules that are encoded in Babette enable it to learn about the pattern or commonality in things, not to model human theories of the nature of language. Whether the hypothesis is true or not, evaluating such a model will have implications for computer and human problem solving, interfacing and mental modelling.

References

Brown, R. 1973. A First Language. Harvard University Press: Cambridge, MA.

Collier, R. 1994. An Historical Overview of Natural Language Processing Systems that Learn. Artificial Intelligence Review. 8(1): 17 - 54.

Cottrell, G. W. 1989. A Connectionist Approach to Word Sense Disambiguation, Pitman Publishing: London.

Crain, S. 1991. Language acquisition in the absence of experience. Behavioural and Brain Sciences. 14(4): 597-612.

Elman, J. L. 1990. Finding structure in time. Cognitive Science 14(2): 179 - 211.

Ervin, S. 1964. Imitation and Structural Change in Children's Language. New Directions in the Study of Language. E. Lenneberg. MIT Press: Cambridge MA.

Gold, E. 1967. Language Identification in the Limit. Information and Control. 16: 447 - 474.

Hanson, S. J. and Kelg, J. 1987. PARSNIP: A Connectionist Network that Learns Natural Language Grammar from Exposure. *The Ninth Annual Conference of the Cognitive Science Society,* 106 - 119. Seattle, Washington. Lawrence Erlbaum: Hillsdale, NJ.

Joshi, A. K. 1991. Natural Language Processing. Science. 11(4): 1242 - 1249.

Kuczaj, S. A. 1977. The Acquistion of Regular and Irregular Past Tense Forms. Journal of Verbal Learning and Verbal Behaviour. 16: 589 - 600.

Manaris, B. Z. and Slator, B. S. 1996. Interactive Natural Language Processing: building on success. Computer 29(7): 28-31.

Meier, P. R. 1991. Language Acquisition by Deaf Children. American Scientist. 79(1): 60 - 70.

Newell, A. and Simon, H. A. 1976. Computer Science as Empirical Inquiry: symbols and search. Communication of the ACM. 19(3): 113 - 126.

Pollack, J. B. 1990. Recursive Distributed Representations. Artificial Intelligence. 46: 77-105.

Rich, E. and Knight, K. 1991. Artificial Intelligence., McGraw-Hill, Inc., New York, NY.

Rumelhart, D. E. and McClelland, J. L. 1986a. On Learning the Past Tense of English Verbs. Parallel Distributed Processing, Volume 2: Psychological and Biological Models. J. E. McClelland and D. E. Rumelhart, 2: 216 - 271. MIT Press: Cambridge, MA.

Sejnowski, T. J. and Rosenburg, C. R. 1987. Parallel Networks that Learn to Pronounce English Text. Complex Systems. 1: 145 - 168.

Sejnowski, T. J. and Rosenburg, C. R. 1987. Parallel Networks that Learn to Pronounce English Text. Complex Systems. 1: 145 - 168.

Waltz, D. L. and Pollock, J. B. 1985. Massively Parallel Parsing. Cognitive Science: a strongly interactive model of natural language interpretation. 9: 51-74.

Wermter, S. 1995. Hybrid Connectionist Natural Language Processing., Chapman and Hall: London.

Wermter, S. and Weber, V. 1996. Interactive Spoken-Language Processing in a Hybrid Connectionist System. Computer 29(7): 65.

Notes

[1] Characters 91 and 93 are reserved for feature detection processing. Characters 126 and 47 are used later in Babette. They are implementational conveniences, not model-theoretic requirements.
[2] This is not a model-theoretic constraint, it is limitation of the software environment (Visual Basic).

14 A Responsive Dialog System

N. Ward and W. Tsukahara

1 Motivation

Modeling language as people really use it is an elusive goal. Today, thanks to advances in speech recognition, dialog systems capable of understanding the meaning of user input and replying with appropriate information exist, but there are as yet no systems which interact naturally with humans. Two problems are:

1. Priority is given to understanding and responding accurately; but for human dialog, being responsive and interactive is also important.
2. The granularity of interaction is the sentence; but for human dialog, interaction happens more frequently, in real time, often with overlapping utterances;

Given that such responsiveness is important to human language use, the question arises: how do we build systems with these abilities? The obvious approach is to add these abilities to a meaning-based speech system. An alternative approach is to take these abilities as a basic foundation, and to layer meaning-based processing on top of this, subsumption-style (Ward, 1997).

2 Phenomenon

Back-channel feedback, also called "listener responses", is produced by one participant as a response that does not interfere with utterances by the other participant (Ward and Tsukahara, submitted). In American English 'yeah', 'mm' and 'uh-huh' are typical back-channel feedback. In Japanese 'un' is most typical.

To be a good conversation partner, production of back-channel feedback is essential; if it is lacking the conversation tends to die out. Back-channel feedback is an example of "responsiveness", which is important in spoken dialog between humans, and probably also in human-computer systems (Johnstone and Berry et al., 1995; Ward, 1997).

3 Analysis

Many have sought for the perceptual clue that tells a participant "it's now time to produce back-channel feedback". It has often been speculated that this clue from the speaker would be prosodic, rather than involving meaning.

In search of this clue we looked at the prosodic environments of back-channel feedback in corpora of natural Japanese and English conversations. Potential clues considered included pitch contours, vowel lengthening or speaking rate slowdown, volume increase or decrease on final syllables, a low pitch point, and gross energy level changes, following suggestions in the literature, as discussed by Ward (1996) and Ward and Tsukahara (submitted). None of these appeared to have a strong correlation with whether back-channel feedback was produced or not.

However, there was one good clue: a region of low pitch. While we have no real proof yet that this is actually a trigger for a reflex response in people, this is certainly usable in spoken dialog systems.

It is commonly thought that silence (at the end of a speaker's turn) is a major clue for back-channel feedback. This is probably important in business-like transactions between strangers, but not for more casual interactions. In the latter the low pitch cue accounts for both back-channel feedback which is produced after the speaker paused and stopped, and that which overlaps the speaker's continued utterance.

4 Results

Using correspondence to corpus data as the criterion, we sought for the rule which best models human behavior. For Japanese, the best we have found so far is as follows:

Upon detection of a region of pitch less than the 28th-percentile pitch level and continuing for at least 110 milliseconds, coming after at least 700 ms. of speech, providing you have not output back-channel feedback within the preceding 1.0 seconds, 350 ms. later you should produce back-channel feedback.

Testing the predictions of the above rule against the corpus of human conversations gives a coverage of 56% (half of the back-channels were predicted) at an accuracy of 34% (a third of the predictions were correct), over all speakers and all dialog types. Performance was better for friendly, attentive listeners and for conversation portions that involved narrative or explanation. 44% of the false predictions seem to be due to inter-speaker differences; thus the rule does much better when judged as a model of a specific speaker (Ward and Tsukahara, submitted).

For English speakers, the best prediction rule has somewhat different parameters: Upon detection of a region of pitch less than the 26th-percentile pitch level and continuing for at least 110 milliseconds, coming after at least 700 ms. of speech, providing you have not output back-channel feedback within the preceding .8 seconds, 700 ms. later you should produce back-channel feedback.

For the English corpus, this achieved a coverage of 48% at an accuracy of 18%.

5 Experiments

We built a system to find out how well the above rules would perform in live conversation. There were two critical issues.

One issue was which back-channels to produce. For Japanese, it turned out to be acceptable to always produce 'un', the most common and most neutral back-channel, in a falling pitch. For English 'uh-huh' and 'mm' were acceptable. Since always producing the same token sounded mechanical, we used two in alternation, or three with random selection.

Another issue was how to get people to try to interact naturally with the system. The only solution was to fool them into thinking they were interacting with a person. Hence we used a human decoy to jump-start the conversation. For the initial experiments we used a partition so that the subject couldn't see when it was the system that was responding; later we ran the system over the telephone. The outputs of the system were recordings of decoy-produced samples, not synthesized. To make it impossible for subjects to distinguish between the decoy's live voice and the system's contributions, we distorted both slightly by over-amplifying them.

We hypothesized that back-channel feedback produced according to the rule would sound natural, and permit the conversation to proceed normally. Conversely, we hypothesized that inappropriate back-channel conversation would seem unfriendly or unnatural, be annoying, or kill the conversation.

We found that back-channel feedback in response to low pitch regions did indeed sound natural. In one run of twenty-odd Japanese subjects, only two suspected that the back-channels were artificial; the vast majority was surprised when told that the decoy had handed the conversation over to the computer. Unfortunately this was not significant, since even in the control experiments, with back-channels produced at random, most subjects did not notice anything odd or different, no matter how hard we probed in post-conversation interviews. Indeed, in many cases they hadn't even noticed whether back-channels were present.

However, third party judges listening to the conversations generally could distinguish the low pitch based back-channels from the randomly produced ones; the former sounded natural and the latter sounded odd, with clear cases of inappropriate back-channels and of inappropriate silences when a back-channel was called for.

We surmise that our subjects were generally so busy speaking that they had only minimal attention to pay to back-channel feedback. Also, to the extent that they do notice back-channel feedback, there is probably a human tendency to be generous and uncritical in interpreting a dialog partner's responses and response patterns. It is of course possible that more sensitive metrics, either subjective, such as impressions of how interested or friendly the listener was, or objective, such as average utterance length, would reveal a difference between the effects of appropriate and inappropriate back-channel feedback on the speaker. However this will not be easy, since the effects of manipulating back-channel feedback are complex and context-dependent (Siegman, 1976).

We also tried a different experimental procedure, where the subject knew that his partner might be a machine, and had to guess, in any trial, whether it was a human or a machine. We found here that slight differences of sound quality between the live and pre-recorded back-channels, more than timing, were what people were sensitive to. Also, the problem of factoring out the effects of variations in topic across runs made it difficult to get meaningful results.

It is interesting to note that people in general are not prepared to chat naturally with a machine. In demonstrations, where subjects knew that their conversation partner was a machine, we sometimes found that the subject, after putting on the microphone, would challenge the system to respond, with no result, and then turn to the experimenter and make some comment, only to have the system them chime in with a perfectly appropriate back-channel.

In experiments with a couple dozen subjects in English run over the telephone as part of the Elsnet Speech System Olympics at EuroSpeech 97, we found two main factors affecting the success of the system. The first was the ability to get the other person talking; this depended on whether the subject was talkative and on the decoy's success at putting them at ease and leading them on to a suitable topic of conversation. The other factor was native language; the system generally worked poorly or not at all for speaker's whose native language was not a Germanic one.

Here are transcripts of two sessions. D is the decoy, S is the subject, and C is the computer. Computer responses are also decorated with asterisks.

```
D: Okay, so let's see, I'll hit return. Say something.
S: Nani ga iimasu.
D: Okay, great, let's just speak English, because all
I want is your pitch range.
S: Yeah that's fine.
D: And let's talk for a minute and um.
S: Okay, because I think my pitch range is
. . .
S: Shall I keep on talking?
D: Yeah, please. So how's the weather, in England? Is
it better than here?
S: It's certainly cooler, that's for sure.
C: *mm*
S: Probably it's better, I don't know. I saw the um
forecast on the TV last night,
C: *mm*
S: and it's something like 15 centigrade, which is on
the cooler side I think, isn't it.
C: *mm*
S: I'm not sure what it is here for us
C: *mm*
S: 59, 58 something I think, about that. Fairly cool.
C: *mm*
But um, over here I find, I have to pace myself
carefully, because I start sweating,
C: *mm*
S: before I get tired.
```

C: *mm*
S: [laughs]
D: Well that's the humidity more than the, uh temperature, I think.
S: Yeah, that's right, yes
. . .
D: Okay, so we have your pitch down. So, um that was, like a normal English conversation?
S: I think so, yeah.
D: Nothing strange about it.
S: No. Except the fact we can't see each other, but that's nothing. And I'm being videotaped of course. [laughs]
D: Okay, great. So in fact, in about 10 places, it's that the system said 'mm', and that was produced by the system.
S: Oh right. I didn't notice, I didn't notice
. . .
The next transcript is of a failure. This was perhaps because the subject was not a native speaker, and perhaps because she was suspicious from the start.

Example 1

D: Okay, so. So tell me, is Rick Alterman still there? I guess.
S: Is who?
D: Rick Alterman.
S: Oh yeah definitely, because he's in the department.
C: *mm*
D: So what's he up to?
S: It's really hard to say
C: *mm*
S: I don't think I
C: *mm*
S: can really quite define his work,
C: *mm*
S: but um,
C: *mm*
S: you know he's. Why are you doing that?
C: *mm*
S: [laughs] What's that sound?
C: *mm*

Example 2

6 Significance

We have demonstrated a system that can keep up its end of a conversation, without doing speech recognition or understanding. More generally, the impression of naturalness in spoken conversation can be achieved, in large part, by simply following the prosodic and gaze-given cues of the interlocutor, as other work also found (Schmandt, 1994; Thórisson, 1994; Iwase, 1998).

We are planning to look for more such cues. So far we have tentatively identified some of the factors that affect the choice of which word or grunt to produce as back-channel feedback (Ward, 1998; Tsukahara, 1998).

Ultimately we plan to combine simple reflex-type responsiveness with recognition and understanding. Our near-term aim is to build a system that will interact truly naturally with people in a simple verbal game.

Acknowledgements

We thank the many students who have helped with this work, and the Sound Technology Promotion Foundation, the Hayao Nakayama Foundation, and the Japanese Ministry of Education for support.

References

Iwase, T. 1998. Yuza ni awaseta Taiwa Peesu no Chosetsu (Adjusting the Pace of Conversation to Suit the User). in Proceedings of the 4th Annual Meeting of the (Japanese) Association for Natural Language Processing, pp. 472-475.

Johnstone, A., Berry U., Nguyen T. and Asper, A. 1995. There was a Long Pause: Influencing turn-taking behaviour in human-human and human-computer dialogs. International Journal of Human-Computer Studies, 42, pp. 383--411.

Schmandt, C. 1994. Computers and Communication. Van Nostrand Reinhold: New York, NY.

Siegman, A.W. 1976. Do Noncontingent Interviewer Mm-hmms Facilitate Interviewee Productivity? Journal of Consulting and Clinical Psychology, 44, pp. 171--182.

Thórisson, K.R. 1994. Face-to-Face Communication with Computer Agents. Working Notes, AAAI Spring Symposium on Believable Agents, pp. 86--90.

Tsukahara W. 1998. Purosodi oyobi Bunmyaku Joho o Mochiita Ooto no Sentaku/Chosetsu no Kokoromi (Selecting and Adapting Confirmations in Response to Prosodic Indications and Contextual Factors). Proceedings of the 4th Annual Meeting of the (Japanese) Association for Natural Language Processing, pp. 468-471.

Ward, N. 1996. Using Prosodic Clues to Decide When to Produce Back-channel Utterances. International Conference on Spoken Language Processing, pp. 1728--1731.

Ward, N. 1997. Responsiveness in Dialog and Priorities for Language Research. Systems and Cybernetics, 28, pp. 521--533.

Ward, N. 1998. The Relationship between Sound and Meaning in Japanese Back-channel Grunts. Proceedings of the 4th Annual Meeting of the (Japanese) Association for Natural Language Processing, pp. 464-469.

Ward, N. and Tsukahara, W. (submitted). Prosodic Features which cue Back-channel Responses in English and Japanese. Journal of Pragmatics.

15 Situated Communication with Robots

J.-T. Milde, K. Peters and S. Strippgen

1 Introduction

A human-computer dialogue can be compared to a telephone conversation. Such a conversation is constrained by the fact, that the participants are not situated in the same environment. During their communication, they can only refer to parts of the dialogue but not to current events or objects in their surroundings. As a consequence, the syntactic structure of occurring sentences may be complex, but the semantic interpretation of a sentence is normally based on past and current utterances.

This differs from situations, where both conversation participants share the same environment. Consider the case where an instructor and an executive cooperate in a construction task. Here the use of natural language is dominated by the given task, the possible and allowed interactions between instructor and executive as well as the manipulative and sensoric abilities of both. Rather than describing a complete action in full detail, natural communication during cooperative construction is constrained by the situation and the perception of the common environment. The instructor gives hints on suitable actions to perform or describes objects to be used. Possible feedback by the executive are questions to solve situative ambiguities or short descriptions of what the executive perceives.

Natural language used in such a setting tends to have a simple syntactic structure, but nevertheless is very hard to be interpreted. Utterances found in an instruction situation include phenomena such as ellipses, indirect speech acts and situated object or action reference. Because of the complex interplay between language, perception and action, a correct semantic interpretation of these phenomena can only be achieved by integrating extralinguistic information. Furthermore, form and content of instructions and answers depend on the current situation. Quite often utterances can only be understood if background knowledge of the sequence of actions needed to achieve a given goal is considered.

In the following we want to analyse selected phenomena of situated communication that are typical for instruction situations and introduce a hybrid architecture, which integrates language, perception and action in order to cope with those phenomena. Testbed for the architecture is a simulation of a robot manipulator (Puma 260), which can be directed by typed natural language instructions. The arm manipulates Baufix elements, a toy construction system. Examples of Baufix elements are coloured wooden bolts, nuts, connecting bars and cubes. The manipulator is equipped with an arm mounted camera and a two finger gripper.

2 A situated dialogue

First we want to show some typical phenomena of situated communication on the basis of an example dialogue. The scenario, in which the dialogue takes place, is the following: The robot is standing on a work surface, where the assembly parts, like bolts, connecting bars, and screwing cubes, are also lying. Depending on its position, the camera allows the robot to see a part of the environment.

Figure 1 depicts the situation at the beginning of the following dialogue. Figure 2 shows the current snapshot of the robot's camera, i.e. what the robot perceives at this moment.

(1) *Put the red screwing cube on the connecting bar.*[1]

The robot moves towards a red cube in order to grasp it.

(2) *No, the other one!*

The red cube the human interlocutor refered to in (1) is different to the one the robot chose. After processing the intervention the robot moves towards the other cube and grasps it. Now it looks for the connecting bar on which it should lay the cube.

(3) `On which connecting bar?`[2]

(4) *On the left one!*

The robot, with the cube in its gripper, moves towards the left connecting bar. Then it gets closer to the middle hole of the bar.[3]

(5) *More to the left!*

The robot moves to the left along the connecting bar. Due to the current position of the bar (see fig. 2) the robot's movement is a diagonal one. Then the robot stops.

(6) `Here?`

(7) *Yes.*

The robot puts the cube down in this place.

(8) *Put the short connecting bar on top of it!*

The robot looks for a short bar, finds and grasps it. It moves to the cube, which it put down before, and puts down the bar. However, the bar doesn't remain lying on the cube but falls off.

(9) `The connecting bar fell down.`

(10) *Once again!*

The robot tries again to put the bar on top of the cube. This time it succeeds.

(11) *Do you see the red bolt?*

The robot looks for the red bolt and after finding it moves towards it. Then it stops above the bolt.

(12) `Do you mean this one?`

(13) *Take it and use it to connect the parts!*

The robot approaches the bolt thread.

(14) `I can't grasp it.`

(15) *The other way round!*

The robot approaches the bolt from the other direction. Now it is able to grasp the bolt head and picks it up. Then the robot tries to screw the bolt into the cube.

(16) `It doesn't work!`

(17) *Try it again!*

The dialogue considered in isolation, i.e. without including the whole situation, is ambiguous, or perhaps even incomprehensible, in many places. Without the description of the agent's actions and the knowledge of the objects' position it isn't clear what is meant by both the robot and the human interlocutor. Understanding and production of utterances in cooperative, action-oriented dialogues are extremely dependent on the situation, which they are located in (see Fiehler, 1993).

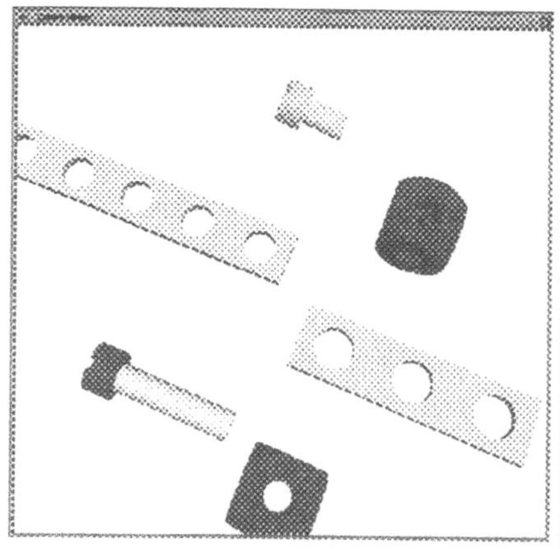

Figure 1: The simulated robot

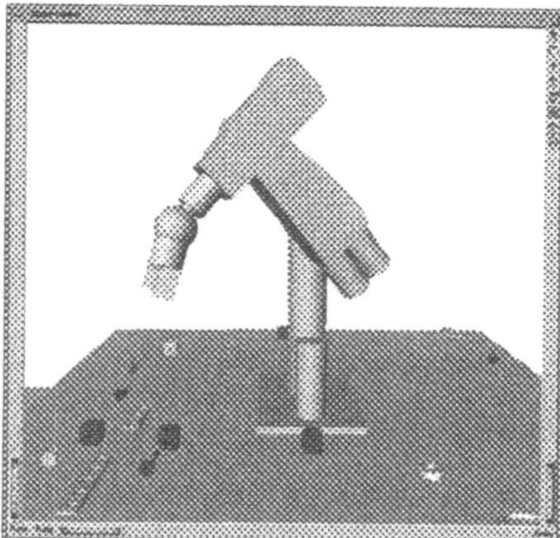

Figure 2: Snapshot of the camera

Utterance (2) refers to an object, but neither specifies which kind of object is meant nor what should be done with this object. The missing information arises out of the current action of the robot, which moves towards a red cube. To which 'the other one' refers, depends on the cube the robot chose, or rather the one it didn't choose. This is an example of the type of phenomena which is called situated object reference.

Spatial relations have to be interpreted depending on the current situation as well, e.g. in (4) and (5). (5) can be interpreted as a hint or correction in order to find the bar (see (3) and (4)). Since the robot found the bar already, the given direction can only refer to the place where the cube should be put down. This place has to be somewhere on the bar (see (1)). Deictic expressions, like in (6) and (12) are only produced and comprehended in a concrete situation.

(10) refers to an already completed action, which is not specified. In order to interpret this utterance the hearer has to recognize the action or sequence of actions that should be carried out. This does not depend on the last directive in all cases but on what is useful in the whole context of actions. This type of phenomena, which can also be seen in (15) and (17), is called situated action reference. If (15) didn't immediately follow (14), i.e. if something happened in the meantime, there could also be other possibilities of interpretation. One possible meaning might refer to the direction from which the bolt approaches the cube. Another meaning concerns the direction of rotation during the process of screwing.

An indirect speech act is seen in (11) or (14). Since (11) is uttered in an instructional context, it has been interpreted not only as a question but, in the case of not-seeing the object, as a demand for searching for the object. (14) informs the human interlocutor of the current problem and therefore indirectly asks for assistance. To produce and understand this, the knowledge, that a bolt that should be screwed has to be grasped first, is necessary on both sides. The ability to carry out certain directives and communicate about them requires higher-level knowledge about actions.

Action-oriented dialogues are characterized by elliptical utterances, which contain situated references to actions and objects. Considered on their own as well as in the dialogue context, it seems as if the information contained is incomplete. However, in connection with perception and action they are complete utterances, which are easy to comprehend and very well suited to the situation of communication. This results in a form of communication, similar to that between humans.

3 Related work

The processing of natural language instructions is a central topic in miscellaneous research projects. Torrance (1994) presents a hybrid system, consisting of a symbolic and a behavior-based level, for the navigation of a mobile robot. After preprocessing, natural language instructions control the robot via a planning component.

Chapman (1991) describes a behavior-based system, which controls a video game autonomously. A human observer can influence the system by natural language instructions. The instructions are send to the behavior system directly, where they are treated like other sensor data.

Stopp and Blocher (1997) introduce a natural language user interface for controlling a robot equipped with two manipulators. The main focus of their work is the processing of spatial expressions.

The project AnimNL (Webber et al., 1992) deals with the animation of anthropomorphic agents in simulated technical environments. The actions, which should be carried out by the agents, are initiated by natural language instructions.

4 The hybrid architecture *CoRA*

In order to be able to process action directives on different levels of complexity, the hybrid architecture *CoRA* (Förster et al., 1995; Milde, 1995) has been developed (see fig. 3). *CoRA* contains a deliberative system, which models higher cognitive competences, and a behavior-oriented[4] base system, which integrates language, perception and action on a lower level. This hybrid architecture allows the optimal distribution of the necessary competence and therefore the tasks of the whole system onto both subsystems. The deliberative system is responsible for the sequentialization of complex actions into simple basic actions and schedules the execution of these actions. However, because of the complexity and uncertainty of the real world, a fully detailed plan of robot movements cannot be provided by the deliberative system. The behavior system on the other hand is embedded in the real world by means of sensors and actuators, which enable it to detect changes in the world and react to them immediately. It has the necessary competence for the autonomous execution of basic actions, but cannot aim at fulfilling given goals by itself. It is only through the coupling of the behavior system with a deliberative system, that the accomplishment of tasks can be realized by the interplay of goal-directed and reactive behavior.

As a consequence of the hybrid architecture, two types of action directives are distinguished: Complex directives - called instructions - influence the deliberative system and only in the second step the behavior system, simple directives - called interventions - can manipulate the behavior system directly.

Instructions cannot be processed by the base system directly. They provide resources for planning goals or action sequences and guide the planning process. First, instructions are parsed by a dependency parser that builds up typed attribute-value pairs. The semantic part of those structures - based on the work by Jackendoff (1990) - is passed on to the deliberative system, which is responsible for keeping track of long-time goals. The deliberative system uses this semantic part to initialize a corresponding action scheme. Action schemes contain explicit knowledge about the decomposition of higher level actions into basic actions. The resulting information blocks of an action scheme can be mapped one after the other onto so-called internal sensors, which provide the basis for the communication between deliberative system and behavior system. Thus the necessary sequentialization of control parameters to initialize the corresponding basic actions in the behavior system can be produced. Suitable feedback from the base system allows the deliberative component to monitor the activity state of the behavior system and feed in the control parameters that are needed for the completion of the next subtask just in time. In the current prototype of the architecture, the production of robot utterances is realized in a straightforward manner. Based on the feedback of the behavior system, the action schemes initialize corresponding templates in the generator, which produce the suitable language output.

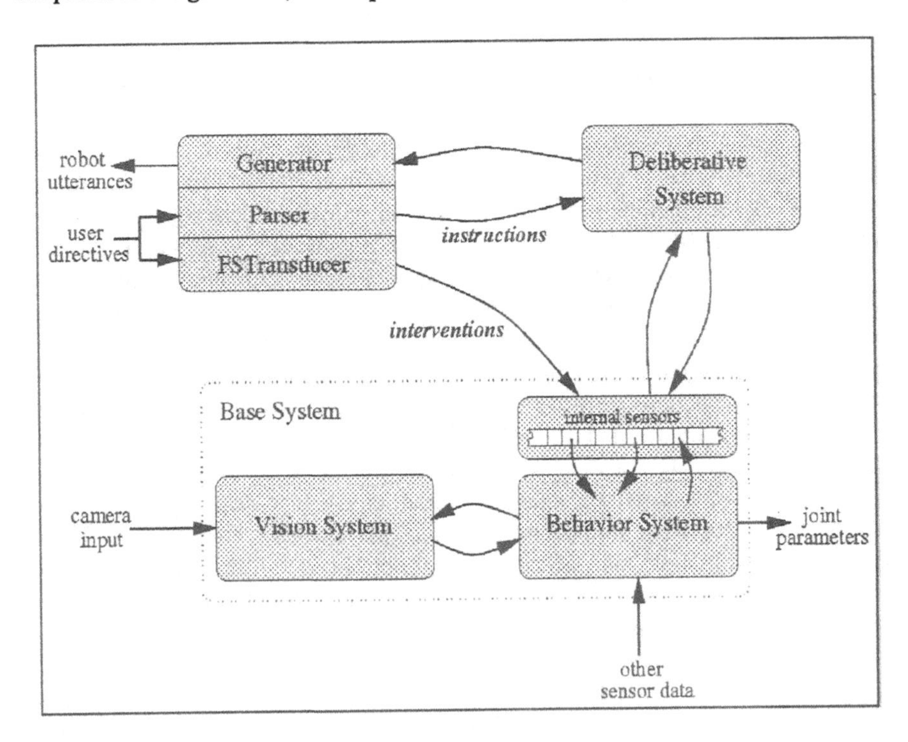

Figure 3: The hybrid architecture *CoRA*

The behavior system is partly autonomous. It can carry out basic actions and react to unexpected events without the help of an external control, but it is still controllable by a 'higher' system: The selection of basic actions is initialized by the deliberative system - as explained above - or through user interventions. Interventions refer to the direction and velocity of a robot movement or to simple object-oriented actions. They are fed into the behavior system directly, thus they allow the immediate manipulation of the ongoing behavior. Interventions are processed one by one by a finite state transducer (FST) which recognizes valid input, extracts the relevant information and generates simple attribute-value pairs which are filled into the internal sensors of the behavior system. The behavior system is responsible for the situated and time-adequate translation of sensor input into actuator output, treating information from the internal sensors just like any other sensor data. The integration of the different sensor inputs allows the situated interpretation of directives. As a consequence the processing of elliptical utterances like situation-dependent object references and indexicalic expressions, which can only be comprehended in the current context of sensing and acting, is made possible.

The behavior system consists of a hierarchy of behavior modules, each of it specialized for a certain task, which it can fulfil autonomously. In contrast to traditional, knowledge-based robot control, action related knowledge is not represented in a model of the world, but is distributed among all behavior modules. This leads to a reduction of complexity, because an error does not cause global re-planning or the intervention of higher system components, but only local reactions inside the relevant behavior module. The modularization of the behavior system is motivated by the requirements concerning reactivity and autonomy of the behavior system on the one hand and by the expected user directives on the other hand: All possible linguistic sub-directives must be depictable to a - as small as possible - set of corresponding behavior modules. For the current prototype of the system, the following set of behavior modules turned out to be suitable: INSERT, PUTDOWN, GRASP, MOVE. The behavior modules are composed of object- or manipulator-oriented behavior routines, which manage the coupling of sensors and actuators. These behavior routines work on aspects of the task the module is responsible for. Within one module, all routines work in parallel, thus producing the overall functionality of the module. As an example, the behavior routine VELOCITY controls the velocity of a robot movement, taking into account sensor data from internal sensors, tactile sensors and the vision system.

A non-traditional control architecture requires a non-traditional vision system. Therefore an integrated, task-oriented vision concept has been developed, which provides a basis for active and selective perception. Instead of extracting unused information from every incoming picture, the vision system delivers information only on request from the behavior routines. Requests are not always formulated in the same order and with the same parameters, as a consequence the visual processing can also be seen as selective and situated.

5 Examples of processing

The architecture presented in section 4 is well suited to process the phenomena presented in section 2, which will be illustrated by the following two examples. First we will have a closer look at the processing of an instruction, which initiates an action:

(a) *Put the red cube on the bar.*

As mentioned above, instructions are parsed by a unification-based dependency parser. The semantic representations generated by the parser are passed on to the deliberative component. These representations are used to choose and initialize so-called action schemes. As a result of the instruction (a) the action scheme PUT is chosen (see fig. 4). Action schemes contain explicit knowledge of actions on a higher level of abstraction than the (implicit) one in the base system. One part of an action scheme is the 'head', which, at its most simple, corresponds to a semantic representation and is used for the selection of the scheme. Other parts refer to the pre- and postconditions of the actions specified by the action scheme. These conditions can be used to process corresponding instructor's utterances (e.g. *Put the parts on top of each other, so that they form a right angle.*) The most important part of an action scheme is the decomposition of the complex action into a sequence of basic actions. So the 'put'-action is decomposed into a sequence of a 'grasp'-action and a 'put-down'-action. These basic actions allow the coupling of deliberative and base system.

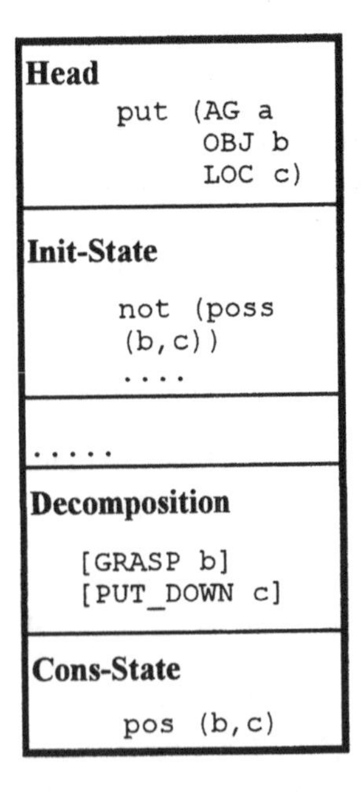

Figure 4: The action scheme PUT

The information about the basic actions and the objects involved are passed on to the internal sensors. The accompanying informations (translated into attribute-value pairs) of the first action of the sequence in our example is:

action	:	grasp
det_obj	:	+
obj_colour	:	red
obj_type	:	cube

These values are fed into the internal sensors of the base system (see fig. 5). They cause the activation of the behavior module GRASP ensuring, together with other sensor data, the situated execution of the grasping of the desired object. If this action has been completed successfully, positive feedback flows back to the deliberative system. Then the second basic action (put-down) can be initiated by transmitting the corresponding attribute-value pairs to the base system.

If the action's execution wasn't successful, a negative feedback is generated including the reason why the execution failed (e.g. the failed identification of the red cube). This feedback is used to generate a natural language message to inform the human instructor. This message can be a question or a statement, which usually requests the instructor's help.

During the execution of a basic action, which may have been initiated by an instruction or an intervention or which can be a part of an autonomous action, the instructor is allowed to intervene. An example of such an intervention is:

(b) *The other one!*

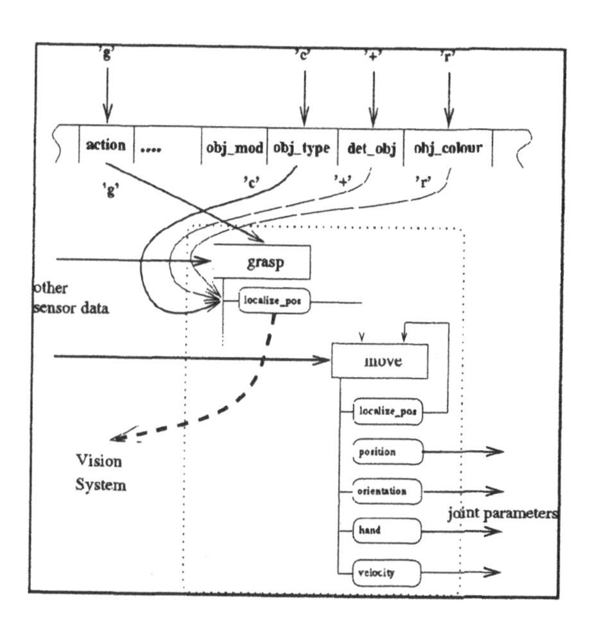

Figure 5: Initialising the first partial action of PUT

The question, which object this utterance refers to, can be answered only by taking the current situation into account. It should be an object that shares some of the features of the currently focussed one. First, the intervention mentioned above is processed by the FST (see section 4), which generates the following output:

det_obj	:	+
obj_mod	:	other

These values are immediately passed on to the base system, where they are fed into the internal sensors (see fig. 6). The missing information about what should be done with this object is extractable from the currently executed action of the robot. When the intervention is uttered the robot is moving towards a red cube in order to grasp it. Therefore the last utterance refers to the 'grasp'-action, which should be continued with the new (*other*) object.

The changed information in the internal sensors concerning the object is used by the behavior routine LOCALIZE_POS, which provides the identification of objects. In interaction with the vision system, LOCALIZE_POS uses the internal sensors' values together with information on the focused object to identify the object the instructor refered to. Thus the behavior system uses different types of information, i.e. language data, perceptual data, and data of the ongoing activity, to enable a situated interpretation of elliptical utterances.

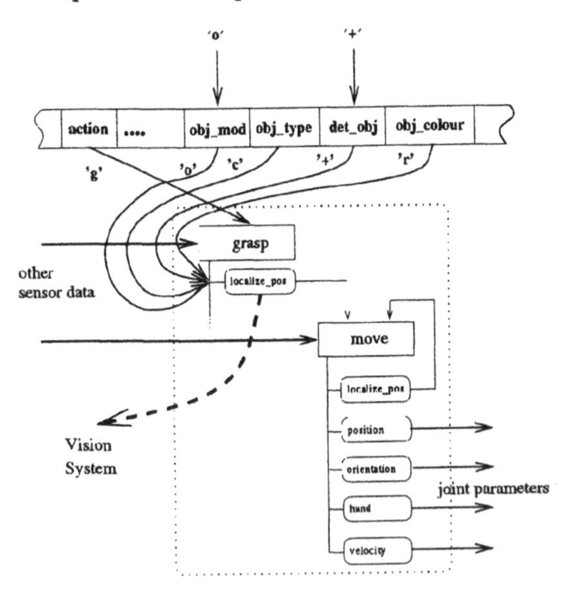

Figure 6: Intervening by uttering *The other!*

6 Conclusions

Face-to-face communications between humans are characterized by elliptical utterances, which contain situated references to actions and objects and cannot be interpreted on the basis of the dialogue context alone. Those - often incomplete - utterances can only be comprehended in connection with perception and action. Traditional human-computer dialogues circumvent those phenomena - a computer is not situated in its environment - but if a human and a machine sense and act in a common environment, new methods of language processing are needed. In this paper we analysed phenomena of situated communication that occur in human-robot instruction situations and introduced a hybrid architecture that integrates language, perception and action in order to cope with those phenomena. The behavior-oriented base system is responsible for the situated and time-adequate translation of sensor input into actuator output. It treats language input just like any other sensor data. Because of this feature, the behavior-based control architecture proved to be very well suited for the situated interpretation of directives. The deliberative system is responsible for the sequentialization of more complex directives into basic actions. It is through the coupling of a deliberative system and a behavior-oriented base system, that the interpretation and flexible execution of all kinds of directives can be realized by the interplay of goal-directed and reactive behavior.

Acknowledgements

The hybrid architecture has been developed in the project 'Communicating Agents'[5] at the University of Bielefeld. The project is part of the Collaborative Research Center 'Situated Artificial Communicators' (SFB360)[6] which is funded by the German Research Foundation (DFG).

References

Brooks, R.A. 1991. Intelligence Without Representation. In Artificial Intelligence, 47, pages 139-159.

Chapman, D. 1991. Vision, Instruction, and Action. MIT Press. Cambridge, MA.

Fiehler, R. 1993. Spezifika der Kommunikation in Kooperationen. In H. Schröder, editor, Fachtextpragmatik. Gunter Narr Verlag, Tübingen.

Förster, S. Lobin, H. and Peters, K. 1995. Hybride Architekturen als Grundlage natürlichsprachlicher Steuerung. In L. Dreschler-Fischer and S. Pribbenow, editors, 19. Deutsche Jahrestagung für Künstliche Intelligenz, KI-95, Bielefeld. Gesellschaft für Informatik e.V.

Jackendoff, R. 1990. Semantic Structures. Current studies in linguistics series, 18. MIT Press, Cambridge, MA.

Milde, J-T. 1995. A hybrid control architecture for a simulated robot manipulator. In Proceedings of the 13th IASTED International Conference on applied informatics.

Steels, L. 1994. The artificial life roots of artificial intelligence. In Artificial Life Journal, volume 1,1. MIT Press, Cambridge MA.

Stopp, E. and Blocher, A. 1997. Spatial Information in Instructions and Questions to an Autonomous System. Technical Report Memo Nr. 63. SFB 378 - Ressourcenadaptive Kognitive Prozesse.

Torrance, M.C. 1994. Natural Communication with Robots. Master's thesis. Department of Electrical Engineering and Computer Science. Massachusetts Institute of Technology.

Webber, B., Badler, N., Baldwin, F.B., Becket, Di E, W.B, Glib, C., Jung, M., Levison, M.L., Moore, M. and White, M. 1992. Doing What You're Told: Following Task Instructions In Changing, but Hospitable Environments. Report MS-CIS-92-74, LINC LAB 236. Computer and Information Science Department. University of Philadelphia.

Notes

[1] The human's utterances are written in italics.

[2] The robot's utterances are written in courier.

[3] All spatial expressions are interpreted from the robot's point of view.

[4] A detailed description of the characteristics of behavior-oriented architectures can be found in (Brooks, 1991) and (Steels, 1994).

[5] http://coli.lili.uni-bielefeld.de/D1/D1.html

[6] http://www.techfak.uni-bielefeld.de/sfb/sfb.html

16 LEAP: Language Enabled Applications

B. Alabiso and A. Kronfeld

1 Introduction

1.1 Project Goals and Major Components

The goal of the LEAP project is to provide a Software Development Kit (SDK) that enables application developers to add a natural language interface (including speech) to their products. When it is successfully attached to an application, LEAP converts spoken utterances into function calls that are dispatched to an application for execution as user requests.

LEAP contains two major parts: an *authoring* system and a *run-time* system. By *authoring* (or *customization*) we mean all development activities that are required to connect LEAP as a natural language interface to a particular application (see Section 2 below). The *run-time* system includes the following sub-systems:

1. The *Advanced Speech Recognition* engine (ASR, a.k.a. Whisper).
2. The *Natural Language Processor* (NLP).
3. The *Text To Speech* generator (TTS, a.k.a. *Whistler*).
4. The *LEAP Semantic Engine* (LSE).

The first three sub-systems were developed at Microsoft Research and are now mature enough to be used. LSE is in its early architectural and prototyping stages. Figure 1 shows the relationships among the four components. In a nutshell, ASR (Whisper) takes continuous speech as input and provides a text lattice as output. NLP takes a text lattice as input, parses each sentence in it and produces multiple logical forms as output. LSE converts the output of NLP to Application Interface (API) calls, and finally, Whistler generates speech from text to close the conversation loop.

An important sub-goal of LEAP is to integrate these distinct sub-systems into a coherent unit. Work is now being done to guarantee a smooth flow of data from one component to another. We have also conducted several usability studies to examine important features of man-machine communication. This was carried out by simulating an imaginary application, the *Personal Voice Assistant* (an integrated communication and schedule manager), which uses speech almost exclusively as its input/output channels. The data collected from the tests (speech and text transcripts) are used as points of reference for the design of the system as well as test data for the prototype.

While the integration of the sub-systems is crucial, the main focus of LEAP is the LEAP Semantic Engine (LSE), which is the topic of this paper.

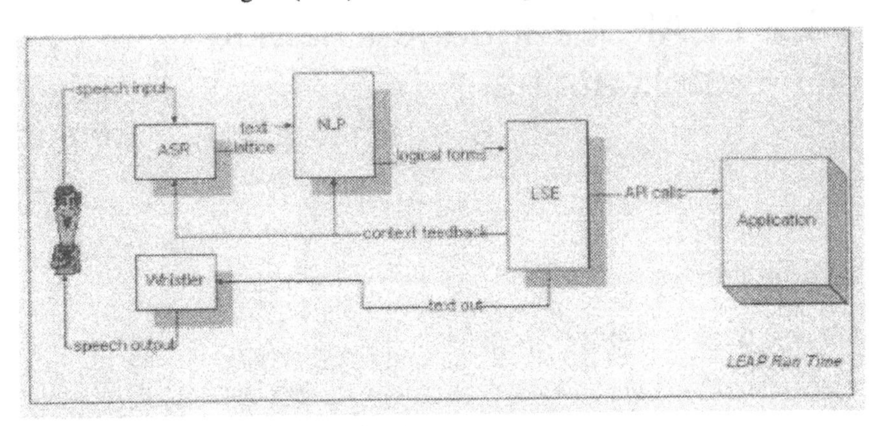

Figure 1: The LEAP run-time system

2 LEAP Authoring

2.1 The General Approach

LEAP is intended to be a general tool which should be accessible to any developer who wants to add natural language capability to her product. Given this objective, it is clear that the process of *customizing* or authoring LEAP (that is, the ability to tailor a general NLP tool to a specific application) is crucial. Without a well thought out and effective authoring methodology, LEAP has little chance of success.

Traditionally, one can distinguish two general approaches to the problem of authoring a natural language (NL) application:

Let the developer do it --- A general interface to a NL system is provided. It is the responsibility of the developer to map general semantic structures onto her application. The advantages of this approach are that the customization is done by the person who knows best the application (and its intended users). However, the (prohibitive) disadvantages are that customization requires NLP knowledge which most developers do not have; the learning curve is steep; and development time is unreasonably long.

We do it all for you --- Customization teams are dispatched as consultants to help developers add a NL component. With this approach, NLP customization is indeed done by NLP experts, but it takes time for these experts to learn the precise requirements of the application itself. In addition, many developers feel that the consulting solution is simply not feasible economically: consulting time is too expensive and the prospect of long term dependency on outside maintenance is too risky.

Let's do it together --- The optimal approach should have all the advantages and eliminate the disadvantages. The main idea is simple enough: the developer specifies the semantic domain of the application in an author's file. Then the LEAP Semantic Engine (LSE) dynamically uses the specification of the semantic domain to interpret logical forms and matches utterances to tasks that the application can execute. However, although the basic idea is simple, its implementation is nothing but. In particular, requiring the author to specify the semantic domain may be dangerously close to the old "let the developer do it" approach. We have to be careful not to ask of developers something they neither know how to do, nor have any interest in learning. In other words, the customization process must follow a familiar paradigm of development. It may require knowledge of programming, a strict testing and debugging discipline, and an understanding of users' needs (and language). But the customization process cannot require a developer to have a Ph.D. in Computational Linguistics, nor can it presuppose the ability or willingness to learn a totally new way of thinking about computational problems.

Our approach to LEAP customization design follows several basic principles:

1. An intuitive way of thinking about the world is in terms of entities (or objects), their properties (traits), and the relationships they participate in.
2. Object Oriented programming is a programming methodology that encapsulates such a view of the world and is already taken to be the accepted programming paradigm.
3. As English utterances are, roughly, about entities (nouns), their properties (adjectives), and their relationships (verbs), the application domain should specify the entities, properties and relationships that make sense in the context of the application.
4. Entities are the kind of things that the application is expected to "know about" (e.g. persons and messages in an email systems). Entities may have names and/or id numbers.
5. Properties (or traits) of entities are characterizations of entities, for example, the length of a message or the sex of an employee. Traits can be interpreted as functions from entities to values.
6. Relationships hold among entities.
7. Relationships can be expressed in two major ways:
   a) Task-oriented --- when one or more entities participate in a complete speech act (e.g. "send a message to Bruno").
   b) Referential --- when two or more entities are combined together to form a noun. For example, "the red square to the left of the circle".[1]

8. When relationships are encoded in the author's file, they specify both which entities participate in the relationship and the role each entity plays there. [2]

The main idea, then, is for the author to map the functionality of her application into an object oriented domain which LEAP can read from the author's file and incorporate into the knowledge base. Incoming utterances are than matched with the object-oriented domain, which in turn is matched with specific API functions.

2.2 An Example: The Bunny Express

The *Bunny Express* is an application that allows children to create lines, rectangles, ellipses and text boxes in different colors on a screen, using the following set of function calls:

```
Pen(color)                // Select the color of lines and text
Brush(color)              // Select background color of shapes
                          // and text.
Line(x1, y1, x2, y2)      // Draw a line from (x1,y1) to
                          // (x2,y2) using the current pen
                          // color
Ellipse(x1,y1,x2,y2       // Draw an ellipse bounded by the
)                         // rectangle whose top-left corner is
                          // (x1,y1) and whose bottom-right
                          // corner is (x2,y2). The ellipse is
                          // drawn with the current pen color
                          // and filled with the current brush
                          // color.
Rectangle(x1,y1,x2,y2)    // Draw a rectangle whose top-left
                          // corner is (x1,y1) and whose
                          // bottom-right corner is (x2,y2).
                          // The rectangle is drawn with the
                          // current pen color and filled with
                          // the current brush color.
Erase(x1, y1, x2, y2)     // Erase the shape (and/or line)
                          // defined by (x1,y1) and (x2,y2)
Text(x1,y1,x2,y2,text)    // Write text starting at (x1,y1)
                          // using the current pen color.
Grid(bool)                // If bool is TRUE, display a grid on
                          // top of the drawing area.
```

In its simplest form, the Bunny Express may be seen as a tool for teaching children how to construct complex figures out of simple shapes. For example, Figure 2 shows on the left a subset of the commands that produced the picture on the right. [3] However, the manufacturers of the *Bunny Express* would like to add speech capability to their application. Perhaps inspired by a famous scene in the movie *Blade Runner*, they believe that there is a future for the manipulation of graphic objects by voice[4]. If nothing else, the *Bunny Express* may serve as a prototype on their way to bigger and better things.

2.3 Object Oriented Design

How would a developer go about specifying the semantic domain of the Bunny Express in a way that LEAP can use? To begin with, she should recast her set of functions into an object model containing classes, attributes (data) and methods, as follows:

```
class CDrawingTool
   attributes:
      COLOR
   methods:
      MakeDefault(Color)
class CPen : CDrawingTool
   methods:
      MakeDefault(Color)
class CBrush: CDrawingTool
   methods:
      MakeDefault(Color)
class CGraphicObject
   attributes:
      COLOR ForegroundColor
      COLOR BackgroundColor
      CPoint FirstPoint
      CPoint SecondPoint
   methods:
      Erase()
class CLine :  CGraphicObject
   methods:
      Draw()
class CTextBox : CGraphObject
   attributes:
      text
methods:
      Write()
class CRectangle : CGraphicObject
   methods:
      Draw()
class CEllipse : CGraphObject
   methods:
      Draw()
class Cpoint
   attributes:
      x
      y

class CApplication
   methods:
      ShowGrid()
   DontShowGrid()
      EraseAll()
```

```
Brush: gray
Ellipse(132,93,168,73)
Brush: white
Ellipse(143,84,152,78)
Brush: black
Ellipse(162,85,169,80)
Brush: blue
Pen: yellow
Text(5,5,Frank the bunny faces West)
Pen: red
Text(175,60,"Yo, Herman!")
```

Frank the bunny faces West

Figure 2: The Bunny Express

Once the object model of the application is clear, the next step for the author is to map this model into a semantic domain consisting of entities, properties and relationships. This should not be too difficult (at least in the initial stage) since there is an intuitive correspondence between elements of the object model and elements of the semantic domain:

Object Model	**Semantic Domain**
Classes	Entity types
Attributes (data)	Properties (traits)
Methods	Relationships

Of course, since the semantic domain serves as the bridge between user's utterances and the object model, the domain must contain additional (linguistic) information. However, the organization of the semantic domain follows closely the object model.

2.4 Define Entities

First, the author needs to define the entity types in the domain. The following "forms" present an outline of such definitions.[5]

2.4.1 Drawing Tool

```
entity: DrawingTool
  instances: none
  Properties: COLOR
```

The value of the "instances:" field is either 'none', 'one' or 'many'. It indicates the number of instantiations that this entity type can have. When the value is 'none', this is a "virtual" entity type. That is, there will be no instances of this entity (very much like an abstract class in C++), but there may be entities that are derived from it.

The DrawingTool entity type has one property, namely COLOR. Derived entities also inherit (or override) the properties of the parent entity.

2.4.2 Pen

```
entity: Pen
   word: pen
   synonyms: foreground color,
   default foreground color,
   current foreground color
   isa: DrawingTool
   instances: one
   properties-with-defaults:
      COLOR
```

The Pen entity is derived from DrawingTool (as indicated by the isa: field). The fact that the value of the instances: field is 'one' indicates that only a single instance exists. This helps LEAP resolve references to "the pen". It also means that a single instance of this entity type is created by LEAP at startup time, independently of any specific task.

The linguistic information provided by the word: field is used as the very basic bridge between English and the domain. The link between the domain and the application itself will be given by the task-oriented relationships, as we shall see. Note that synonyms are supplied. This would enable LEAP to treat "make the pen red" and "make the foreground color red" as equivalent.

The properties-with-defaults: field simply indicates that the application supplies a default value. This means that a request to use the Pen may be successful even if the user did not specify a color.

The definition of the Brush entity is virtually identical and we will not repeat it here.

2.4.3 Graphic Objects: Line and Label

```
entity: GraphicObject
   instances: none
   Properties:
      FOREGROUND_COLOR
      BACKGROUND_COLOR
      FIRST_POINT
      SECOND_POINT

entity: line
   word: line
   isa: GraphicObject
   instances: many

entity: label
   word: label
   synonyms: text box
   isa: GraphicObject
   instances: many
   Properties:
      TEXT
   condition:          FOREGROUND_COLOR != BACKGROUND_COLOR
```

GraphicObject is another "virtual" entity. It merely serves as a carrier of properties that can be inherited.

Line is a derived entity (from GraphicObject). It has the same properties as GraphicObject. However, since the value of instances: is 'many', instances of this entity are created on the fly depending on the conversation. A label is a GraphicObject with an additional property: TEXT. Note that a label must satisfy a condition that is necessary if the text is to be readable.

2.4.4 Graphic Objects: Shapes

```
entity: rectangle
   word: rectangle
   isa:  GraphicObject
   instances: many

entity: square
   word: square
   isa: rectangle
   instances: many
   condition:
   (FIRST_POINT x - SECOND_POINT.x) = (FIRST_POINT.y - SECOND_POINT.y)
```

Note how the use of the word: isa: and condition: fields allows the author to define a square as a special case of a rectangle. A declaration for an ellipse allows a special definition of a circle along similar lines.

2.4.5 Point and Application

```
entity: point
   word: point
   isa: NULL
   instances: many
   Properties:
      LABEL
      X
      Y

entity: application
   word: Bunny Express
   instances: one
```

The LABEL property on a point allows attaching a name to the point (as in "point A"). The X and Y properties specify the coordinates. Finally, the application itself is an entity.

2.5 Define Properties

The next step is to define the properties that each entity can have.

Most properties have English names that can be used in sentences (e.g. "the <u>color</u> of the line"). Properties also have values, but the status of these values depends on two related factors:

1. Within the context of the application, is the set of possible values for a property open or closed?

2. Are specific values of a property likely to appear in sentences that LEAP is expected to understand?

Color in the Bunny Express is an example of a property whose values both form a closed set (only pre-defined colors are recognized), and these colors are likely to appear in sentences ("draw a blue circle"). The set of measurement values (e.g. the length of a document) or the set of proper names are open sets. Still, values of these properties are expected to be understood by LEAP (e.g. "print all documents whose length is less than 4,000 words"). Other open sets (for example, the set of possible messages that can be sent) are not expected to appear as speech parts in sentences at all. Finally, some closed sets will not appear in sentences either, depending on the application (for example, if colors are assigned randomly by the application, the set of colors is indeed closed, but LEAP does not have to worry about understanding color names).

If LEAP is expected to understand values of properties in sentences, the author must provide the means of doing so. If the set of values is closed (and relatively small), the author can simply enumerate it. Otherwise, the author must provide a method of identifying these values (e.g. by providing a function). The following examples show the kind of information that the author encodes about properties.

```
property: COLOR
   property of: DrawingTool
   word: color
   preposition: of <DrawingTool>
   property values:
      red, blue, green, black, white, yellow, cyan,
      magenta, gray
   value speech part: adjective
```

The word: field specifies the name of the property. The preposition: field specifies the preposition that can be used to relate the property with the entity ("the color of the brush").[6] Since the set of recognized colors is closed and is expected to be used in sentences, the possible colors are enumerated. In addition, it is indicated that each value of the COLOR property is to be used as an adjective. This will allow LEAP to recognize structures like "above the red circle" and "make the color of the Pen blue".

Some properties inherit their linguistic attributes from other properties:

```
property: FOREGROUND_COLOR
   property of: GraphicObject
   isa: COLOR

property: BACKGROUND_COLOR
   property of: GraphicObject
   isa: COLOR
```

A property can be in itself an entity. For example, FirstPoint and SecondPoint are both instances of the entity Point, and properties of GraphicObject. In this case they inherit some of their attributes from an entity.[7]

```
property: FIRST_POINT
   property of: GraphicObject
   isa: Point
   word: first point
   preposition: of <GraphicObject>
property: SECOND_POINT
   property of: GraphicObject
   isa: point
   word: second point
   preposition: of <GraphicObject>
property: LABEL
   property of: POINT
   word: label
   preposition: of <point>
property: X
   property of: POINT
   word: x coordinate
   preposition: of <point>
property: Y
   property of: POINT
   word: y coordinate
   preposition: of <point>
property: TEXT
   property of: label
   word: text
   preposition: of <label>
```

2.6 Define Tasks

Tasks are defined as special relationships. Since the language of tasks expresses relationships either between entities ("send a message to Bruno") or between entities and properties ("Paint the box blue") the task arguments can be either entities or propertiesA definition of a task has three parts:

Required entities and properties: These identify both the entities that are relevant to the tasks and the properties that are needed to make the function call.

Command phrases. This is a crucial part that is used to help LEAP match an incoming sentence with a task. Since the number of variations that can be expected is virtually indefinite, it makes no sense to specify all possible sentences in advance. Instead, the author specifies a set of templates, each corresponding to a class of sentences that can be used to initiate a task. The method, in a nutshell, is this:

1. Elements of the template are either **verb: arg:** (for arguments of tasks), or const: (for linguistic constants such as prepositions, conjunctions, etc.)
2. The value of arg: can be either an entity or a property
3. Complex noun phrases are handled by the entities, the properties and the referential relationships.[8]

The following is an example of a command phrase template:

```
verb:  make
arg:   DrawingTool
arg:   DrawingTool.Color
```

This template corresponds to any of the following commands: "make the Pen blue," "make the Brush green," "make the Pen gray," etc.

Execute. The third part of the definition of a task is the execute field. The value of this field is code that LEAP is able to execute. A special function in the execute: code is **SEND**, whose argument is sent to the application.Here, then, is the definition of the task "Make Default Color" in the *Bunny Express*:

```
task: MakeDefaultColor
    required properties: DrawingTool.Color
    command phrases:
      // Example: "make the pen red"
   verb: make arg: DrawingTool arg: DrawingTool.Color
      // Example: "make the color of the pen red"
   verb: make arg: COLOR arg: DrawingTool.Color
      // Example: "Change the pen to be red"
   verb: change arg: DrawingTool const: to be arg:
         DrawingTool.Color
      // Example: "change the color of the pen to be
         red"
   verb: change arg: COLOR const: to be arg: COLOR
 execute:
      if (DrawingTool == Pen)
   SEND(Pen(DrawingTool.Color))
      else SEND(Brush(DrawingTool.Color))
```

Note the difference between DrawingTool.Color and COLOR. The former is a particular value of a color(e.g. "red"). The latter is the property COLOR itself in relation to an entity (e.g. "the color of the pen").

Defining entities, properties and tasks is only the first step in defining the semantic domain of the application. The next step is to define referential relationship and provide the mechanism that allows LEAP to handle singular references to specific entities in the course of the conversation, as well as to define *events*. But this is beyond the scope of this paper.

3 The Run Time System

How does LSE map generalized logical forms, which are the output of NLP, with specific API calls to an application? In this section we present an overview of the process.

3.1 Types and Conversations

At startup time, LEAP reads the author's file and creates *types* for each entity, property and task that is defined there. Each of these types (entity type, property type and task type, respectively) will serve as a template for particular *instances* of each category (see Section 3.2 below).

LEAP takes a strict goal-oriented approach to discourse: it assumes that the point of each and every interaction between man and machine is simply to make the application *do* something. We distinguish between the task itself and the conversation that takes place in order to achieve it. Each task, therefore, defines a discourse segment. But the discourse segment are represented in LEAP as *conversation templates* and *conversation instances.* A conversation template in LEAP is a data structure that encapsulates both the knowledge about a particular task and the model of conversation that allows the acquisition of such knowledge. For example, suppose that the application enables a user to announce a meeting. The conversation template associated with this task will contain, on the one hand, the knowledge that a meeting must include a date (and time), a duration and a list of people who need to attend. On the other hand, the conversation template will contain a conversation model that allows LEAP to ask for these items of information if the user does not supply them in her initial utterance. Both aspects of the conversation template are generated from the author's file, but this does not necessarily mean that the author must declare a new category, namely, the category of a conversation template. Rather, the generation of the conversation template is done automatically out of information contained in the definitions of entities, properties and relationships.[9]

The conversational aspects of LEAP include a *mixed initiative* model. The initiative is always assumed to start with the user. When LEAP needs to prompt the user for additional information, or to ask for clarification, it grabs the initiative 'token', and follows a conversation model biased towards potential answers to its requests. The user may choose to accept this subordinate role by supplying the missing information, or she may insist on regaining the initiative token by starting a different conversation. In the latter case, LEAP tries to match the new utterance to a different task, perhaps after confirmation. This may result in incomplete conversations, which LEAP leaves hanging around for a pre-specified amount of time. If the user chooses to refer back to an incomplete conversation at a later time: LEAP will resume the conversation at the point of interruption

The *conversation manager* holds a list of conversation templates, each with its associated task. If the user has the Initiative Token, the conversational manager matches the incoming input (that is, the logical form that it gets from NLP) with a specific task type, and once this is done, the appropriate conversation template is recognized.

One important resource used by LSE is *MindNet*. This is an internal element of *NLP*, which contains a semantic net corresponding to the lexical definitions of the *Longman Dictionary of Contemporary English*. This resource allows LSE to expand its search capabilities by providing the ability to measure "conceptual distances' between a potential matching target and the input semantic form.

3.2 Instantiations

Once a task and its corresponding conversation template are matched with the input, the following sequence takes place:

- A *task instance* is derived from the task type.[10]
- A *conversation instance* is derived from the conversation template.[11]
- Each entity and property that are required for the task are instantiated.
- The conversation manager attempts to associate constituents of the logical forms with instances of the relevant entities and properties.[12]
- Using the *Reference Monitor* (see Section 3.4), the conversational manager attempts to see if the newly created instances of entities and properties should be unified with already existing instances.
- If any entities and/or properties that are required for the completion of the task are still missing, or if verification of defaults is needed, the conversation manager takes control of the Initiative Token and attempts to get the missing information from the user (using the conversation instance and its embedded conversation model).
- When all the information required for the task is present, the conversation manager takes control of the Initiative Token (if it does not have it already) and sends the task to the application for execution, using the code provided in the author's file. Post execution feedback from the application is passed on to the user in an appropriate form. The Token of Initiative is returned to the user for subsequent requests.

Figure 3 shows a schematic description of the system following a request to set an appointment.

Note that a conversation instance does more than guide the information gathering process. In a sense, a conversation instance encapsulates the *context* of the current discourse segment. In addition to the static conversation model that underlies the exchange, the context also contains representations of all participating entities, their properties, the way the user has referred to them and so on. For this reason, the content of the active conversation instance is exposed to both NLP and ASR so that it can be used for disambiguation, anaphora resolution, etc. The current conversation instance (also known as the *context object*) is, therefore, part of a continuous internal feedback loop where the output of each component both modifies and is being modified by it.

Conversation instances are organized as a stack. New tasks cause new conversation instances to be pushed onto the stack and when a task is completed its corresponding conversation instance is popped. This allows the possibility that a new task may begin before an old one is. As a structure of context objects, the stack of conversation instances contain two special members: the very root of the stack is the *global context* which contains general LEAP information that can be used independently of the application. The second element of the stack is the *application context* which contains general information about the application that can be used independently of any particular task.[13] The global context is provided by LEAP, while the application context is provided by the author. These two elements of the stack are pushed at startup and popped when the application and LEAP terminate.

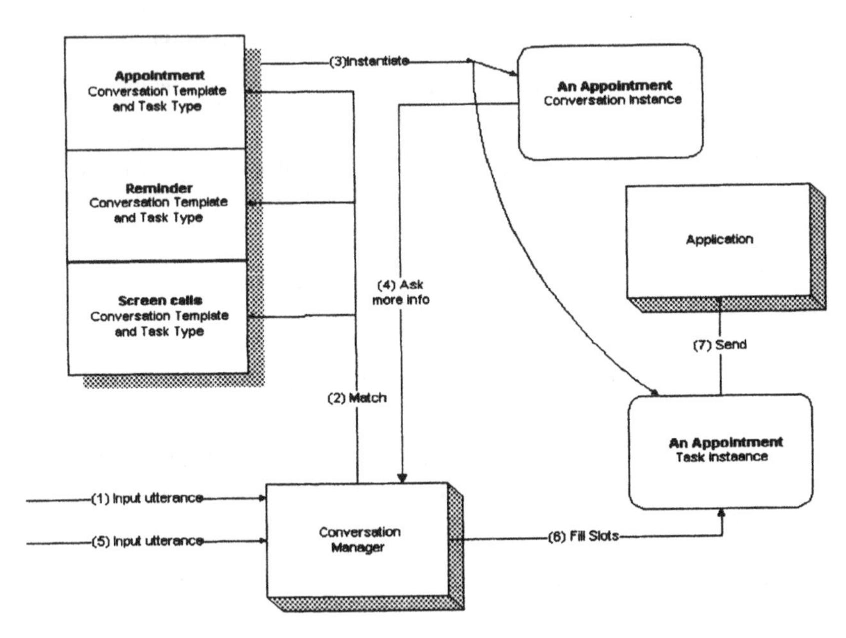

Figure3: From logical forms to API calls

3.3 Discourse Structure

Following Grosz and Sidner[14] we take discourse to be a composite of three interacting components: the linguistic structure of the utterances, the participants' discourse intentions and the attentional state consisting of the entities, properties and relationships that are salient at each point of the exchange. The discourse itself is broken into *discourse segments*, depending on the changing goals of the participants. In the context of LEAP, the linguistic structure is simply the user's utterances and their NLP analysis, the discourse intentions are encapsulated by the tasks that the user intends to execute and the attentional state is the collection of entities, properties and relationships that are relevant for the tasks. Each discourse segment is defined by the task it is supposed to accomplish.

LEAP's conception of the discourse structure is complicated by the fact that each task may be divided into *sub-tasks*. A sub-task may be an application task itself[15] but most likely a sub-task is a capability of the application which may not be exposed to the user as a task but which nevertheless requires it's own conversation instance. For example, suppose the task is expressed by the sentence: "Remind me three days before Jane's birthday that I should get her a present." Let's suppose that the REMIND task must have two arguments: a date and a message, and let's suppose that the content of the message is already understood by LEAP to be "Get a present for Jane". An additional sub-task is for the system to compute the absolute date that the expression "three days before Jane's birthday" refers to. Note that the sub-task itself is broken into two parts (finding Jane's birthday and computing three days prior to that), and that in the course of managing the sub-tasks, LEAP may need further clarification from the user (e.g. "do you mean three business days before Jane's birthday?") In other words, some sub-tasks may require their own conversation instances and if this is the case, the sub-task will be a full member of the discourse. Its conversation instance will be pushed into the conversation stack when the sub-task is initiated, and it will be popped when the sub-task is done.

3.4 Reference Resolution

As new entity instances are created, the system must determine which of them should be unified with entities that exist already. One aspect of this problem is anaphora resolution --- especially when pronouns are concerned --- but this is only a special case that is handled, to a large extent, by NLP (while taking the context object into account, of course). The real problem for LSE is more general. For example, consider the command

```
Erase the red ellipse.
```

In the context of the Bunny Express, this requires the identification of a red ellipse that may have been created, perhaps, 25 sentences earlier. It is surely a stretch to call this a case of anaphora resolution and require the parser to handle it. Even simpler cases are a serious problem for a parser. For example, consider the following request:

```
Please print the file kp.doc.  The document is in the
Temp directory.
```

LEAP must understand that the entity referred to by "the document" is the same as the one referred to by "the file kp.doc".

The approach that LSE takes to solve this problem is similar to the one taken by Kronfeld in his BERTRAND program[16]: Entities are represented by *individuating sets*, which are collections of "presentation modes" that the entity uniquely satisfies.[17] Individuating sets are constructed dynamically as new noun phrases are interpreted. In constructing individuating sets, LSE uses a combination of *logical* and *pragmatic* strategies. The first strategy exploits various logical properties of the relation *belonging to the same individuating set*. Specifically, LSE concludes that two presentation modes p1 and p2 should belong to the same individuating set in one of the following ways:

1. Directly --- i.e., when the referring expressions "R1" and "R2" are associated with p1 and p2 respectively and it is knows that R1 is R2.

2. Recursively using transitivity --- i.e., when, for a presentation mode p3, it can be shown that both p1 and p3, as well as p2 and p3, belong to the same individuating set.
3. Recursively using substitution --- i.e., when p1 and p 2 are identical, except that the first contains a constituent xi exactly where the second contains a constituent xj, and xi and xj belongs to the same individuating set.

The logical strategy has two major drawbacks: First, if we identify presentation modes with referring expressions, the logical strategy implies that two identical tokens of a referring expression must refer to the same entity, which is obviously wrong. In addition, the logical strategy is useless for the case in which "the file 'kp.doc'" and "the document" are supposed to refer to the same object. This is where the pragmatic strategy kicks in. The pragmatic strategy is based on the notion of a *focus stack*[18] which is part of Grosz and Sidner's notion of an *attentional state*. According to Grosz and Sidner the attentional state is modeled as a stack of focus spaces, each of which is associated with a discourse segment. Each focus space records the entities, properties and relationships that are in focus in each particular segment of the conversation. Focus spaces in LSE are associated with conversation instances and in particular, LSE maintains a dynamic stack of individuating sets representing those entities that are in focus in each conversation.

The focus stack is used to solve some of the problems that the logical strategy cannot handle. To see how this is done, we need the concept of *subsumption*. One description *subsumes* another when from the assumption that an entity satisfies the first it follows that it also satisfies the second[19]. This notion of subsumption can be extended to hold between individuating sets and presentation modes. An individuating set *I* is said to subsume a presentation mode p when *I*, taken as a conjunction of referring expressions, subsumes p.[20]

Now, whenever a new referring expression is processed, LSE must decide whether it should be included in some pre-existing individuating set. First, the logical strategy is applied (although the substitution rule must be used with caution to avoid the conclusion that two identical tokens of a description are necessarily used to refer to the same entity). If the logical strategy fails, then each individuating set in the focus stack is examined in order. The new referring expression is added to the first individuating set in the stack that subsumes it. If none is found, then a new individuating set is created, containing the new referring expression. This strategy provides a way to overcome the afore-mentioned problems. First, two tokens of the *same* referring expression are considered as referring to the same entity only if both are subsumed by the same individuating set in the focus stack. Second, two *distinct* referring expressions may still be considered as referring to the same object even when the logical strategy fails to show this, provided that both are subsumed by the same individuating set in the focus stack.

References

Grosz, B. J. 1978. Focusing in Dialogue, in TINLAP-2, pp. 96—103, University of Illinois, Urbana-Champaign, IL.

Grosz B. J. and Sidner C.L. 1986. Attention, Intentions, and the Structure of Discourse, Computational Linguistics, 12(3), pp. 175-204.

Kronfeld, A. 1990. Reference and Computation: an Essay in Applied Philosophy of Language, Cambridge University Press, Cambridge.

Notes

[1] Some referential relationships are derived from task-oriented ones. For example, 'the message that Ami Sent to Bruno'.

[2] The line between properties and relationships may not be sharp. For example, the address of a person may be taken either as a property or as a relationship between a person and a location. To begin with, it should be up to the developer to decide whether an address is only a property or a entity in its own right. In addition, for the purpose of this paper we allow one entity to serve as a property for another, as we shall see later on. But this may change in the future.

[3] The Bunny Express is a slight modification of the program DDEExec which was written by Herman Rodent to illustrate DDE capabilities. Microsoft Developer Network, 1992.

[4] In the scene, the character played by Harrison Ford is manipulating a photograph using speech.

[5] The semantic domain is specified here by an abstract declarative language. Needless to say, an actual author will not be exposed to such a language at all. Instead, she will use an interactive tool where the methodology is encapsulated in an interview mode, with an appropriate graphic interface.

[6] In the case of 'of', the preposition implies a possession relation, so that structures such as 'the brush whose color is red' are also recognized.

[7] But see footnote 2.

[8] Complex noun phrases are beyond the scope of this paper.

[9] In the short term, LEAP uses 'canned' requests for information. For example, if the user says 'Please draw a circle whose center is point A,' the response ('OK. What should the background color of the circle be') is derived from a predefined sentence template whose only variable is a place holder for 'circle'. The template itself is supplied by the author. In the future, this may be automated using a language generator.

[10] A task instance has the same structure as the task type, but each instance will be different. For example, the task instance that results from the request 'Draw a blue circle' would be different from the one resulting from 'Draw a red rectangle'. But both are instances of the same task type.

[11] As is the case with tasks, a conversation instance has the same structure as a conversation template while different instances will have different content. But there is an important difference between conversation and task instances. Task instances differ only in their corresponding entities (and the traits of these entities). Conversation instances, on the other hand, guide and record the task-oriented discourse itself.

[12] For example, if the request is 'Make the Brush blue,' the conversation manager uses the command phrases from the author file to determine that the Drawing Tool for this task is the Brush and that the color of the drawing tool should be blue.

[13] For example, in the Bunny Express, the Pen entity is a constant element of the application context.
[14] See (Grosz, 1978) and (Grosz and Sidner, 1986).
[15] For example, in the Bunny Express application, the task of drawing a circle requires a sub-task of defining a point, which is itself a task.
[16] See (Kronfeld, 1990) pp. 144-149.
[17] For present purposes a presentation mode is identified with a referring expression in the context of a conversation instance. This is obviously an over-simplification.
[18] The concept of a focus stack as a computational tool for modeling discourse was developed by Grosz, B.J. and later by Grosz and Sidner, C.L.. See references in footnote 14.
[19] For example, 'the green metal box' subsumes the description 'the metal box'.
[20] For example, let I be the individuating set containing the descriptions 'the green expensive box' and 'the heavy metal box,' and let p be the description 'the green metal box.' Then I subsumes p since whatever is a green expensive heavy metal box cannot fail to be a green metal box.

17 CONVERSE: a Conversational Companion

B. Batacharia, D. Levy, R. Catizone, A. Krotov and Y. Wilks

1 Introduction

Empirical and theoretical investigations of the nature and structure of human dialogue have been a topic of research in artificial intelligence and the more human areas of linguistics for decades: there has been much interesting work but no definitive or uncontroversial findings. the best performance overall has probably been Colby's PARRY (Colby,1973) since its release on the (then ARPA) net around 1973. It was robust, never broke down, always had something to say and, because it was intended to model paranoid behaviour, its zanier misunderstandings could always be taken as further evidence of mental disturbance rather than the processing failures they were.

Colby actually carried out a version of the Turing test (Turing,1950) by getting psychiatrists to compare blind PARRY utterances with those of real paranoids and they were unable to distinguish them—indistinguishability results are never statistically watertight, but it was, nonetheless, a very striking demonstration and much longer ago than many now realise.

CONVERSE was intended not to be based on any scientific research but on hunches about how to do it, together with taking advantage of some recent methodological shifts in computational linguistics. The main hunch was derived directly from PARRY's impressiveness when compared with its passive contemporaries like ELIZA (Weizenbaum,1976): PARRY had something to say, just as people do, and did not simply react to what you said to it. It could be said to rest on the hunch that a sufficient condition for humanness in conversation may be what Searle (Searle,1983) calls intentionality: the apparent desire to act and affect surroundings through the conversation, which is a strong version of what we am calling "having something to say" since a computer program without prostheses can only create such effects through speech acts and not real acts on physical objects.

The extension of this hunch as far as Turing test—i.e. fooling people that the system is human—situations is concerned is that if the computer can get to say enough, to keep control of the conversation, as it were, through being interesting or demanding enough that the human plays along, then there is correspondingly less opportunity for the human interlocutor to ask questions or get responses to an unconstrained range of utterances that will show up the system for what it is. Naturally enough, this hunch/heuristic, must be tempered in practice since a system that will not listen at all, which will not be diverted from its script no matter what is said, is again inevitably shown up. The hunch/heuristic is simply a tendency—be as active and controlling in the conversation as possible, subject to necessary and unavoidable interruptions and topic shifts driven by the human. RACTER, PARRY's only real rival over the last 30 years, worked on the principle of being so interesting and zany that many humans did not want to interrupt it so as to intrude new topics or demands of their own. Others were less charmed of course, but it was one very effective strategy for operating this key hunch and one not involving actual clinical madness.

The original features of CONVERSE are probably as follows:

1. top down control of conversation by means of a range of scripts, plus an active bottom up module seeking to answer questions etc. against a set of data bases on individuals.
2. control and interaction of these features in 1 by means of a weighting system between modules that could be set so as to increase the likelihood of one or other of these modules "gaining control" at any given point in the conversation.
3. the use of large scale linguistic data bases such as thesaurus nets giving conceptual connectivity—for dealing with synonyms---and large proper name inventories that allowed CONVERSE to appear to know about a large range of people and things not in either the scripts, the data bases, or the semantic nets, though this information as formally mapped to the structures of the semantic network and the databases.
4. a commercial and very impressive text parser, based on trained corpus statistics. This however had been trained for prose rather than dialogue which meant that much of its output had to be modified by us before being used. We also made use of large scale patterns of dialogue use derived from an extensive corpus of British dialogue that was recently made available.

The last takes advantage of recent trends in natural language processing: the use of very large resources in language processing and intermediate results obtained from such resources, like the dialogue patterns. It meant that CONVERSE was actually far larger than any previous Loebner entry, and that much of our effort had gone into making such resources rapidly available in a PC environment. So, although not based on specific research, CONVERSE was making far more use of the tools and methods of current language processing research than most such systems. Its slogan at this level was "big data, small program" which is much more the current trend in language processing and artificial intelligence generally than the opposite slogan which had ruled for decades and seen all such simulations as forms of complex reasoning, rather than the assembly of a vast array of cases and data.

CONVERSE, although, it has some of the spirit of PARRY, does in fact have data bases and learns and stores facts, which PARRY never did, and will allow us in the future to expand its explicit reasoning capacity. The weighting system would in principle allow great flexibility in the system and could be trained, as connectionist and neural network systems are trained, to give the best value of the weightings in terms of actual performance. We will continue to investigate this, and whether weightings in fact provide a good model of conversation—as opposed to purely deterministic systems that, say, always answer a question when it is posed. In the end, as so often, this may turn out to be a question of the application desired: a computer companion might be more appropriate weighted, since we seem to like our companions, spouses and pets to be a little unpredictable, even fractious.

On the other hand, a computer model functioning as a counsellor or advisor in a heath care situation, advising on the risks of a certain operation or test, might well be more deterministic, always answering a question and always telling all it knew about a subject when asked.

2 The CONVERSE Personality and Characterization

The character of CONVERSE is Catherine, a 26 year-old female editor for Vanity Fair, who was born in the UK, but currently lives in New York. The details of Catherine's character are stored in a database, known as the Person DataBase (PDB). The kinds of things that we store about Catherine are the details of her physical appearance, her birthday, astrological sign, some of her likes and dislikes, whether she has a boyfriend, where she works, etc. For the most part, things in the PDB are all related to facts about Catherine. We can also store information about other people in the PDB, in particular people that are related to Catherine in some way, mother, father, friend, boss, etc.

The scripts are the driving force of the program and whenever possible, we aim to keep control of the conversation, by posing a question at the end of a system utterance. The scripts cover a range of 80 topics, but can be extended (within the limits of the hardware). Currently, some of the topics covered are crime, racism, religion, 'The Simpsons', mobile phones, abortion, travel, food and violence. The method for acquiring the scripts is done in a two stage process. First, a script writer sketches out the script on paper and secondly, the scripts are entered into the system via a script editor. The script editor establishes the flow of control through the script based on the user's responses to each script utterance.

3 System Modules

3.1 Overview

CONVERSE consists of a number of independent software modules which are co-ordinated by a shell structure. The total size of the code is approximately 600 kbytes, plus 28.8 mbytes of data. The software can currently converse on a variety of 60 different topics, using the knowledge of several thousand people and places. In addition it can provide answers to questions using the same knowledge base. CONVERSE is implemented in C and C++ and runs under Windows95. It employs a parser written by Prospero Software, a UK company, and a lexical database called "WordNet" created at Princeton University under the direction of George Miller (Miller, 1990).

Very briefly, the system works as follows (see Figure 1). First, user input is read and passed through the input modules. Then, a dispatcher calls up action modules to see if they can do anything with the processed input. Then, it collects the text generated by the action modules, chooses the most appropriate and passes it through the generator, which prints out the output message. Meanwhile, action modules read and update the data in data modules. When the output has been printed, the system waits for the user input and the entire cycle starts again. The remaining part of this section will describe in detail how each of the components operates.

3.2 Architecture

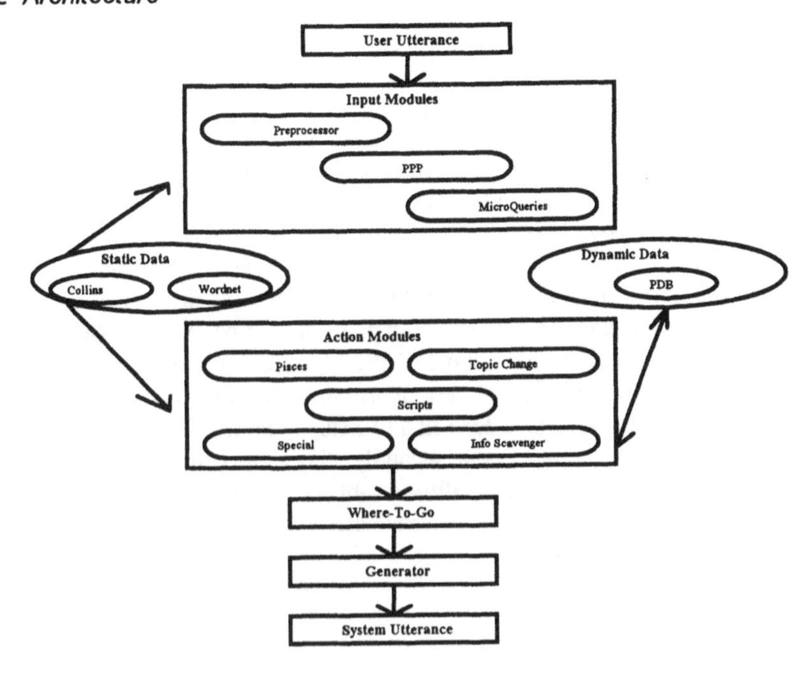

Figure 1

3.3 Input Modules

Input modules deal with the user input. Their function is to extract any useful information from the input and present this information to action modules.

First of all, the utterance is pre-processed in order to correct grammatic imperfections, spelling mistakes and to identify proper and place names. Then, the corrected utterance is passed to Prospero parser and to the parser post-processor (PPP). Finally, the microquery module provides an interface which other action modules use to access the output of PPP.

3.3.1 Pre-processing

Pre-processing includes the following modules: spell checker, elision expansion module, name tagger, and trivial punctuation correction module. Using a large dictionary, spell checker corrects the user's spelling. Elision expansion replaces abbreviations such as 'I'll', 'they've', 'it's' with their full forms (I will, they have, it is). If the input contains any place names or proper names, they are identified by the name tagger. First names are augmented with a sex (or as being unisex). Place names are augmented with extra place information data. In a similar manner the tagger marks dates and arithmetic expressions. Name, place, date, and arithmetic information is used by action modules through the microquery module. For example, if 'John' was typed in response to 'What is your name?', we can tell that the user is probably a man called John. Similarly, we can look for the user's birthdate and birthplace and say something clever about the latter.

Finally, trivial punctuation correction module rectifies a problem where the user input is not terminated with a punctuation sign. The module decides whether the input is a question or a statement and puts the appropriate punctuation sign at the end.

3.3.2 Prospero and PPP

Prospero Software's syntactic parser is used to determine the sentence structure. It gets the pre-processed input, tags it with the part-of-speech information, and then parses. The output of the parser is passed to the Parser Post-Processor (PPP).

The PPP's tasks are two-fold: it simplifies and flattens the parse tree and also corrects the deficiencies of Prospero. For example, given a sentence 'My name is Mary', PPP can tell that the verb of this sentence is "be" and the object is "Mary". PPP also knows that 'Mary' is a female name (from the information supplied by the pre-processor). PPP breaks the input into sentences and determines whether each sentence is a command, question or a statement.

3.3.3 MicroQueries

Microquery module is a front end to the PPP. Each action module queries the processed user input using the list of microqueries. A microquery defines a set of patterns posed as 'questions' to the input in order to filter and extract relevant information. For example, one pattern can determine if there are any proper names in the input. Individual patterns are connected to each other with logical functions.

They can access the elements of input as well as Wordnet functions (synonym sets and hierarchies) and built-in functions such as string matching.

Action modules can decide what to do according to what answers the microQueries returned. Microqueries can also input and return values and use variables. For example, a microquery can determine a command "Tell me X" and pass the value of X to the action module for further processing.

3.4 Data Modules

3.4.1 Person DataBase (PDB)

This is the module which is responsible for storing all the information for each user, as well as information about the system's own persona - Catherine.

Pisces answers most questions by fuzzy matching with the Person DataBase. A potential tagset will be formed from the user's utterance. This tagset will be passed to the fuzzy-matching portion of the PDB, which will attempt to find a "closest match" tagset within the database. Given a good enough probability that the tagset matches, Pisces will then be able to supply a response, hopefully answering the question.

This is the module that will be responsible for storing all information for each judge.

Information will be stored with associated tags - it will not be arranged as a slot-filled table. Information that can be stored may be numerical (in either integer or floating-point format) or a text-string. Tags will be passed as text strings. The order of fields is unimportant. There is, also a mechanism for allowing lists. There are procedures to allow for the entire set of the current user's data to be exchanged for another user's data. This is useful in a multiple user environment.

3.4.2 Wordnet

Wordnet is a lexical database created in Princeton under the guidance of Professor George Miller. It stores words and their definitions as well as synonym sets (complete, finish) and hierarchical information (e.g. wine is a kind of a drink). Wordnet is used by PPP, MicroQuery module (for synonym and hierarchy functions) and Pisces (for word definitions).

3.4.3 Collins

We are using the Harper-Collins dictionary of proper nouns for identifying famous people and places. This resource is accessed primarily by the question-answering module, Pisces.

3.4.4 MicroQuery providers

Each action module and each script maintains its list of microqueries. Individual microqueries are stored as text, and are different from the MicroQuery module which applies these microqueries to user input. For example, Pisces (the question answering module) has microqueries filtering out only questions and determining the type of a question. Special case module has microqueries looking for rude words. Some script lines have microqueries extracting sentences specific to that script line.

3.5 Action Modules

3.5.1 Where-To-Go Module

The "Where-To-Go" (WTG), or dispatcher module decides which of the action modules handle the input utterance. The analogy that is the most powerful is that of dispatcher acting as an auctioneer, holding each piece of input up for bids by each of the action modules.

The Dispatcher presents input to each action module in turn, keeping track of the bids. An action module returns a bid describing that module's confidence that it has a valid response to the current piece of input. This bid lies between 0 (no bid—I can't say anything about this) and 100 (I understood completely what the user said and I can respond to it). A piece of input is then 'won' by the module which returned the highest bid. In some cases, there can be more than one winner.

The calculation of a bid depends on each individual action module. They are described in detail in later sections.

After the bidding is complete, dispatcher decides which parts of input will be presented to which action modules. Some parts of input may not be processed at all, in which case the information scavenger module is activated. If an action module wins a bid, then it may extract data from the input and store it in the Person Database.

3.5.2 Pisces

Pisces is the module that answers questions. Pisces functionality is broadly divided into two tasks: question recognition and question answering. The question recognition module tries to identify the type of question asked based on a typology of about 20 different question types. Once the question type is identified, a response to the question is given. The response is formed by looking first in the Person DataBase (using a synonym matching algorithm with Wordnet) to see if we have an accurate response to the question. If this fails, we produce a filler that corresponds to the users question type. If we fail to recognize the question type, a general filler is given. Pisces also handles user requests. All of the request/question type identification is done using microQueries. Both Wordnet and Collins are referenced by Pisces for definitions of people, places and things.

3.5.3 Special Cases

This module handles exceptional cases such as rude language, illogical birthday or age, talk about sex, violence. Once a special cases situation arises in the program, we trigger a response taken from a canned set of phrases that correspond to the situation at hand.

3.5.4 Scripts

Script module guides the conversation through a network of script lines. It keeps track of the "script pointer" pointing to the current script line. Each script line has some canned text, branches pointing to other script lines, and a set of Microqueries together with other information. When the conversation reaches a certain script line, the canned text is passed to the generator, and the system awaits user response. User input is then run through the set of Microqueries to determine how relevant input was to the script line, which branch to follow next, and what information should be extracted from the person database. A bid is then passed to the dispatcher.

Script module keeps track of what lines have been visited by the user. In case conversation comes back to the same line, the person database should have the previous user's response to the script question. If the response is known, the relevant branch is simply followed. Also, if user input does not match the current script line, another matching line can be found.

3.5.5 Information Scavenger

The function of this module is to extract any possible information from the given clause if the clause is a statement. This module is the penultimate one called by the Dispatcher. It is called only if no other action modules have extracted information from the current clause.

3.5.6 Topic Change Module

Topic Change module controls the flow of conversation. It decides in what order the available 60 topics should be presented to the user. Catherine starts with the introduction, and then switches to a new topic whenever it runs out of the previous one. However, if the user wants Catherine to move to a different topic, the topic change module switches to the new topic before the old topic is exhausted.

In order to control what topic comes next, topic change mechanism guesses what the user wants to talk about. This is done by monitoring user input and trying to match it with the content words of the available topics. If there is a good match, the matched topic is put on the "topic stack" for later use.

3.5.7 Generator

The Generator takes the results of the action modules and assembles them into a coherent utterance which is then output to the user. Variables from the Person DataBase are referenced where necessary. Finally there are connectives added where needed to ensure a smooth flowing response. There is a final module, SenGen, which adds variety to an utterance by randomly choosing among various ways of saying the same thing.

4 Conclusion

4.1 Testing and Limitations

CONVERSE runs under Windows95 responding to each user utterance within a few seconds. At the last stage of development, the system was thoroughly tested. Testing included several tasks such as microquery testing, script testing, entire system testing. For each of these tasks a separate shell was created so that each task could be done individually without loading the entire system.

CONVERSE was tested by an independent person for bugs and for the quality of output. He then suggested possible improvements to the script lines, script logic, which topics are good and which are not so good, and provided us with other useful comments.

One of the main limitations of the system is the present parser. Prospero was designed to parse prose, not dialogue, which meant that some simpler utterances became unparsable, or were parsed incorrectly. That fact, along with the general rigidity of syntactic parsers (e.g. one misspelled word or a wrong tag can set off the entire system) calls for a better dialogue parser. The new dialogue parser along with the 'requests' module (modified MicroQuery module) will be geared towards recognising patterns in the input rather than looking for syntactic elements in the sentence.

Another limitation of CONVERSE is our failure to take advantage of previous utterances in formulating a response to the user. Although we have a dialogue history as such it is not used by any of the action modules. We plan to incorporate the dialogue history in the near future. One obvious use is to spot when the user repeats himself. In this case, we will notice and respond accordingly.

4.2 Future Directions

CONVERSE is fun to use and as such it will find many applications as recreational software. Data can be written to enable it to talk about many more topics. It can be linked to a text-to-speech package and to a speech recognition package so that the user can conduct a conversation without the need to type on the keyboard (it is already working with speech output).

Amongst the recreational applications which are foreseen for CONVERSE, foremost is the idea of using it as a virtual friend. CONVERSE's Person Data Base can be augmented with data for different personalities, enabling the user to talk, on one day, to a virtual elderly English gentleman and on another occasion to a virtual 20-year-old punk music fan from the Bronx. Eventually the user will be able to describe the personality with whom he wishes to talk, and there will be a module to create a suitable Person Data Base conforming with the user's specification.

Commercial applications are already being considered. Typically, CONVERSE will be provided with data to enable it to talk intelligently about a variety of customer applications. For example, a local government office could have a version of CONVERSE which can deal with questions about the schools in the neighbourhood. A travel agency might want a version of CONVERSE which was an expert of various vacation destinations, hotels, etc. One use for CONVERSE would be as front end for a relational database. CONVERSE can also be used as the front end for almost any type of software application which requires regular interaction between user and program, e.g. a "Help" system within a popular package such as a Word Processor or Spreadsheet.

Acknowledgements

We would like to thank our colleagues, David Fulford-Brown, Jill Govier, Kenny Guy, Pete Oakley, and Paul Woods whose contributions to the system were invaluable. Any mistakes are, of course, our own.

References

Colby, K. 1973. Simulations of Belief systems. In Schank and Colby (Eds.) Computer Models of Thought and Language. Freeman, San Francisco, CA.

Searle, J. 1983. Intentionality. Cambridge University Press, Cambridge.

Turing, A. 1950. Computing Machinery and Intelligence. Mind vol. LIX.

Weizenbaum, J. 1976. Computer Power and Human Reason. Freeman, San Francisco, CA.

Ballim, A. and Wilks, Y. 1991. Artificial Believers. Erlbaum, Hillsdale, NJ.

Miller G. A. (Ed.), 1990. WordNet: An on-line Lexical Database, International Journal of Lexicography.

Appendix: CONVERSE Output from Loebner Competition

PROGRAM[10:18:04]Hi, my name is Catherine, what's yours?
JUDGE04[10:18:32]My name is Elliott.
PROGRAM[10:18:34]Well, it's nice to meet you, Elliott.
PROGRAM[10:18:48]Did you see that story on CNN last night about the lesbian
PROGRAM[10:19:04]couple who came out at a White House party on Sunday?
JUDGE04[10:19:55]Yes, I did. I think it may all be a publicity stunt for Ellen.
PROGRAM[10:20:01]Ellen Degeneres was one of them - she was kissing her lover
PROGRAM[10:20:11]in front of Bill Clinton. Do you think he was very
PROGRAM[10:20:25]embarrassed?
JUDGE04[10:21:00]I think he want the gay vote. He will do anything to get it and keep it.
JUDGE04[10:21:15]He does not have a conservative base.
PROGRAM[10:21:21]
PROGRAM[10:21:21]Are you still a Friend of Bill Clinton?
JUDGE04[10:22:20]I am not sure if he has any real friends. He has achieved alot and has
JUDGE04[10:22:31]left alot of people behind.
PROGRAM[10:22:35]You really don't like the guy—well, at least that's
PROGRAM[10:22:50]definite—I thought most people were just indifferent or
PROGRAM[10:23:02]numb by now.
JUDGE04[10:23:34]I think we could have a more honest and dynamic leader. One able to
JUDGE04[10:23:55]face the real dangers facing the country and address them with
JUDGE04[10:24:26]courage and intelligence. Rather then listening to public opinion polls.
PROGRAM[10:24:30]I guess that means you really think there's serious behind
PROGRAM[10:24:56]Whitewater, the Special prosecutor and all that stuff?
JUDGE04[10:25:58]We have two dead people, Brown and guy who commited suicide, we have lost
JUDGE04[10:26:36]papers. And we have Clintons people willing to tell all. I think that
JUDGE04[10:26:55]Hillary will be found guilty of something.
PROGRAM[10:26:58]But how do you actually feel about him, now in the number
PROGRAM[10:27:09]two term?
PROGRAM[10:27:15].
JUDGE04[10:27:44]He is too smart to get caught. He deserved to named hotel manager of the 43dxc
JUDGE04[10:27:47]year.
PROGRAM[10:27:49]OK, but what happens now—does it all drift on, with
PROGRAM[10:28:01]everyone waiting to see how much his friends have said about
PROGRAM[10:28:17]him under threat of lots and lots of jail-or will something
PROGRAM[10:28:32]dramatic actually happen?

Index

D

E

F

G

H

I

J

K

L

M

N

O

P

Q

R

S

T

U

V

W

X

Y

Z